LOVE
AND
THE LAW

by
Gail Koff
FOUNDING PARTNER OF
JACOBY & MEYERS LAW OFFICES

SIMON AND SCHUSTER

New York   London   Toronto   Sydney   Tokyo

Simon and Schuster
Simon & Schuster Building
Rockefeller Center
1230 Avenue of the Americas
New York, New York   10020

Designed by Irving Perkins Associates, Inc.
Manufactured in the United States of America

1 3 5 7 9 10 8 6 4 2

Library of Congress Cataloging in Publication Data

Koff, Gail J.

Love and the law / by Gail Koff.
p.   cm.
Includes index.
1. Domestic relations—United States—Popular works.   I. Title.
KF505.Z9K58   1989
346.7301'5—dc19   88-39100
[347.30615]   CIP

ISBN 0-671-64608-7

DEDICATION

To my husband, Ralph Brill, who helps me reach my dreams

Contents

Acknowledgments

I would like to thank Charles Salzberg for his inestimable help and good humor in the preparation of this book.

I would also like to thank the following attorneys at Jacoby & Meyers offices throughout the country for their invaluable assistance in the preparation of this book.

Stephanie Baynon
Howard Benick
Mitchell Berman
Randy Bisson
John Boll
Michael Brady
Dean Despotovich
Steven P. Dragna
Fred Emmer
Charles Fishbein
Michael F. Geary
Scott Gilmore
Gerald H. Horowitz
Ellen Huffine
Jeffrey Kirsch
Karl Kramer
Richard LaNave
Dick Lanai
Don Latzer

Michael Latzes
Harry Lenaburg
James Lia
Gregory Messer
Thomas G. Moshier
Francine Moss
Sharon O'Brien-Reyes
Margaret O'Hara
Don B. Panush
Raymond Pilch
Richard Ribakove
Patricia Riley
Raymond Riley
Richard Rocco
Gary M. Rose
Richard Stein
Marilyn Sternstein
Conrad Strabone
Mart Susi

Finally, I would like to thank Dean John Feerich of the Fordham Law School for allowing us the generous use of the Fordham Law School Library, and John Howard of Citibank.

INTRODUCTION

It should come as no surprise that in the past twenty years or so there have been a number of fundamental changes in the mores of our society which have had a dramatic impact on the way we live. In many cases the traditions we've clung to have either vanished or evolved to such an extent that they are hardly recognizable. Our basic patterns of living have been decidedly altered as a result. In short, whether we like it or not, the good old days are gone.

Perhaps nowhere is this more evident than in our relationships with the opposite sex. Though some may look back nostalgically to those days when the man majestically ruled the roost, today basic philosophical and practical changes have resulted in a balancing of the roles of men and women. For one thing, more women than ever are making their way in the work force; and many of these women are performing an intricate juggling act between family and career. Add to this the growing number of scientific advances that affect sexuality and reproduction—astoundingly accurate methods of blood testing, *in vitro* fertilization, and surrogate parenting—and you can see why the old rules no longer apply.

A generation or so ago, for instance, a couple living together prior to marriage was rare; the idea of that couple living together with no intention of marrying was even rarer. Furthermore, the notion of bringing suit against a sexual partner for spreading venereal diseases, some with such dire consequences as Acquired Immune Deficiency Syndrome (AIDS), was purely in the realm of fiction. Yet today these are only two of many such situations that face us nearly every day.

In response to these changes, the law has also been forced to evolve. Some might accuse the legal system of being the turtle rather than the hare, and indeed the law does evolve slowly, having to wait for the results of social change. Take, for instance, the laws concerning divorce. Twenty years ago if a spouse wanted a divorce he or she would have to show cause, perhaps citing adultery, abandonment, or mental cruelty. But today every state has instituted some form of no-fault divorce. And in response to the changes in the divorce laws that have eliminated fault, the system has developed equitable distribution and community property laws, which are meant to deal with the changing view of marriage. Marriage, in turn, which heretofore was primarily looked upon as a "life" partnership between husband and wife, has now evolved into what might best be considered an economic partnership between a man and a woman, with the possibility of divorce a very real one.

Coincidentally, at just about the same time the rules of the game began to change, we established the law firm of Jacoby & Meyers. Founded on the principle of providing accessible, quality legal services at reasonable fees, we believe in making law accessible to the middle-income "legal niche." We also believe that the law ought to be demystified and that one of the ways to best serve the public as well as the legal system was to have an educated client.

At Jacoby & Meyers it has always been our feeling that it's in the public's best interests to be informed not only of any changes in the law but also how these changes affect our lives on a daily basis. If we can help you accomplish this, you will have the capability of knowing how to take control of your life and at the same time protect yourself. The more you know about how the law works, the more opportunity there is to save time and money, and perhaps most important, alleviate potential emotional pain. Think of this, if you will, merely as a form of "preventative" law.

So there, in short, is the reason for and the aim of this book: to impart information in the hope that it will help prevent legal problems and help you to control your destiny. In the method we've chosen, presenting cases that have been handled through our offices, as well as precedent cases, we hope you will be able to more closely identify with the kinds of problems we all face and, as a result, feel less isolated.

Arguably, love is one of the most important forces in our lives. At any one time we all seem either to be looking for love, in love, in the process of falling out of love, or trying to get over a love turned sour.

Whether you realize it or not, the law is an integral part of "love." The state not only has an interest in the institution of marriage (a state-issued marriage license must be obtained before a valid marriage can take place and, similarly, a divorce must also be sanctioned by the state) but also in family, which includes the relationship between parent and child. The law touches upon just about every facet of love, and it is probably well that it does. After all, it was Publilius Syrus who wisely said, "A god could hardly love and be wise." In other words, our judgment is often beclouded by love, and it is not unusual when love fades to have to rely on the law to solve our problems.

We all know the foolish things that have been done "for love." How often have you heard stories of men or women getting involved in foolish financial situations as a result of love? Certainly the following poem, written by John Godfrey Saxe, cynical as it may be, rings true:

I asked of Echo, t' other day
(Whose words are few and often funny),
What to a novice she could say
Of courtship, love, and matrimony?
Quoth Echo, plainly: — "Matter-o'-money."

Since our firm does so much work in this area—literally from conception through living together, marriage, divorce, and finally death—it seemed natural to address this book solely to the universal subject of love.

Due to the societal changes I mentioned earlier, there is now far more flexibility in the law. As a result, in many areas today we have an opportunity to use this flexibility to structure our lives accordingly. In order to do so we must first be familiar with the law in order to let it work for us.

An example that comes immediately to mind is the case of an unmarried couple living together. Neither party is protected by the same laws that pertain to a married couple. They must therefore, if they choose, take appropriate steps to protect themselves. This means clarifying individual rights, and one way to do this might be either to draw up, or at least discuss the possibility of, a cohabitation agreement. This agreement, a preventative measure, can save money, time, and perhaps most important, emotional anguish.

But whether or not you choose to make these clarifications, it's always best to be aware of your options, even if you choose never to take advantage of them. If nothing else, education provides us with the opportunity to make an informed choice.

In this book I've tried to cover just about every legal issue that has an impact on "love." There are sections on living together, marriage, divorce, children, and even the more contemporary issues such as the right to die, surrogate parenting, and organ transplants. Individual topics range from annulments to child abuse; from battered spouses to palimony; from the rights of homosexuals to prenuptial agreements.

Though this book is meant to take a close look at these sometimes controversial issues, it should by no means be considered comprehensive. In fact it should be noted that at best I could only touch upon each topic; in point of fact an entire book could well be written on each of the subjects covered here. I've tried instead to offer as much broad-based information as concisely and as easily understandable as possible.

At this point I'd like to take a moment to explain the methods used in putting this book together. At Jacoby & Meyers we see over one hundred seventy-five thousand new clients each year and have seen more than 1.5 million clients since we founded the firm in 1972. As a result we get a chance to see a wide variety of cases. I took advantage of this asset in putting together this book. Believing that it's always easier to understand a concept by presenting interesting anecdotal examples, I contacted dozens of our attorneys, in all parts of the country, and asked them to offer pertinent cases on the various subjects to be covered. They did just that. Though the names, certain details, and the locations have all been changed to protect the privacy of those involved, the basic facts and the legal questions involved are all based on actual cases handled by our attorneys. These cases are used to illustrate particular points of law, all of which I have tried to convey in plain language rather than the often indecipherable hieroglyphics of "legalese."

Beyond the actual cases from our offices I made liberal use of primary and secondary sources such as newspapers, magazines, law journals, trade publications, and standing case law. In addition, whenever possible, I tried to relate experiences in my own life when they were appropriate to illustrate a point.

Obviously it would be impossible to write a book like this without resorting to generalizations. There are fifty states in this country with fifty different sets of laws. Though many states do have similar statutes on the books, each has the right to interpret them according to the state's precedents. And some states are more progressive than others. Also, decisions often depend on the particular judge involved or on the jurisdiction in which the case is heard. For these reasons it is impossible to provide the reader with absolutes. Rather, I've tried to give a generalized account of the law in order to educate. This book is not meant to take the place of an attorney, nor is it meant to be a textbook. Instead it should be used as a tool to help inform people in order that they may make the intelligent decisions that will enable them to better structure their lives.

I would be remiss if I didn't offer one piece of essential advice: Always consult with a qualified attorney regarding any of these matters, at the very least in order to find out what the law is in your state or community. No matter how much you read on the subject, you wouldn't try to fill your own tooth when suffering from a toothache, and for much the same reason you shouldn't represent yourself in any legal matter.

LIVING
TOGETHER

CHAPTER 1
Legal Ramifications

In the past two decades more and more unmarried couples in this country have chosen to live together. As of 1970 there were barely five hundred thousand unmarried couples living together. By the mid-1980s, however, this number had more than quadrupled, to 2.2 million, and it is likely this figure will continue to rise dramatically over the next decade.

It happens every day. Two people, either of the opposite or the same sex, fall in love and decide to move in together. Soon their lives become intertwined. They share confidences, possessions, friends, even money. They are, in effect, partners. Yet they aren't married and therefore are vulnerable to a plethora of potentially thorny legal problems that may make their lives much more complicated than they bargained for.

It is paradoxical that when people try to keep life simple by not marrying, they end up further complicating it instead. In the absence of marriage we are left without the support system of a governing body of rules. We can't look to the state for protection because, without a marriage contract, the state is not involved. This is one reason people are finding it necessary to consult attorneys more often.

The first area of conflict may involve a shared house or apartment, something as simple as who has the rights to the place where you reside. If it's a house and it wasn't purchased with the names of both parties on the deed, who owns it? What rights does the non-owning partner have if he or she contributes money toward the maintenance of the house? If there is shared ownership, what happens if the couple breaks up? Who gets the house? Must it be sold? If it is sold, how is the money to be divided?

All too often people neglect to face questions like these, questions that may conjure up unpleasant situations and eventualities. Some people are superstitious, thinking that to discuss potential problems will only make them real. And yet, as a rule, it's always better to be prepared for the worst, even while expecting and hoping for the best.

KEEPING THE HOME FIRES BURNING

When two people live together for a long period of time without benefit of marriage, one problem that inevitably arises is each person's interest in a house they shared. This was the case with Harvey and Joyce, an unmarried couple who lived together for fourteen years in a home they purchased just outside New York City, during which time they had a child. Due to an error the deed was made out in the name of Mr. and Mrs., as if they were husband and wife. This made them tenants in entirety; this meant they shared an undivided interest in the house, and neither one could sell it without permission of the other.

After a dozen years the relationship began to fall apart. Harvey consulted one of our attorneys because he was concerned about the status of the house, especially since the bulk of the money used to pay for it came from him. At the same time Joyce retained a lawyer and counterclaimed for child support and palimony.

The palimony issue does not concern us here (it will be discussed fully in Chapter 2), but New York, like most states, does not recognize this concept. As for the child support (which will also be dealt with later), Harvey is responsible, regardless of marital status. The state's position is that it is in its own best interests to see to it that the welfare of a child is taken care of. Since Harvey is an adult, it is his responsibility, married or not, to support his child.

Rather than go to court we negotiated a settlement concerning the house. Joyce was allowed to live there until their child, Anthony, who at the time was thirteen years old, finished high school. During this period she was responsible for maintaining the residence and paying for the utilities and the general upkeep of the house, although Harvey agreed to pay some of the bills, including the taxes and the mortgage. After Anthony graduated, the house would be sold and the proceeds split equally. (It should be noted that it would have been possible for Harvey to instigate proceedings against the attorney who had mistakenly prepared the deed. However, this might have been a costly and time-consuming procedure.)

Although they would still have needed an attorney, all this trouble could have been avoided if Harvey and Joyce had been married. Then, regardless of whose name was on the deed, the house would have been considered the property of both, and in the divorce settlement, under either the doctrine of equitable distribution or community property, Joyce would have been entitled to up to fifty percent of the house, in addition to a portion of Harvey's business and other assets.

But this was not the case. Instead, an error on the deed allowed Joyce to eventually get half the value of the house since Harvey and Joyce purchased it as a married couple. In other cases, the theory of constructive trust could have been applied, meaning the house was to be shared regardless of how much money was put into it.

A constructive trust is an equitable remedy in which the court looks at the facts of a situation and says, in effect, "This isn't fair." A trust is created against one who has perpetrated fraud or has used questionable means to hold property, thereby being unjustly enriched. It's a theory the court uses to give someone rights he or she otherwise would not have. For instance, if a piece of property is acquired in one person's name but a second party has also contributed money toward its purchase, that second party is meant to have an interest in it. This constitutes a constructive trust, and the courts may decide the proper percentage of the property due each party.

Another example of a constructive trust is the case of a man with his own business who decides it is in his best interests to transfer title of their home to his wife in order to protect it against possible business debts. Although the house is in his wife's name, if they should divorce he might try to show that in transferring title he had established a constructive trust, meaning it was always the couple's intention that the house was theirs despite the fact it was in her name alone.

However, although it is relatively simple to file for this remedy, it is quite difficult to prove.

A couple may live together in a house that has been paid for by the man, is in his name only, and is maintained solely by him. If this is the case, and the relationship ends, does the woman have any rights to the house? Unless she can prove she acted as a wife, raised children, contributed to his business either directly or indirectly (entertained business clients, helped with mailings, gave advice, made telephone contacts with potential clients), it is highly unlikely she can stake a claim to the property.

In fact, if she hadn't had her name on the deed to the house, this would have been the case with Martha, who lived with Sam for twenty-three years and had three sons with him. Although they occasionally discussed getting married, they never did. There were always the same arguments against it: Sam didn't want to add to his life the legal complications he thought would come with a marriage certificate; he was frightened of the commitment, which seemed too permanent. Martha, who had been married before, also shied away from the idea of marriage because she was afraid it would somehow ruin their relationship.

One day Sam, who ran a successful plumbing supply business, decided he wanted to end their relationship, and he consulted an attorney in one of our offices. Sam was under the mistaken impression that because he lived with Martha for so many years, theirs was a common-law marriage. (Their three sons believed their parents were married.) Our attorney informed him, however, that in New York, as in most states today, there is no such thing as common-law marriage.

Nevertheless, because their children believed them married, Sam and Martha decided to tell their family that they were getting a divorce. The primary property they owned was a house, the deed to which was in both their names, but since Sam and Martha were never actually married, Martha had no legal right to any property other than what she could actually prove was hers, nor did she have the right to alimony. In fact, because they were unmarrieds living together, she didn't even have a right to share in his pension, which was considerable. Thus, when the relationship ended, Martha was entitled only to half the house because her name was on the deed.

Martha and Sam thought that by not being married they would avoid legal complexities but, ironically, this was not the case. If they had been married, Martha would have protected herself more effectively. She would have had the right to up to half his plumbing business, under either community property or equitable distribution. She also might have received maintenance until she could be trained to hold a job of her own. On the other hand, as it turned out, Sam benefitted by not being married because Martha received far less than she would have.

YOUR PLACE OR MINE?

Jane and Betsy were good friends who, after an extensive search, found and moved into a large two-bedroom apartment. Both women signed the lease as co-tenants. After a short time Jane asked her boyfriend John to move in with her. Shortly thereafter Betsy asked her boyfriend Richard to move in also.

It wasn't long before the two couples found they couldn't get along. Their life-styles were totally in conflict. John and Jane enjoyed listening to loud rock music and throwing raucous parties for a host of friends. Betsy and Richard preferred a quiet night home alone, listening to classical music. After a while the situation worsened to the point where the two couples weren't even speaking to each other.

Finally, the situation reached an intolerable point, and John and Jane consulted a lawyer to attempt to evict Betsy and Richard from the apartment. Confused as to where they stood, Betsy consulted an attorney in one of our offices. He represented them and formed a legal position that it was inappropriate for one tenant to try to evict the other, that only a landlord has this remedy.

The attorney was basing his argument on the origin of the concept of property ownership as we now know it. This means that today a tenant may hold land or occupy space in a building for a definite term or on a month-to-month basis, while the landlord reserves the right to eviction if certain provisions are not met. It is the landlord who retains control of his property, not the tenants.

After a hearing the court upheld the argument we set forth on behalf of the defendants, Betsy and Richard, and refused to evict the couple. Unfortunately, the situation between the couples had completely deteriorated, and this decision did not solve the problems between them. Their lawyers finally negotiated a settlement in which John and Jane agreed to pay Betsy and Richard a lump sum of $10,000 for the rights to their lease.

WILL YOU STILL LOVE ME TOMORROW?

In their attempt to keep things simple, people sometimes fail to plan ahead. They believe nothing bad will happen to them. In general, people don't take the time to organize their lives. I know, because I have occasionally been guilty of this. I'm an attorney, yet it wasn't until I was forty-three years old with two children that my husband forced me to deal with the issue of making a will.

When people are in love, good sense sometimes flies out the window. You wouldn't enter into a business relationship without a proper agreement, and yet when it comes to matters of the heart, people are reluctant to take the same precautions.

The lack of a proper legal agreement between two people living together may spell disaster for one of the parties. This was the case for Mary who, after going out with Gary for nearly a year, moved in with him in an apartment over the garage of his parents' house. Mary and Gary became engaged and, with the provision they would marry within one year, Gary's mother and father added both Mary and Gary to the deed to the house. Part of the agreement was that Gary's parents would refinance the house and the additional mortgage would be paid for by Mary and Gary.

After living together for nearly a year and a half, Gary and Mary decided to call off the wedding and end their relationship. Gary convinced Mary to sign a quitclaim deed (an instrument that transfers all one's legal interest in a property), with the understanding she would receive a $10,000 settlement. After signing away her rights to the property, she moved out west.

Several months passed and she failed to receive the promised check for $10,000. Upset and desperate for the money that she was counting on to help her begin a new life, she contacted Gary's parents who said, "You never really owned any part of this house. Your name was put on the deed only with the understanding that you and Gary got married. You didn't, so any money you paid toward the mortgage was really rent."

As a result, Mary came to one of our offices looking for relief. Unfortunately, there was little we could do for her. Since she had signed the quitclaim deed and had no proof of any kind of agreement with Gary and his family to receive the $10,000 payment, her case was very weak. By not being married, she had forfeited all rights to the house. We told her she could possibly argue that she was a victim of fraud (having been told she would get a settlement for signing the quitclaim deed), but this would be very difficult to prove.

Mary should have consulted a lawyer before signing the quitclaim deed and negotiated a settlement. In addition to the amount she was to be paid, this agreement would have stipulated when the payment was due as well as what rights she'd have if Gary defaulted.

Mary was naive. She trusted and depended on the good will of Gary and his parents. The reality is that when a person is faced with circumstances in which someone once close is now lost to him or her, a situation that may be fraught with anger and resentment, there is a natural, human tendency to rationalize behavior. If you rely on the good will of others, as Mary did, you run the risk of harming yourself.

APARTMENT TO LET

The same thing can happen when you're dealing with rentals as opposed to an ownership situation. We've already learned what can happen if a relationship ends and both names are on the lease (they have equal rights to the apartment), but what if only one person's name is on the lease? What rights does the other partner have? And in the case of a cooperative apartment, who is entitled to the insider rights or any other rights related to possession or resale of the property?

These are the kinds of questions that may arise, especially in highly populated urban areas where housing is scarce. In many cities across the country rental apartments are being converted into cooperative units. Those already living in these apartments are offered "insider rights," which allow the renter a substantial discount on the market value upon purchasing the apartment in which he or she lives.

This opportunity becomes more complicated when a couple lives together but only one person's name appears on the lease. If the building goes co-op, who has a right to the insider price?

Legally, it's the person whose name is on the lease. If both people are paying rent, however, the person whose name is not on the lease might be entitled to a remedy by going to court and asking for equity. His argument would be, "I paid half the rent for this period of time; therefore, I ought to have an equal right to buy the apartment at the insider's price." Using this argument a judge might find in favor of the person whose name was not on the lease, even awarding that party a right to part of the profits if the apartment was resold. It should be noted, however, that it is expensive to litigate, with no guarantee of success.

There is a more effective way to ensure that matters don't go this far. If you are living with someone, it's best to insist that you be allowed to add your name to the lease. (It should be noted that because a lease is a contract between the renter and the owner of the property, landlords are under no obligation to honor this request by adding another party to an already existing contract.)

Another good reason for getting both people's name on a lease becomes apparent in the event of the death of one partner. With both names on the lease, the rights of the surviving partner will be protected, not only in the case of insider rights but also in the continuation of the right to rent. I have a good friend who lived with a man for three years in a great apartment with a very reasonable rent. Unfortunately, the man was killed in an automobile accident, and because her name was not on the lease she wound up on the street. Today she lives in an apartment that is not half as nice and costs nearly four times as much.

THE INSIDE SCOOP

Even if an agreement is made between two parties either to share in the insider rights or to purchase an apartment together, problems can still arise.

Frank and George, a homosexual couple, agreed to buy their apartment in partnership. In an effort to protect each one's rights, they came to our office and had one of our attorneys draw up an agreement which stated that Frank, who had a well-paying job, would provide the down payment for the apartment. If the apartment were to be sold in the future, he would be entitled to the return of the down payment, and the remaining profits would be shared equally.

Keep in mind that modifications may always be made to such agreements. For instance, let's say Frank and George decide to split the maintenance equally, but at some point George is unable to come up with his share. In order that the apartment not go into default, possibly resulting in its forced sale, the maintenance must be paid. Realizing this, Frank takes up the slack and pays all monthly costs. He might then want to modify the original agreement to reflect this added responsibility. It might now read that if the apartment is sold, Frank would not only be entitled to the return of the down payment but also the additional money he provided to pay George's share of the maintenance.

YOURS, MINE, AND OURS

When two people move in together, they often pool resources, buying what's needed for the apartment or house, sharing expenses, even chipping in for high-price-tag items such as televisions and automobiles. Who retains the right of ownership if the relationship ends?

If an item such as a house is purchased jointly and meant to be a fifty-fifty proposition, co-ownership papers, which assume the property is held equally, are adequate. If the couple is not to share ownership equally, then it is best to get some kind of written agreement specifically outlining the terms of ownership. This may be accomplished by having a cohabitation agreement (a sample of which is produced in the Appendix). This agreement should discuss how property accumulated during the relationship is to be divided in the event of a breakup.

One case that illustrates this potential dilemma concerns Marcy and Jim who found an apartment and lived together in it for three years. During this time Marcy held a high-paying job in an advertising agency while Jim, a musician, spent much of the time looking for work. As a result Marcy was the main support of the household, providing the funds for furniture and an expensive stereo system. Although paid for by Marcy, these items were actually purchased by Jim, who would shop during the day while Marcy was at work with cash Marcy had given him. He kept all the receipts, which were made out in his name.

One day Jim approached Marcy and told her he was bringing another woman in to live with them, Sheila, whom he represented as his cousin. In truth, Sheila was not Jim's cousin but another girlfriend. It didn't take long for Marcy to catch on, and she confronted Jim. There was an argument. Marcy lost her temper, struck Jim, then went after him with a knife.

Jim retained a lawyer, and they went to family court, where he was able to attain an order of protection against Marcy. A week or so later Marcy returned home from work to find that her apartment had been cleaned out. Sometime during the afternoon Jim and Sheila had filled a moving van with nearly $15,000 worth of items from the apartment. Marcy tried to locate Jim, but he'd disappeared.

At this point Marcy came to us looking for legal relief. Unfortunately, because she and Jim were not married, there could be no matrimonial action. She was told she could try to find him and serve him with papers, but it would then be necessary to prove all the items he had taken were actually purchased by her and were therefore her property. What made the situation even more complicated was that Marcy had been too busy to sign the apartment lease; it was in Jim's name, which made it look as if she'd moved in with him.

Marcy had very little recourse; it would have been virtually impossible, since the receipts were in Jim's name and the items had been purchased with cash, to prove she was the actual owner of the property. If she had possessed better proof, she might have been able to go to the police for help. But even if she had, this kind of case would have had a low priority. Another available remedy might have been to litigate on the grounds of a constructive trust but, again, this would have been a difficult road to take.

What Marcy should have done was make sure all the purchases were in her name alone, or perhaps she should have forced Jim to sign a cohabitation agreement that would have outlined who owned what property. On the other hand, if Jim and Marcy had been married, she could have recovered at least up to half the value of the furniture he took, regardless of whether or not the receipts were in her name.

Some couples maintain a joint bank account and pay for items by splitting costs in some equitable fashion. Because funds are commingled, it is virtually impossible to establish who pays for what. With a proper cohabitation agreement, however, couples may avoid potential problems by being as specific as they like, even down to establishing who gets which record albums.

The first thing a cohabitation agreement might list is the property owned exclusively by each party on entering the relationship. If the woman moves into the man's house, the agreement might state this; for example, "The parties agree that the condominium in which they live, at 355 Main Street, is owned by Robert. The furniture and furnishings of this residence are also owned by Robert, with the exception of those listed earlier as owned by Sheila." The agreement might also include a clause stating that each party is to pay one-half of their joint living expenses; that a joint checking account will be established for such payments; that all medical, dental, drug expenses, et cetera, shall be the sole responsibility of the person incurring them; and so on.

And remember, these contracts can be periodically updated to reflect new purchases or new areas of agreement.

This approach can be extremely helpful, as illustrated by the couple who buys an expensive stereo system. The woman pays for half, but the man puts it on his credit card, thus his name appears on the receipt. If the relationship ends, it will be extremely difficult for the woman to prove she contributed half the price of the stereo equipment.

This ceases to be a problem, however, if there is a cohabitation agreement stating that "everything we buy during this relationship is to be split equally, no matter whose name is on the receipt." In fact, you may even list exceptions, that is, property that is to remain in the hands of one of the parties.

Without this sort of agreement, one's rights are severely limited since oral contracts are difficult to prove in court. A cohabitation agreement should be signed by both parties. It can be executed without an attorney, but is probably strongest if both parties consult an attorney after they have drafted an initial agreement.

I would recommend using our sample agreement as a basis of discussion, then composing your own draft. Using this as a model, you won't need an attorney, other than to review the agreement and raise pertinent issues. The most conservative couple might each be represented by their own attorney, but in my opinion this is overkill. Remember, ethically an attorney can only represent one of you. Although a witness is not necessary, it does strengthen the agreement to have one. This way neither party can argue he or she didn't understand it or that it was signed under duress.

In recommending a cohabitation agreement I don't mean to frighten people into thinking that everything must be in writing and that to trust others would be a mistake. As a matter of principle, however, it might be considered a mature approach and could possibly save a lot of time, money, and heartache in the future.

BETTER LATE THAN NEVER

The ultimate protection is, of course, marriage. This was the eventual choice of Sarah and Mac, who lived together for thirty years and had a son. Why marriage after thirty years? Because Sarah wanted to be protected in order to share in Mac's inheritance after his death. If they remained unmarried, their son would inherit everything. And what about a will? Wouldn't it be just as simple for Mac to name Sarah a beneficiary? Not really. A will can always be changed, or challenged, but in this sense at least, marriage is forever.

HOW MUCH IS THAT DOGGIE IN THE WINDOW?

Another matter that sometimes arises when an unmarried couple splits up is who gets custody of the pet. As heartless as it might seem, the courts have usually deemed pets as property; therefore, the person who actually bought the animal or brought it into the home is the one who gets custody. In our experience, however, some courts, in the spirit of enlightened humanism, have actually granted visitation rights to a pet. (This situation is not limited to unmarried couples.)

COMMON KNOWLEDGE

If a married couple has irreconcilable differences and decides to divorce, the law is relatively clear as to the rights and financial responsibilities of each party. But if an unmarried couple chooses to end the relationship, the matter is somewhat more complicated even though the couple has lived together as man and wife.

For instance, let's say a man and woman live together, have children, and accumulate property, all of which is in the man's name. After ten years they decide to separate. What rights does the woman have in these circumstances? Is she, after all this time, a common-law spouse? Is she entitled to the same benefits as if she were married?

Common-law marriage is a form of marriage entered into by two people who live together, announcing they're married but without benefit of a marriage ceremony or license. Common-law marriages are recognized in Alabama, Colorado, Idaho, Iowa, Kansas, Montana, Nebraska, Ohio, Oklahoma, Pennsylvania, Rhode Island, South Carolina, and Texas.

As an example, Robert and Marilyn live together in a state that does not recognize common-law marriage. They live in that state for ten years and have a child together. Everything is in Robert's name. They split and the child stays with Marilyn. Marilyn is entitled to nothing but child support and any property that she can prove is hers.

But let's change the facts a bit. Let's say Robert and Marilyn live together for eight years as husband and wife in Oklahoma, which recognizes common-law marriage. Now they decide to move to California, which does not recognize common-law marriage. They live in California for two years and then decide to split up. Is Marilyn entitled to anything?

In this case an attorney might successfully argue that their common-law marriage is valid since it met the requirements of the state from which they came, a state they lived in for eight years. If this argument was accepted by the court, Marilyn would be entitled to all the rights that accrue from being married. Common-law marriage is treated the same as any marriage and so it is handled as if the couple was married—adhering to the rules of individual states.

Something very much like this happened recently in a New

York case although, as you'll see, it did stretch the point almost to an absurdity. Rita and John Kellard lived together as man and wife for almost thirty years. In 1985 Mrs. Kellard filed for divorce, but Mr. Kellard claimed a divorce was unnecessary since there had been no marriage. New York does not recognize common-law marriage but does recognize them if they are "contracted in a sister state" where they are considered valid.

The judge in this case decided that since the couple had held themselves out to be man and wife during overnight trips to South Carolina and Georgia where they stayed in motels while driving to and from Disney World in Florida, the State of New York would consider them to be common-law spouses. "Neither state," the judge held, "has a residency requirement nor proscribes any particular length of stay in its jurisdiction in order to consummate a common-law marriage. . . . The lengthy history of the parties' relationship, the defendant's registration of himself and plaintiff in the [motel] register as husband and wife, and sleeping overnight together and indulging in sexual intercourse satisfies the law of South Carolina as to the validity of the parties' marriage at common law in that state."

The judge applied a similar finding to the couple's two-night stay in Georgia. The judge applied the principle of "obvious public policy" in reaching this decision. Otherwise, he wrote, there would be "harsh consequences" because "the financial security of the parties is jeopardized and offspring declared illegitimate. For these and other reasons, New York courts have taken an extreme position in extending recognition of out-of-state common-law marriages, requiring a minimum of contact with such state by cohabitants of the opposite sex" claiming such marriages.

I OWE WHO?

When two people decide to live together, there is often the need to get credit, perhaps in the form of a car loan, credit card, or home mortgage. Occasionally, perhaps because one party is not working or has not established a line of credit, the burden falls to the other party.

The most common example occurs when one person in the relationship has a credit card and the other doesn't. The one holding the credit card may apply for an additional card for his or her live-in lover. Regardless of who actually uses the card, the individual whose name is on the account is responsible for the debts. This is the individual the credit card company will go after. In fact, the only remedy the card owner has to collect his or her partner's fair share of the debt is to take the other person to court.

Often, this is impractical, however, as in the case of Janet and Francine, a lesbian couple living together. Janet, an attorney, could easily attain credit, while Francine, in ill health, was unable to work. They enjoyed dining out at good restaurants, and eventually they managed to run up credit card debts, all in Janet's name, totaling close to $25,000.

After a time they ended their relationship. Francine had no money to pay off her share of the debt. In any case, Janet was the one solely responsible for paying them off because the cards were in her name. As a result she was forced to declare bankruptcy.

It's also wise to remember that when cosigning a loan or acquiring any kind of joint credit, the creditor will always go after the one with the most money, the person with the greatest ability to pay off the debt.

Another problem joint credit can bring occurred in the case of John and Susan. They lived together in a rental apartment for several years. Both were working at good jobs, and when their incomes increased to the point where it would put them in a better tax position, they decided to purchase a cooperative apartment. Each put up half of the down payment and split the maintenance equally. Shortly thereafter they decided to end the relationship.

Both were concerned about the payments due on the apartment. They knew if they failed to make them, the apartment would go into default and would be sold, probably at something below market value. As a result they approached one of our attorneys, and an agreement was worked out wherein John, who was making more money, would pay a higher share of the maintenance, and when the apartment was sold, he would realize a greater proportion of the profits.

WHERE THERE'S A WILL . . .

In cases where couples are committed to each other and yet have decided, for one reason or another, to remain unmarried, it is a necessity that they have a will to assure that their assets are properly disposed of at the time of their death. If they fail to do this, their assets will be divided in accordance with the laws of the state in which they live. In most cases this means that surviving relatives will inherit, leaving the surviving partner with nothing. The only exceptions are when both partners' names are on the deed, in the case of property, when they are beneficiaries of each other's insurance policies, or when there is a joint bank account; all of these pass outside of the will.

There may still be problems even when an unmarried couple has drawn up a will. Take the case of Mary and Herbert, both in their seventies who lived together for nearly twenty years. Herbert died, leaving a will in which he stipulated that a piece of property he owned be left to Mary. Unfortunately, the will was an old one and there was a problem probating it, leaving open the possibility that the property would revert to the state since Herbert left no surviving relatives.

The court requires affidavits from all the witnesses, and in this case they were no longer alive. The problem our attorney faced in representing Mary was establishing, first, that all the witnesses were indeed deceased, and then that their signatures on the will were valid. To do this he had to find samples of their handwriting and copies of their death certificates or other proof of their demise, all of which takes time and money.

These problems could have been avoided by attaching to the will what is called a self-proving affidavit; this means the testimony of the witnesses is taken at the time they sign the document, thus making later affidavits unnecessary in many cases.

1. If you're purchasing something together, a piece of property, for instance, make sure both names are on the deed. Or, in the case of rental property, make sure both names are on the lease.

2. Keep a list of separate property that is brought into the relationship. For instance, who owns the stereo, the television, etc.

3. Draw up a cohabitation agreement which would include individual property ownership, who pays for what items in the relationship (rent, food, etc.).

CHAPTER 2
Palimony

JUST GOOD FRIENDS

Prior to 1976 Lee Marvin was known simply as a fine actor of the tough-guy school, having starred in such films as *The Dirty Dozen* and *Point Blank*. He also won an Academy Award in 1965 for his role in "Cat Ballou." But in 1976 Lee Marvin's fame took another turn when his name suddenly became synonymous with a legal concept that entered the language as "palimony."

Palimony is really nothing more than a term for alimony paid to a live-in lover or "pal" after the relationship has ended. The logic behind this concept was simple: Since so many more people were choosing to live together instead of getting married, shouldn't the law provide protection for the unmarried partner who was, in effect, filling the role of a spouse? After all, a wife who took care of the home, raised children, and ministered to her husband was, upon divorce, entitled to share in the man's property as well as in the wealth both had accumulated, so why not an unmarried person who performed the same services?

TOUGH GUYS DON'T DANCE

Perhaps the best way to come to grips with the concept of palimony and what it really means is to take a look at the Marvin case and then examine its ramifications.

Lee Marvin and Michele Triola lived together for seven years, between 1964 and 1970. Triola was a divorcee and Marvin was married but separated from his wife at first and finally divorced in 1967. At this time Michele legally changed her last name to Marvin and gave up her acting career. The couple lived together as husband and wife until they separated in 1970. Soon afterward Marvin married another woman. It was at this time Michele Triola retained an attorney and brought an action to force Marvin to provide her with a financial settlement, as if they'd been married and divorced.

Triola argued that while she and Marvin lived together they made an oral agreement that stated they would combine their efforts and earnings and share equally any and all property accumulated. Triola also maintained that it was agreed she and Marvin would present themselves to the general public as husband and wife. Her part of this agreement was to render services as a companion, homemaker, housekeeper, and cook.

In Triola's complaint, filed by her attorney Marvin Mitchelson, she asserted two causes of action, both of which were based on the concept of an express contract. The first action asked the court to determine contract and property rights, while the second action sought to impose a constructive trust on one-half of all the property acquired during the course of their relationship, including motion picture rights worth over $1 million.

At first the trial court dismissed the complaint on the grounds that Marvin was married during part of the time he and Triola lived together; thus, to enforce any agreement between them would be contrary to public policy. What this meant was that the court refused to enforce a contract that would undermine the institution of marriage.

A higher court overturned this decision, however, ruling that Triola did have cause to bring such an action. The Supreme Court of California held that "the fact that a man and woman live together without marriage and engage in a sexual relationship does not in itself invalidate agreements between them related to their earnings, property, or expenses. Neither is such an agreement invalid merely because the parties may have contemplated the creation or continuation of a nonmarital relationship when they entered into it. Agreements between nonmarital parties fail only to the extent that they rest upon a consideration of meretricious sexual services."

The court was saying, in effect, that as long as the agreement—if, in fact, there was one—between Marvin and Triola did not hinge on an exchange of sexual favors, it would be acceptable.

The court further held that any agreement made between Lee Marvin and Michele Triola did not violate public policy by impairing any property rights that might have been held by Marvin's wife Betty because her share of community property was intact, and any recovery by Michele would come only from Lee's share.

The court summarized that "we believe that the prevalence of nonmarital relationships in modern society and the social acceptance of them marks this as a time when our court should by no means apply the doctrine of unlawfulness in a so-called meretricious relationship."

In effect, then, the court held that the fact that two persons live together without being married would no longer invalidate as against public policy any agreement reached between them that provides for support or division of their property.

What most people fail to realize is that the Marvin case did not end here. The case went back to trial, and it was there that the judge finally ruled that *no* express contract was made between Marvin and Triola and, in addition, that none was created by implied contract. This meant that Michele Triola had no contractual claim on any of Marvin's property. Although they may have lived together as if they were married, they were not. Therefore, since there was no contract between them, Michele was not entitled to share in his assets.

The court did award Triola $104,000 "for rehabilitation purposes so that she may have the economic means to reeducate herself and learn new, employable skills or to refurbish those utilized, for example, during her most recent employment and so that she may return from her status as companion of a motion picture star to a separate, independent but perhaps more prosaic existence."

On appeal, the court held that the rehabilitation award given to Ms. Triola was improper because she never raised the issue of rehabilitation in her pleadings.

Though the general impression is that this was a landmark case, the reality is somewhat less dramatic. Michele Triola came away with what was really a minimal amount of money, when the court rejected her claim that she had a contract with Lee Marvin and was therefore entitled to a portion of his assets. What was important about this decision, however, was that it was a step in the direction of protecting people who don't have the protection of marriage. The court, in its decision, held that if Marvin and Triola had had an agreement (which the court held they had not), it would have been enforceable.

What the Marvin case shows us is that unless certain criteria are met, the courts will not give an unmarried partner the same rights as one who is married. In California as in most states, there is no such thing as palimony, which means there is no statutory duty of support for nonmarried people. Instead, if there is to be any support, it must arise out of a contractual agreement made between the two people.

According to the Marvin ruling, the courts should remain free to come up with additional equitable remedies, such as money for rehabilitation. In essence, then, if a woman living with a man gives up her profession to remain at home and performs household duties (or in the unlikely situation their roles should be reversed) in the absence of a written agreement, or with no witnesses to an oral agreement, the man will not be responsible for her support once the relationship ends.

IT AIN'T OVER TILL IT'S OVER

Although the Marvin case effectively did away with the notion of palimony in the absence of a contract, this does not mean that a woman or a man may not make some kind of financial recovery when a relationship ends. What it does mean, however, is that certain criteria must be met:

- EXPRESS CONTRACT: An express contract is founded on a promise directly or indirectly enforceable by law. This contract requires mutual consent of both parties. The usual requirements for this contract include an intent to make a contract and a clear understanding of the meaning of the contract. Unless there is documentation in the form of a written agreement, the burden of proving an express contract is difficult at best.

- IMPLIED CONTRACT: Under the Marvin decision it is possible for a cohabitant to recover the value of household services, provided it's shown that it was the intent of both parties for compensation to be paid. It's interesting to note that in its decision the court said there is no presumption that these services are contributed as gifts. Quite the contrary. There is a presumption that "the parties intend to deal fairly with each other." Courts have followed the line that people cannot make contracts that exchange sexual services for other items: "Of course," the court held, "they cannot lawfully contract for the performance of sexual services, for such a contract is, in essence, an agreement for prostitution and unlawful for that reason."

- QUASI-CONTRACT: Let's say a couple lives together for a long period during which the woman performs services and aids the man in his earnings and property acquisition. During this time it may reasonably be contended that the man has been enriched. If the couple breaks up and the man gets everything, it might successfully be argued that he is being unjustly enriched since she helped him accumulate this wealth. It should be kept in mind, though, that there is no specific precedent yet for this theory of recovery. In the absence of any other argument, however, this one, tenuous as it might be, could be advanced.

- CONSTRUCTIVE TRUST: We've spoken earlier about constructive trusts which the courts may use to require restitution of something that in fairness and in good conscience does not belong to the owner alone. This is especially the case when there is evidence the property was acquired by one party, either directly from the other party or with money supplied by the other party, and that unjust enrichment resulted from either mistake or fraud.

Keep in mind that none of these theories of recovery is guaranteed to work. An unmarried man or woman in this situation could easily wind up with nothing in the absence of some kind of written contract.

PUTTING IT IN WRITING

The best protection for a couple living together, outside of marriage, is a nonmarital cohabitation agreement, a sample of which is reproduced in the appendix. Some items that should be covered in such an agreement are as follows:

1. The agreement should establish the beginning of the term of the relationship. This will effectively do away with any tendency to exaggerate the length of the relationship.
2. The effective date of the agreement should be set

forth, and the parties should define the duration of the proposed relationship (for instance, until marriage or a decision to separate). If possible, the manner in which the separation or termination of the relationship may occur should also be spelled out.

3. The financial position of both parties should be given. Each person should have a complete and understandable explanation of what he or she is giving and what he or she is receiving in return, if anything. To avoid any charge of fraud, the financial position of each party should be disclosed fully.

4. The assets and liabilities of each party should remain separate. This is best accomplished by setting forth who owns what property upon entering the relationship. The parties may also agree on what funds, if any, are to be commingled.

5. A paragraph should be included to assure each party title to gifts or inheritances received by each.

6. Earnings should be considered as separate.

7. A paragraph should be included that concerns how earnings should be applied to cover joint living expenses and purchases.

8. The agreement should spell out that its principal purpose is the mutual promise of each nonmarital cohabitant to provide companionship and home-making services to or for the other, and it should negate the idea that the agreement was made primarily for sexual services.

9. A clause should be included whereby each party waives the right to be supported by the other after separation or termination of the relationship.

10. A confidentiality clause might also be included, to protect the privacy of each party upon the termination of the relationship.

If you do choose to draw up an agreement such as this one, I recommend that each party seek independent advice. (This can be done in a low-key, non-threatening manner.) This way neither person can claim that he or she was taken advantage of by the other. Furthermore, the certification of such an agreement by attorneys for both parties is also important to make sure there are no charges of fraud, undue influence, duress, or other equitable grounds that might be used to set aside the document. Although the law in this area is still in a state of flux, the document has the strongest chance of surviving if each party has been represented by independent counsel.

MARVIN FALLOUT

The ramifications of the Marvin decision, affecting property rights for unmarried couples living together, are just beginning to be felt. It is impossible to predict the outcome of individual cases. It is unlikely that any measure of stability will be seen until the individual states pass legislation to govern the property rights of unmarried cohabitants.

This legislation will have to deal with questions such as the following: How long must the couple have resided together in order to establish a claim? Will recovery be available in same-sex relationships? Will the acquired property rights allow for wrongful death actions? Will recovery be allowed to a non-marital partner under Workers' Compensation? How will non-married couples be treated for insurance purposes? Are unmarried partners entitled to collect Social Security benefits? How will these kinds of relationships be treated for tax purposes? Will support payments be paid upon the conclusion of this kind of relationship?

In the absence of legislation, the Marvin case has opened up a fertile area of litigation that has already made itself felt on the judicial system of this country. I believe we've begun to see only the tip of the iceberg.

CHAPTER 3

Paternity

With more people living together today than ever before, it stands to reason that there are also more pregnancies among unmarried couples. In fact, according to recent government statistics, births to unwed women have increased fifty percent in the last decade, to the point where at least one of every six American babies is born to an unmarried woman.

An unfortunate situation in this country is that mothers often have difficulties collecting child support. This is not only the case with divorced women who have custody of their children but with unmarried mothers as well. However it would be a mistake to think that all married and unmarried fathers routinely shirk the responsibilities of fatherhood. Perhaps in the past, even as recently as twenty years ago, the mere mention of the word paternity conjured up visions of scores of unmarried fathers making a desperate attempt to flee from the responsibility of raising a child, but I don't believe this is always the case any longer. Although the number may be small, there is a growing trend toward fathers embracing their responsibilities.

Times have changed. I have a male friend who slept with a woman who subsequently became pregnant but chose not to tell my friend that he was the father. Some time later, however, when he learned about the pregnancy, he felt as if he'd been raped. Rather than run away from his responsibility, he was ready to embrace it, and by being kept in the dark he felt the woman had denied him this right—had, in effect, exploited him. I think his reaction was not unusual but rather proof of the male's changing role in our society.

In the matter of paternity, we will discuss several potential legal problems. For example, how does a woman go about proving who is the father of her child? What can a mother do to ensure that an unmarried father who denies paternity lives up to his legal responsibilities? What rights does an unmarried father have in regard to his child?

In general, there is one thing to remember: Simply because a couple is unmarried does not mean they and the child forfeit the protection of the law. However, it may be incumbent upon an unmarried father or mother to fight more vigorously for his or her rights; for example, a married father who deserts his wife and child and then returns after, let's say, five years might have a better chance of getting visitation rights than an unmarried father who does the same thing. Yet there is one thing you can count on: The courts will always try to rule in a way that is in the best interests of the child.

WHOSE CHILD IS IT, ANYWAY?

After living with Joe for three and a half years, Sally learned she was pregnant. The pregnancy was unplanned, and when she told Joe about it he became visibly disturbed. For several days he was moody and uncommunicative. Finally he told her he didn't want a child, he wasn't ready. His business was just getting off the ground, and he couldn't afford the expense of a child. He suggested that Sally get an abortion. She refused.

They argued and, after one particularly bitter confrontation, he walked out on her, ending their relationship.

Distraught and emotionally drained, Sally visited one of our offices in southern California, looking for someone who could help answer some of her questions. Meeting with an attorney, Sally told him that not only did she want child support but she also wanted to force Joe to have a relationship with their child.

Her attorney explained to Sally that there was no way the courts could force Joe to have a relationship with his child. At the same time he assured her that Joe was responsible for child support, even prior to the birth of the child, if he acknowledged that he was the father. Sally's attorney also told her, however, that just because Joe was legally responsible for child support did not mean she might not have trouble collecting if Joe refused to pay; collecting child support from an unwilling father in any situation can often be an arduous and painful ordeal. (This will be discussed in detail in the section on Breaking Up.)

If Joe denied paternity, it would then be necessary for Sally's attorney to obtain an order to show cause, requiring that a blood test be administered to Joe. If he refused to take this test, in California as in many states, his refusal could be used against him in court. Courts have ruled that a refusal to submit to a paternity test is tantamount to refusing to testify on the issue and, as a result, the court may draw the strongest inference against Joe on the evidence presented by Sally.

Once Joe realized how the courts operated, he was anxious to negotiate a settlement. He did insist, however, that he would have nothing to do with the child. Joe's stance effectively gave Sally a good argument for receiving a higher level of support since, without Joe being around to lend a hand, it would be necessary for her to spend a good deal more money for services such as babysitting.

In California, as in all states, there is a child support law. This legislation sets forth a formula to be applied to each parent's income. There is a minimum support level, and each parent, according to his or her ability to pay, is required to contribute an amount toward this level. The courts will always order that the minimum be met and, depending on circumstances, often urge a higher amount. Using this formula as a base, Joe finally agreed to a weekly support figure that was acceptable to Sally.

BLOOD IS THICKER THAN . . .

If there is any doubt as to paternity, the first hurdle to overcome is proving who the father is . . . or isn't. This may be accomplished by a series of blood and tissue-typing tests.

With the enactment of Title IV-D of the Social Security Act in 1975, every state has established an agency responsible for assisting mothers in bringing paternity actions and securing child support. Today nearly a dozen states have adopted the Uniform Act on Blood Tests to Determine Paternity, which outlines the procedure, admissibility, and use of blood tests in paternity proceedings.

Over the last several decades the scientific community has developed a great many refinements that have, in turn, had a serious impact on the law. Blood testing for paternity is one of those areas. The three basic paternity blood tests are Level I, which tests only red blood cell antigens using approximately twenty genetic markers; Level II, which tests red blood cell antigens, red blood cell enzymes, and serum proteins, using sixty genetic markers; and Level III, which tests red blood cell antigens, human leukocyte antigens (HLA), and red blood cell enzymes and serum proteins, using ninety genetic markers.

The Level I test produces the least definitive results and therefore, taken alone, is generally deemed unsatisfactory as proof of paternity. Level II is three times the scope of Level I, but Level III is the most definitive test of all. The combined use of all three tests, which is highly recommended, can produce an accuracy rate of up to 99.7 percent.

These strides along with scientific advances such as DNA

fingerprinting have now enabled the courts to accurately determine paternity.

Now that we know something about paternity testing, let's
return to the case of Joe and Sally. If Joe denied paternity and,
as a result, was forced to undergo the combination of blood
tests to ascertain whether or not he was the father, the test
results could show that the probability of Joe's being the father
was ninety-seven percent. If he chose to, he could still fight
Sally's paternity action by taking the matter to trial, either
before a judge or a jury. If he elected this option, with the
probability as high as ninety-seven percent, chances are the
courts would find him to be the father. If the percentage was
much lower, however, let's say in the low ninety percentile,
the burden would then shift to Sally to prove that there was,
in fact, sexual conduct between her and Joe at the appropriate
time.

HE'S MINE, ALL MINE

If a married couple with children divorces, there is no question but that the father, barring complications such as a history
of child abuse, will be granted liberal visitation rights or, if
both parents consent, shared custody. But are these same rights
available to an unmarried father? Generally the standard the
courts use is what is in the best interests of the child. Because
there are so many variables and so many complex situations,
this standard may seem at times to be somewhat oversimplified,
but the bottom line is always how the individual judge feels
the evidence supports the best interests of the child.

Several years ago we had a case in one of our New Jersey
offices that illustrates the kind of problems an unmarried father
may encounter.

Several weeks before she was to be married, Ann bumped
into John, a man she'd gone to college with almost ten years
earlier. They had coffee, reminisced about old times, found
they still had a lot in common, and made a date to see each

other again. Ann was attracted to John and, though she struggled with her conscience, she began sleeping with him. She knew it was morally wrong, but no matter how hard she tried she couldn't get herself to stop seeing John. Despite the fact that she was experiencing grave doubts about her impending marriage, she still chose to go through with it. Nevertheless, the night before she was to be wed, she slept with John for what she told herself was the last time.

Six weeks later John received a call from Ann who told him she was pregnant and that he was the father. He asked, "How do you know?" She replied, "A woman knows these kinds of things."

Months passed. Ann gave birth to a boy and then, feeling more connected to John than ever, resumed sleeping with him. Again she became pregnant. Again she told John he was the father. Again he asked, "How do you know?" He received the same answer: "A woman knows these things."

Although Ann remained married and her husband believed the two children were his, she continued to lead a double life by seeing John whenever she could. John even had contact with the children, seeing them when Ann took them to the park in the afternoon. As it happened, both children looked very much like him—Nordic, blond, and broad-faced, whereas Ann and her husband were dark-skinned, Mediterranean types.

Finally, when the pressure became too much to bear, Ann confessed to her husband that she had been seeing another man, that the children were not his, but that she was ending the affair and wanted to start all over with him. She then told John that she never wanted to see him again, nor would he be allowed any contact with the children.

John was distraught. The children were his and, though his contact had been limited, he'd still become quite attached to them. Although he knew it was over between him and Ann, he didn't want to give up contact with his children, and so he came to an attorney in one of our New Jersey offices to see if he could force Ann to grant him visitation rights.

The first thing the attorney did was see to it that John underwent a paternity test. It established the remarkably high probability that he was indeed the father of both children. Nevertheless, a judge refused to grant him visitation rights, saying that to do so would not be in the best interests of the children because it would establish too disruptive a situation for them.

Our attorney continues to litigate this matter on behalf of John, but the outcome is far from guaranteed. John faces years of litigation and high legal fees. As we can see by this unfortunate situation, John's rights were severely limited because he was not married to Ann and, in fact, she was married to someone else. If this had not been the case, barring extraordinary circumstances, he would certainly have been granted visitation rights.

THREE'S COMPANY

A man who is not married to the mother of his child is not necessarily denied visitation rights. In fact, we had an opposite conclusion in the case of Paul, a California man who, although married to Ellen, was having an affair with Tracey. Tracey became pregnant. Ellen found out about Paul's affair and that he was the father of Tracey's child but, bizarre as it may seem, she agreed to allow Tracey, who was six months pregnant, to live with her and Paul.

Not surprisingly, this odd arrangement was soon destroyed by incredible tension in the household. Paul and his wife already had a child together, and a second child in the house resulted in a change of behavior in Paul's first child. He began to vie with the infant for attention. Normally an even-tempered child, he became prone to throwing violent temper tantrums. Naturally, there was also jealousy between Tracey and Paul's wife. Finally, by the time Tracey's daughter Susan reached the age of six months, things had gotten so bad she knew she had to leave. Without telling Paul, she took Susan and left.

Paul searched for Tracey but was unable to find her. He finally approached an attorney in our Los Angeles office to see if she could help find Tracey and get him visitation rights to his daughter. Our attorney first recommended that Paul hire a private investigator to find Tracey. Simultaneously he went to court to file an order to show cause, asking for temporary custody of the child even though Paul sought only visitation privileges. Our attorney's strategy was to ask for more than Paul wanted, custody, in order to negotiate for what he really did want, visitation rights.

Paul agreed to this approach, and a search for Tracey and Susan was set in motion. Finally, after several thousands of dollars in legal and private investigation fees were run up, Tracey was found and served with court papers.

The court then granted Paul visitation rights, but it was only a matter of days before Susan, who was displeased with the judge's ruling, disappeared again, taking the child with her. At this point, because a court order had been disobeyed, the district attorney's office became involved. Although this involvement did help somewhat, the reality is that when the authorities get involved in what they consider a family matter, they don't invest much time or effort in the search. Still, it did give Paul the weight of the state on his side.

Once again Paul hired a private investigator, but a year passed before Tracey and Susan were found again. Along with his private investigator and the police, Paul stormed the house where she was living with the child, now about eighteen months old. This time, because Tracey had a history of running away, when Paul went into court he received exclusive custody of Susan until a final court hearing was scheduled.

One month later at the final court hearing Paul agreed to a shared custody arrangement. Six weeks passed without incident, but then Tracey called the police and accused Paul of sexually molesting his own daughter.

The law can be used as a sword or as a shield. At this point Tracey, who felt she was being abused by the system, took the

offensive in the only way she knew how, on the only grounds
that would allow her full custody of Susan: by showing that
Paul was an unfit father.

The police launched an investigation, and Paul was told that
while this was under way the child would have to be placed
either in foster care or in the custody of her mother. Because
he did not wish to see his daughter in foster care, Paul did what
he thought was best for the child and agreed to put Susan in
Tracey's custody.

After a thorough investigation, the police found there was
absolutely no truth to Tracey's charge, and the child was returned to the same shared custody arrangement. (Paul could
have gone on to sue Tracey for slander or abuse of process,
but that would have involved an expensive and difficult litigation).

Unfortunately, the story did not end there. Six months passed,
and Tracey got married. Her husband's job was transferred to
a city several hours away from Los Angeles, and Tracey asked
for full custody of Susan. The courts do have the right to reg-
ulate where a child goes. They generally will allow the custodial
parent to move the child if there is a valid reason, such as job
relocation. In the case of an older child, however, courts have
been known to keep the child in the same area where they've
been living for some time, thus awarding custody to the parent
who remains.

Although this case has not yet been fully adjudicated, because Tracey has a record of trying to stay away from Paul,
the chances are very slim that she will win full custody of Susan.
The laws in California, as in most states, try to promote frequent and continuing contact for a child with both parents. If
one parent attempts to limit this contact, as appears to be the
case with Tracey, the courts usually will decide against that
parent.

As you can see from this case, the courts generally treat
married and unmarried parents similarly, but an unmarried
person still carries a heavier burden. The fact remains that

society is not neutral; it still favors the married over the unmarried.

THE ULTIMATE WEAPON

Just because a couple isn't married doesn't mean there is any
less emotion when they break up. Bitterness, when it comes,
often manifests itself in a power struggle over a child. This is
exactly what happened with Craig and Liz, who had lived together for several years and had a child.

Two years after the child was born, they split up. Both were
angry, but it was Liz who felt she was the injured party. It
wasn't long before she realized she had a very potent weapon
to use against Craig—their child Carolyn. She even went as
far as to say to Craig, "The hell with you, I'm going to control
this child."

Craig, fearing that Liz would make it impossible for him to
see Carolyn, approached one of our attorneys to find out what
his rights were as far as the child was concerned and how to
enforce them.

Our attorney discussed with Craig what his aims were. Craig
said he would be satisfied with visitation rights. His attorney
nevertheless encouraged him to press for shared custody, again
as a negotiating tool, even though he was willing to settle for
less.

Shared custody, a relatively recent development in the law,
came in response to the argument that the mother was having
automatic custody while the father was always relegated to
visitation rights. Ideally, shared custody means that the child
will spend half the time with each parent. Technically, however,
this means thirty percent or more with one parent, although
this is often negotiated down to twenty-five percent.

Basically, there are two kinds of custody: legal and physical.
Legal custody entails making decisions concerning the child's
life, such as education, nonemergency medical treatment, and

extracurricular activities. Physical custody means that at least thirty percent of the time will be spent with one parent. In California, as in many other states, the preference is for shared or joint custody.

When making a decision the court will look at the time each parent spent with the child prior to the breakup. If the father never changed a diaper, never took the child to the doctor, and generally paid little attention to the child, the courts are not anxious to grant shared custody.

In this case Craig's attorney asked for an order to show cause, which is a request that the court give his client a hearing on the issue as soon as possible. Within four to six weeks a hearing would be scheduled. At that time the court would issue an order that would be in effect until the time of trial, which can be anywhere from six to twelve months.

In California, however, before the hearing goes forward the court requires both parents to attend counseling, called Family Court Services. The object of this enlightened approach is to help both parents to resolve their custody dispute through mediation. About sixty percent of the cases are resolved in this manner. Also, most attorneys will try to facilitate a settlement. Unfortunately, there are still too many cases where the bitterness remains and the parents cannot resist the temptation to use their child as a pawn. It is then left up to the judge to resolve the matter.

CHAPTER 4

Gay Rights

It has been only a decade or so since homosexual rights advocates have become openly vocal by lobbying in city, state, and federal governments for gay rights legislation; running for and winning public office; holding gay pride marches in many major cities; and generally trying to make the public more aware of the serious problems resulting from the deep, ingrained prejudice they encounter each day.

Sometimes the bias is blatant, such as when homosexuals are fired from jobs or denied a place to live simply because of their sexual preference. Other times it is more veiled, such as when they are not hired for a particular job though eminently well qualified or when they are ostracized socially.

The social stigma of being gay has and probably always will be with us, but now, added to this, is the public's fear of AIDS (Acquired Immune Deficiency Syndrome), a terrifying disease that is closely identified with the homosexual community.

Many of the problems experienced by homosexuals have been exposed in the past ten years, and as a result a growing number of people in the straight community have become somewhat more sensitive to the plight of gays. Perhaps nowhere is this more evident, symbolically at least, then in the fact that finally, in 1987, the *New York Times* capitulated and began using the term "gay" in place of homosexual in news stories (and, incidentally, at the same time the newspaper also allowed the use of the term "Ms." in place of Mrs. or Miss).

This growing public awareness of the problems experienced by homosexuals has had an impact on the law, which is in the midst of undergoing an upheaval in an attempt to deal with the changes occurring in the social arena. Cases now reaching the court system promise to have a long-lasting effect on how homosexuals are treated under the law. Further complicating the situation, however, is the fact that in many areas homosexuals are not only considered social pariahs but are also subject to archaic laws that have been on the books for one hundred years or more which make their sexual practices illegal.

BREAKING UP IS HARD TO DO

Homosexual couples living together are susceptible to the same problems that can plague heterosexual couples when they choose to end their relationship. Unfortunately, gay couples are not always entitled to the same remedies. They cannot, for instance, protect their interests by getting married. And yet the situation is far from hopeless.

Take the case of Jim and Fred who lived together for seven years. Jim was the wage earner while Fred took care of the household duties. Together they accumulated property including a Jaguar, a Lincoln Continental, and a house. The property was registered in both names.

After a terrible argument one day, culminating in a violent fight in which Jim physically assaulted Fred, Fred was thrown out of the apartment. With few assets of his own, Fred visited one of our offices in southern California to see if he could get his fair share of the property he and Jim had accumulated while living together.

Our attorney informed Fred that since both his and Jim's names appeared on the ownership papers of the property in question and since there was no marriage nor could there be, they would have to ask the court for a partition agreement. (The concept of partition comes to us from the days when this country's western territories were being settled. Two ranchers might pool their resources and purchase property of, say, forty acres. Subsequently, if they couldn't get along and took their grievances to court, the courts would often move to partition the property, giving twenty acres to each rancher. This simple remedy has carried over to today.)

In the case of Jim and Fred there is no way to split a house in half, so the courts may order it sold and then apportion the proceeds accordingly. (Litigation usually results in a buy-out agreement.)

In many localities a case like this could take as long as five years to get to court. Consequently, it may be wisest, if possible, to work out some kind of equitable agreement. Taking his attorney's advice, Fred agreed to a negotiated settlement that gave him one of the cars, and Jim paid him a fair amount for his share of the house.

Even if property is in both parties' names, it might still be a good idea to get some kind of written agreement. The reason is that having the house in both parties' names does nothing to help the person without funds in terms of the expense of litigation if it is necessary. Many contracts between two people in a relationship can include a clause concerning attorney's fees. This is helpful especially in a state like California where the prevailing party in a lawsuit is not entitled to attorney's fees. In addition, this would give the nonworking party some leverage, making it easier for him to find an attorney willing to take his case.

Another possible alternative for a homosexual couple living together and sharing property is, in the case of a house, to take title as joint-tenants with the right of survivorship. In this case, if one party dies, the property goes to the surviving partner.

TILL DEATH DO US PART

It is especially important for homosexual couples to have wills, primarily because the law will not treat them as a married couple.

The necessity for a valid will is apparent in the case of Howard and Terry. They had been living together for nearly five years when Terry found that he was suffering from AIDS. With the realization that he was dying, Terry had a will drawn up, leaving everything he owned to Howard. After months of lying ill, trying to fight off the several diseases that attacked his body, Terry finally died.

Grieving over his lover's death, Howard was totally unprepared for what happened next. Terry's parents, who could never accept the fact that their son was gay, decided to contest the will, arguing that the disease he suffered from made him incompetent at the time he wrote it. Terry's parents had no interest in Terry's money or his property per se. They were motivated to take this action because they were extremely disturbed with their son's palpable admission—which took the form of his generous bequest to Howard—that he was a homosexual.

The case has not yet gone to court, but if and when it does, Terry's parents will have an extremely difficult time challenging the will primarily because the doctor who cared for Terry can testify that his patient was competent at the time he wrote it. This case points out the necessity for a valid will. If Terry had died intestate—that is, without a will—all his possessions would have passed to his parents or, if he had no parents or close relations, to the state.

HOME IS WHERE THE HEART IS

As we've seen in an earlier chapter, sometimes a problem may arise in the case of a rental apartment when only one party's name is on the lease. The matter that concerns us here is not who has rights to the apartment if the relationship breaks up but rather what happens when the partner whose name is on the lease dies.

If a couple is married and the man dies, the woman, as his wife, retains the right to the apartment. But this is not necessarily the case with a homosexual couple, or for that matter a heterosexual couple living together without any kind of agreement. There has been some litigation in this area recently, but the results have not been clear-cut.

For instance, in 1987 a New York Appeals Court in Manhattan ruled that a homosexual whose lover died of AIDS had no right to the rent-stabilized apartment the two men shared because his name was not on the lease. In another case the same year, however, also in Manhattan, a judge ruled that a homosexual had as much right as a heterosexual to take over the lease of a deceased lover.

As can readily be seen, this is yet another area of the law that is in flux, one in which legislation will probably be necessary in order to make clear the rights of those involved.

WILL HE OR WON'T HE?

Miguel Braschi and Leslie Blanchard met in 1976 and eventually moved into an apartment in Manhattan. The two men worked together in Blanchard's hair salon and shared bank accounts, income, expenses, and a credit card, and generally lived together as "life partners" until Blanchard died in the fall of 1986. In his will Blanchard left Braschi his entire estate, amounting to almost $5 million. The will was contested by Blanchard's family.

This case, according to New York Supreme Court Justice Harold Baer, Jr., "demonstrates that a nontraditional unit [can] fulfill any definitional criteria of the term 'family.' "

There have been, of course, other cases regarding wills made by homosexuals that referred to particular and unique state laws. One such was the case of Danny Washington of New Orleans who was left property worth from $400,000 to $750,000 in the will of his lover, Samuel Wilds Bacot, Jr., which was written ten days before Bacot died in 1984. Louisiana has what is called a "concubinage" law which limits the bequests that two people living together but only "pretending" to be married can leave each other. This limit would have allowed Washington to inherit only one-tenth of Bacot's "movable property" and none of his real estate.

The judgment of the lower court was to turn over the bulk of Bacot's estate to a son he'd adopted two years before he died. However, the appellate court reversed that decision, ruling that the concubinage law did not apply to a homosexual relationship because the participants could not be said to be pretending to be married since marriage by two people of the same sex is illegal in Louisiana. In this case, then, the will written by Bacot was honored.

Undoubtedly the Braschi and Washington cases, like many others, will be appealed, and perhaps no definitive answer to questions such as these will be available until local and state legislatures are forced to deal with these matters. In the meantime, it's best to check the law in your area.

MODEL BEHAVIOR

In the past, the mere fact that one parent was an admitted homosexual meant that he or she stood a good chance of being denied custody of a child. The sexual orientation of a parent was often used to show that that parent would be an unsuitable role model for the child.

In many areas of the country this is still the rule rather than the exception. And yet today courts are beginning to ignore the sexual orientation of a parent and instead focus on the real issue: the ability to be a good parent.

In some states the courts, supported by expert testimony offered by psychologists, are rejecting the argument that a parent's sexual orientation should be the deciding factor in a custody battle. Instead they are using the criterion of "the best interests of the child," which might, under certain circumstances, be better served by the homosexual parent.

Still, homosexuals are being ruled out as custodial parents in many areas of the country, especially in those states that still have sodomy laws. In Virginia, for instance, where sodomy is outlawed, the state supreme court decided in the 1985 case of Roe versus Roe that a homosexual man was "an unfit and improper custodian as a matter of law."

What has helped liberalize the attitude of some courts in these cases is testimony by psychologists and other experts. One anonymous psychologist called as a witness in a Massachusetts case said, "There is no difference in the minor children and no evidence of sexual dysfunction to a minor child reared by a single homosexual parent." Furthermore, a 1985 survey concerning homosexual parents and their children, prepared by Dr. Robert J. Howell, a professor of clinical psychology at Brigham Young University, found that "while custody decisions have tended to reflect stereotyped beliefs or fears concerning . . . the detrimental effects of homosexual parenting practices on child development, a review of the research consistently fails to document any evidence substantiating those fears."

And finally, as reported in an article in the *New York Times* of January 21, 1987, Nan D. Hunter, director of the Lesbian and Gay Rights Project of the American Civil Liberties Union, said, "We are fighting very hard to establish the principle that a parent's behavior should not be considered by the court unless it has a negative impact on a child. It is a simple due-process principle, but it is amazing how difficult it has been to convince judges of it."

It's interesting to note that the courts in some states have become somewhat more liberal in this area. In New York State's Suffolk County, for instance, a judge recently granted custody of a child to a homosexual father.

WHO'S THAT KNOCKING AT MY DOOR?

As difficult as it may be to believe, in some states homosexuality per se is against the law. These statutes, most of them on the books for over a hundred years, make sodomy a crime. In fact, these statutes raise the basic issue of the right to privacy. Though these laws are rarely if ever enforced, the mere fact that they may be used constitutes a Damoclean sword over the heads of homosexuals. Sometimes, as you will see in the following case, that sword actually does some damage.

On August 3, 1982, an Atlanta police officer appeared at the home of Michael Hardwick to serve him with a warrant, issued because Hardwick had failed to pay a fine for public drunkenness. The man answering the door was asked by the officer if Mr. Hardwick was at home. He replied that he wasn't sure but the officer could check the house if he liked.

The officer then walked down a hall to a bedroom where the door was ajar. Inside he saw Michael Hardwick and another man performing oral sex. The officer immediately arrested both men and charged each with sodomy, a felony under Georgia law punishable by up to twenty years in prison.

Thus began a case that eventually made it all the way to the Supreme Court; the controversial 1986 decision will undoubtedly have far-reaching effects on the right to privacy of homosexuals and heterosexuals alike.

Most Americans have always been under the impression that

what we do in the privacy of our own home is just that, private. But with this decision the court chipped away at this concept by ruling that the constitutional right to privacy is not as all-encompassing as we might have thought or liked. Several authorities have even gone as far as to say that the decision in the Hardwick case was nothing less than a disaster for homosexual rights advocates.

Interestingly enough, the charges were never actually brought against Hardwick because the Fulton County district attorney refused to submit the charge to a grand jury unless there was further evidence. Nevertheless, Hardwick's attorney, Kathy Wilde, argued that this "left Michael in never-never land. The charge of sodomy could be reinstituted at any moment. That was the point at which he decided to challenge the law."

Michael Hardwick challenged his arrest for sodomy, which is defined by law as "any sex act involving the sex organs of one person and the mouth or anus of another," asserting that his rights of privacy, due process, freedom of association, and freedom of expression were abridged by his arrest.

A federal district judge initially dismissed the case on procedural grounds, but a three-judge panel of the United States Court of Appeals, taking up the case, ruled in May 1985 that the Georgia antisodomy law was unconstitutional. "The Constitution," the court held, "prevents the states from unduly interfering in certain individual decisions critical to personal autonomy because those decisions are essentially private and beyond the reach of a civilized society."

But the case did not end there; the State of Georgia chose to appeal, arguing that sodomy is an unnatural act and a crime against the laws of God and man. The state further argued that the law would help reduce the spread of AIDS.

The Supreme Court chose to hear the case and, on June 30, 1986, in a 5–4 decision, the Court ruled that the Constitution does not protect homosexual relations between consenting adults even in the privacy of their own homes. Furthermore, the Court held that the Georgia law that forbade *all* people to engage in

oral or anal sex could be used to prosecute such conduct between homosexuals.

In effect, this landmark ruling rejected what Justice Byron
White characterized as the view "that any kind of private sexual
conduct between consenting adults is constitutionally insulated
from state proscription." Justice White also noted that until
1961 all fifty states outlawed homosexual sodomy and that twenty-
four states as well as the District of Columbia still do.

Justice White further explained that the Hardwick case "does
not require a judgment on whether laws against sodomy between consenting adults in general, or between homosexuals
in particular, are wise or desirable. . . . The issue presented is
whether the federal Constitution confers a fundamental right
upon homosexuals to engage in sodomy and hence invalidates
the laws of many states that still make such conduct illegal and
have done so for a very long time." He, along with the majority
of the Court, felt the Constitution does not.

WHERE WE STAND

Today there are twenty-six states that have decriminalized
sodomy, and five of the twenty-four that still make homosexual
sodomy a crime have decriminalized heterosexual sodomy, at
least in some contexts.

Those states without a sodomy law are Alaska, California,
Colorado, Connecticut, Delaware, Hawaii, Illinois, Indiana,
Iowa, Maine, Massachusetts, Nebraska, New Hampshire, New
Jersey, New Mexico, New York, North Dakota, Ohio, Oregon,
Pennsylvania, South Dakota, Vermont, Washington, West Vir-
ginia, Wisconsin, and Wyoming.

Those states that have heterosexual and homosexual sodomy
laws are Alabama, Arizona, Florida, Georgia, Idaho, Kentucky, Louisiana, Maryland, Michigan, Minnesota, Mississippi,
Missouri, North Carolina, Oklahoma, Rhode Island, South
Carolina, Tennessee, Utah, Virginia, and Washington, D.C.

Those with a homosexual sodomy law only are Arkansas, Kansas, Montana, Nevada, and Texas.

As a result of this split in state laws, as well as the recent Supreme Court decision, homosexuals appear to be far more vulnerable than heterosexuals concerning the regulation of their sexual practices. Thus, for a homosexual couple, living together presents an even thornier set of problems and possible pitfalls, as evidenced by the abridgment of what some might consider one of the most basic of all rights, that of privacy.

Many cities and communities across the country are trying to balance the scales somewhat by passing homosexual rights laws. This is the case in New York City, where the city council, after rejecting a homosexual rights bill for fifteen years, finally enacted Local Law 2 on March 20, 1986. This law bans discrimination on the basis of sexual orientation in housing, employment, and public accommodations.

MARRIAGE

CHAPTER 5
Getting Married

Though statistics tell us that today more people than ever before are living together, this doesn't necessarily mean that couples are avoiding marriage. If anything, marriage seems to be back in style. Pick up a copy of the Sunday edition of any local newspaper and you'll see that it's chock-full of engagement and wedding announcements.

According to the latest statistics released by the U. S. Census Bureau, there were 2.4 million marriages in 1986, a drop of only twenty-five thousand from the previous year. This represents a national marriage rate of ten per one thousand people. This figure puts us somewhere in the middle between the low of 7.9 marriages per thousand during the height of the Depression in 1932 and 16.4 marriages per thousand in 1946, when soldiers returned from World War II.

Thus, in spite of all the changes in the divorce laws of the last two decades, people are still getting married. On average, however, marriages are occurring somewhat later in life as people pursue education and careers.

Couples continue to get married for many reasons, including the desire to make a formal commitment to each other, security, and having a family. But whatever the reason, certain basic criteria must be met in order for the marriage to be legal and binding.

TERMS OF ENDEARMENT

A marriage constitutes a special kind of contract, one that specifies certain rights and obligations of both parties according to state law. What makes this contract special is that, like any contract, it may be dissolved by the mutual consent of the parties involved, but only if it is also dissolved by the sovereign power of the state, which means either through divorce or annulment.

When a couple decides to marry, they are required to go through certain formalities that, taken together, constitute the marriage contract. The first, of course, is applying for a marriage license either from a marriage license bureau, circuit court, or other local agency. In order to obtain this license, the application must be signed and certain requirements met, such as age and, in a few states, a blood test given in order to ensure that both parties are free of communicable syphilis. Recently, additional states, California among them, have pending legislation for pre-marital blood testing due to the growing fear of AIDS. Presently Illinois is the only state with legislation requiring a blood test. This trend might be picked up by other states in order to help stem the spread of deadly diseases such as AIDS, although it appears to be somewhat controversial.

STATE MARRIAGE LAWS: GETTING THE LICENSE

States that now require blood tests include Georgia, Maryland, Minnesota, Nevada, South Carolina, and Washington.

The minimum age for a man obtaining a marriage license without parental consent is sixteen in Colorado and Wyoming; seventeen in Mississippi and Oregon; twenty-one in Missouri, Oklahoma, and Utah; and eighteen in all the other states. The minimum age for a woman is fifteen in Mississippi; sixteen in Minnesota and Rhode Island; seventeen in Oregon; twenty-one in Florida; and eighteen in all the other states.

There is no minimum age for a man with parental consent in Mississippi. The minimum age is fourteen in Kansas, Massachusetts, Rhode Island, South Carolina, and Texas; fifteen in Idaho and Missouri; sixteen in Colorado, Connecticut, Hawaii, Illinois, Maine, Maryland, Minnesota, New York, North Carolina, Oklahoma, Tennessee, Utah, Virginia, and Wyoming; seventeen in Washington; and eighteen in all the other states.

There is no minimum age for a woman with parental consent in Mississippi. The minimum age is twelve in Kansas, Massachusetts, and Rhode Island; fourteen in Alabama, New York, Texas, and Utah; fifteen in Idaho, Missouri, and North Dakota; sixteen in Alaska, Colorado, Connecticut, Delaware, Florida, Georgia, Hawaii, Illinois, Louisiana, Maine, Maryland, Michigan, Minnesota, North Carolina, Ohio, Oklahoma, South Carolina, South Dakota, Tennessee, Vermont, Virginia, West Virginia, and Wyoming; seventeen in Oregon and Washington; and eighteen in the rest of the states.

WE WERE MARRIED IN VEGAS BY AN AUTHENTIC ELVIS IMPERSONATOR

Once the license is obtained, the marriage must be solemnized within a certain time period with a ceremony conducted by a qualified clergyman, judge, or person appointed by the court (a clerk in the marriage license bureau, for instance).

Some states have what amounts to a legislated "cooling off" period between the time you obtain the license and the time you can marry. This is so the couple may have time to think things over, before actually going through with the marriage.

AFTER THE LICENSE: WAITING

The following states allow marriage immediately after the license is issued: Alabama, Alaska, Arizona, California, Colorado, Idaho, Illinois, Iowa, Michigan, Nevada, South Carolina, South Dakota, Texas, Utah, Virginia, and Wyoming.

In North Carolina you must wait one day; one to four days in Delaware; two days in Maryland; three days in Arkansas, Florida, Georgia, Hawaii, Indiana, Kansas, Kentucky, Mississippi, Missouri, Nebraska, New Jersey, New York, Pennsylvania, Tennessee, Washington, and West Virginia; four days in Connecticut; five days in Maine, Massachusetts, Minnesota, Montana, New Hampshire, Ohio, Vermont, and Wisconsin; and seven days in Oregon.

Some state regulations prohibit certain kinds of marriages. For instance, homosexual, incestuous, and bigamous marriages are prohibited in all states. Some states prohibit the marriage of mental incompetents, alcoholics, drug addicts, and habitual criminals. Thirty-two states prohibit marriages between first cousins.

If any state law is violated concerning the establishment of a valid marriage, it is possible that the marriage may not be legal despite the fact that a ceremony is conducted by a clergyman or other qualified official. It's also possible that if this violation is brought to the attention of the court, the marriage may be annulled. If there is any question as to the legality of a marriage, it's best to check the laws of your individual state.

Once you have obtained the license and the ceremony is completed, you are, in the eyes of the law, married.

WHAT'S IN A NAME?

One of the effects of the women's liberation movement is that is has become more common for a woman to retain her maiden name after marriage. Often this is done for either business or philosophical reasons, or when a woman marries a little later in life, because it would now be confusing to change names.

In forty-eight states a woman has the right to continue to use her maiden name. In Alabama, however, if a woman wishes to use her maiden name after marriage, she must fill out a special form; and in Hawaii the marriage license must be signed with the name you intend to use after your marriage. Generally, a hyphenated last name, combining the wife's maiden name and the husband's last name (such as Brown-Davis), is allowable simply by assuming that last name and continuing to use it. Under normal circumstances it is not necessary to change the name legally as long as both names are used.

NOW YOU SEE IT, NOW YOU DON'T

Occasionally a couple believes they've fulfilled all the requirements that constitute a legal marriage when in fact they have not. In these cases there might be no marriage, despite the fact that both parties believe otherwise.

Ann recently came into one of our offices in Queens, New York, looking for help because her divorce from John was dragging along and she was anxious to get it over with. As it happened, her husband was just as anxious since he was planning to remarry as soon as he was free to do so. Our attorney was able to expedite matters, bringing the divorce to trial quickly.

The divorce was granted by the judge in October; however, in New York a divorce is not final until the written judgment is actually signed by the presiding judge. Unfortunately, the day after the trial was completed the judge fell ill and was away from the bench for nearly a month. As a result the decree was not signed until his return in December.

Unfortunately, their lawyer failed to follow up and inform John and Ann that the divorce was not final. Two days after the divorce trial was over, John, unaware that the paperwork concerning his divorce was never completed and believing he was legally divorced, married Susan.

In late December, Ann called the attorney who had handled her divorce and told him her ex-husband would like to talk to him. The attorney, somewhat puzzled by this unusual situation, arranged an appointment. John told the attorney that after two months of marriage he could see it was not working out and he wanted a divorce. Pleased at how competently and professionally the attorney had handled Ann's case, he was wondering if he could now handle his. The first question our attorney asked was, "When did you get married?" "In September," John answered.

The attorney realized immediately that John was not legally married because he had married before the divorce decree had been signed by the judge. Since the marriage was void from the start, he could obtain an annulment (see Chapter 9 on Annulments).

John was ecstatic at his good fortune. He believed his annulment would mean that he was free of any kind of marital settlement. However, this was not necessarily the case. Though an annulment would normally free him from any kind of spousal maintenance, the courts could, under certain circumstances, require him to make a marital settlement, and any property might be subject to division on the theory of constructive trust.

John petitioned the court and was granted his annulment. As a postscript to this story, John remarried his ex-wife Ann.

WHOOPS!

There are other instances of marriages that are void simply because either the husband or the wife has not obtained a legal divorce from an earlier marriage, which means that he or she is still married. In legal terms this means that bigamy has been committed.

This is exactly what happened to Sam, who came into one of our Pennsylvania offices seeking a divorce from his second wife so he could marry a third. But Sam had never bothered to divorce his *first* wife. When Sam was first married he and his wife were living in Florida. They began having problems, eventually split up, and his wife threatened to divorce him. Before she could bring a divorce action, if in fact that's what she really had in mind, Sam moved to Pennsylvania, hoping that his wife would go through with her threat. As it turned out, she didn't, and so Sam was still married to her. This meant that his second marriage, which he'd been hoping to get out of, was really no marriage at all, so he could simply have it annulled.

Since bigamy—being married to more than one person at the same time—is against the law in this country, one might ask if Sam could be in danger of any criminal prosecution. Theoretically, of course, he could, but unless someone actually filed a complaint, it is unlikely that the authorities would find out about it. In most cases the district attorney's office becomes aware of only highly visible situations.

One of our New York offices had a very similar case, only this time there was a child involved. Joe was not divorced when he married Nancy. They lived together as husband and wife for eight years and had a child. When Joe decided he wanted out of their relationship, he simply filed to nullify a marriage which, in the eyes of the law, had never actually been a marriage. (This is not true in every state; some states would hold that there was a putative marriage since one party actually believed he or she was married.) Nevertheless, even though Joe had the marriage annulled, his child was still considered legitimate, and he was responsible for child support.

Another problem along these same lines may arise when one spouse obtains what he or she thinks is a legal divorce when in fact it is not. This happens frequently with those who answer ads in magazines or newspapers advertising Dominican Republic or Mexican divorces simply by mailing in $25. They send in their money and receive through the mail a document saying they're divorced. This document is worthless since they have never been to the Dominican Republic or Mexico and thus have not fulfilled the legal requirements for the divorce.

This is not to say that a legitimate divorce may not be obtained outside this country. If it is, however, certain criteria must be met. For instance, both parties must actually be present in that country (or, at a minimum, the spouse not present must have given consent), and both must be aware that a divorce is being sought.

LOVE FOR SALE

Though America has long been known as a melting pot, the fact is that we do have immigration laws which limit the number of aliens we allow to live here. In the past several years Congress has passed even stricter immigration laws, making the goal of becoming an American citizen even harder. Consequently, it's not unusual for illegal aliens to try to marry an American citizen solely to obtain a green card which allows them to remain in this country legally.

This is a felony and can result not only in criminal prosecution but also in the deportation of the illegal alien.

The Immigration and Naturalization Service is the government agency in charge of investigating cases where this kind of fraud or collusion is suspected. The authorities are very diligent and will interview each spouse in a separate room, asking each one questions such as, "What did you have for dinner last night?" "What TV shows did you watch last night?" "What's the color of the carpet in your living room?"—all in an effort to see if the couple is actually living together as husband and wife. If the answers they receive are not satisfactory, they will move to take the appropriate action.

A fraudulent marriage is frequently initiated by two willing parties, but at Jacoby & Meyers we've been consulted on many cases in which women were duped into marrying an illegal alien so he could remain in this country.

One case that comes to mind occurred in California. Alicia fell in love with Albert, who had come to this country from South America. He wined her and dined her, sweeping her off her feet, and once she'd fallen in love with him, he dropped the bomb: He was an illegal alien and if found out he would be deported. Alicia, upset by this news, asked if there was anything that could be done. Albert said the only thing they could do would be to get married. That way he could obtain a green card and, after a time, apply for citizenship. Since Alicia was in love, that was little enough to ask.

They were married and Albert obtained his green card, but once he did, his attitude toward Alicia began to change. He stayed out late, became abusive, called her degrading names, and then beat her up. At this point Alicia realized that the only reason Albert had become involved with her was to stay in this country. Angry and confused, she came into one of our offices to see if she could have the marriage annulled. Unfortunately, in this kind of case, annulment was not the appropriate remedy. (Although fraud could be charged, Alicia did marry Albert because she loved him, not simply to allow him to remain in the country.) Instead, our attorney told Alicia that a divorce action would have to be brought, and this is what she did.

YOU'LL HAVE TO SPEAK TO MY WIVES ABOUT THAT

Though there are no federal statutes that prohibit polygamy (having more than one wife at the same time), every state does bar this practice. However, many sociologists have presented persuasive arguments for this practice, including that of allowing polygamy at a time when communal living arrangements among the elderly are increasing and when there are far more older women than men.

Historically, state legislatures in this country have argued that polygamy is per se disruptive to the social order or, as the court in an 1890 case (Davis versus Beason) ruled, that it tends "to destroy the purity of the marriage relation, to disturb the peace of families, to degrade woman, and to debase man. Few crimes are more pernicious to the best interests of society."

While the majority of us might agree that polygamy is disruptive to the social order, this still does not necessarily mean that it is so harmful to society that it ought to be denied as a way of life for those who feel that it justifies their needs.

Nevertheless, at this time polygamy is against the law until such time as state laws are changed (unlikely) or the constitutionality of the ban is successfully argued in the courts (also unlikely).

CHAPTER 6

Prenuptial Agreements

A PERSONAL STORY

When I met Ralph, to whom I have now been married for ten years, he was living in upstate New York and I was living in New York City. We saw each other for two years and developed a very close relationship. Although we did live together for short periods of time, we always maintained separate residences, never actually moving our things into one apartment. After two years we finally decided to get married. When I told my parents they said, "Terrific. Does this mean you two will be living together?"

That wasn't as outrageous a question as it might seem. I was just starting the firm of Jacoby & Meyers in New York City, and Ralph had his architectural, real estate, and venture capital business in the Hudson River Valley. Neither of us was willing to give up our work or life-style for the other, and we didn't see any reason why we should have to. What we needed was compromise, an understanding that would best suit our particular situation.

As recently as twenty-five years ago the rules in marriage were quite clear: The man worked, and the woman usually didn't. And it was difficult to get a divorce, certainly far more difficult than it is now. One of the difficulties today is that there is very little structure to marriage. On the other hand, an advantage is that we now have the opportunity to set our own guidelines which enable us to have a structure to the marriage that suits our individual needs.

In our case Ralph and I had a unique understanding that each would continue to live primarily in his or her own place of residence and try to integrate our lives accordingly. Neither of us demanded that the other relocate. Instead we decided to develop what twelve years ago might have been considered a somewhat untraditional life-style for a married couple. Today it's far more common to have a commuter marriage since marriage itself comes in many forms, including those in which the man remains home to take care of the house while the woman works outside. Marriage as a structure still prevails despite all these wrinkles that only reflect the social changes of the past twenty-five years.

As part of our process in trying to shape what our marriage would be like, Ralph suggested it might be helpful to have a prenuptial agreement which, he said, would help flesh out the issues.

The notion of a prenuptial contract is often a threatening one to many people, and when he first proposed the idea, I must admit I was a little startled, in large part, I suppose, because it never occurred to me. But Ralph had been married before, and he was sensitive to trying to clarify the issues. Since a prenuptial agreement can be an effective tool for communication, I decided it couldn't hurt and that it might even be fun.

In the past several years prenuptial agreements have become far more prevalent. This is probably the result of two major changes that have occurred over the past twenty-five years: There are now more second marriages, and prenuptial contracts have become the accepted tool in terms of inheritance issues involving children from those first marriages. Along the same lines there has been a rise in two-income families, thus there is an interest for some to protect each spouse's individual property. These economic reasons for having a prenuptial contract reflect the growing trend of looking upon marriage not only as an emotional partnership but also as a business partnership.

The other reason for the growth of prenuptial contracts is the many changes in the divorce law. Prior to no-fault divorce, community property, and equitable distribution, the rules of divorce were far clearer. Alimony was almost always granted, for instance. But the new divorce laws are far more flexible, and it's uncertain in many instances how the courts will rule. As a result, in creating prenuptial agreements, people are attempting to formulate the rules of their own marriages and, if it comes to it, their own divorces, at least to a point. Thus, even though it may not be romantic, it is often practical to be clear up front, especially in the case of second marriages or when there is a good deal of property involved.

In general there are two motives for making a prenuptial agreement. The first is purely financial and made in order to protect property that is brought into the marriage. It can also be used to ease relationships with each spouse's family, protecting heirs, for instance. As we'll see later, this kind of agreement is normally used for second marriages where children are involved or for couples who marry somewhat later in life and each wishes to protect some assets. The second kind of agreement is primarily issue-oriented. Sometimes prenuptial contracts are a combination of the two. One might ask why a prenuptial agreement and not a will. Simply put, a will can always be changed unilaterally while a prenuptial agreement, signed by both parties, cannot.

Today prenuptial agreements are generally enforceable if they have been entered into voluntarily, if they were not considered unconscionable when they were executed, and if, before execution of the agreement, both parties have provided a fair and reasonable disclosure of their property or financial obligations.

When Ralph and I decided to get married, neither of us had very much money, so the first type of agreement—financial—wasn't really necessary. Ours dealt more with the emotional and personal aspects.

As I recall, even though I was the attorney in the family, it was Ralph who composed the first draft of the agreement. He brought up issues and then we discussed them. Often we agreed, occasionally we didn't. Those times when we didn't, and when neither one could convince the other, we simply agreed to disagree, noting those disagreements in the contract.

We were married in 1978, but when I began working on this book, it had been three or four years since I bothered to look at our agreement. When I did, some of the provisions surprised me. (In the early years of our marriage we used to amend the agreement annually, but after a number of years this ritual fell by the wayside.)

In any case, I thought it might be interesting to take a look at some of the items we included in our prenuptial agreement and use it not only as an example of the kinds of provisions people might consider but also to illustrate the differences between what we put in the agreement and the reality of what has actually happened in our marriage.

First of all, we agreed that I would keep my surname but that our children would have Ralph's name, Brill. I would use my maiden name in social situations as well as professionally. This is exactly what we've done.

We agreed to maintain residences in both New York City and upstate. We agreed that we would sell the house we owned upstate within three years and that the proceeds would go into the purchase of a new house. We also agreed that after three years, we would make more of a commitment to our New York City home. All these things we have done.

We agreed that in the summer and winter three weekends a

month would be spent upstate and one weekend in New York City. In the spring and fall, if requested by me, two weekends a month were to be spent in the city. If the request was turned down, I still had the right to remain in New York. In reality this became a non-issue since we all like to spend most weekends in the country. In actuality, when there was a question of where I'd spend the weekend, Ralph has always said, "Don't worry about it. Do what's best for you." And so neither of us has imposed unreasonable demands upon the other.

As far as the children were concerned, until they were of school age they would divide their time between the city and upstate. When they reached school age, whether they went to school in the city or the country, neither Ralph nor I would have to commute. This is a perfect example of an unrealistic assumption on our part. It was unreasonable to think that we would want to disrupt our children's lives by shunting them back and forth between the country and the city. Instead, the children stay with me in the city during the week and Ralph comes in a night or two, and on weekends we go up to the country.

Regarding income, each of us would be responsible for our own expenses such as clothing and entertainment. A joint checking account was to be established for mortgages, utilities, and the like. Bookkeeping would be rotated on a yearly basis. This didn't work out quite as planned, however, because Ralph can't stand the way I do the bookkeeping, and he also didn't want to have another bank account to worry about. Instead we did what was practical: Whoever happened to have more cash available would be responsible for the bills. In general, I handle the city and he takes responsibility for the country.

In the event of a divorce, we decided that if there was any disputed property, an arbitration panel would be chosen by us and we would adhere to their decision. Fortunately, thus far we haven't had to test this provision.

In the matter of employment, we agreed that each of us

could work until giving notice of a decision to stop. Whoever wasn't working would then be required to take on additional household duties.

We agreed to have children. A yearly decision was to be made—on my birthday—as to when we would have them, although we agreed to start a family by the time I reached the age of thirty-six. Actually, I did have a child by age thirty-seven but, frankly, by that time I'd forgotten the age stipulation was in our agreement. We had a bit of a problem as to the size of our family, though. Interestingly enough, here's another example of the differences between individual visions and reality. Ralph wanted a large family, as many as eight children, while I wasn't even sure I wanted any, though I finally compromised at two. We agreed to disagree, duly noting this in the contract. Now, interestingly, after having had two, I wouldn't mind having more while Ralph is perfectly satisfied with two. Nevertheless, we are presently expecting our third child!

When the question of vacations came up, we agreed to have two weeks together, but we also allowed for separate vacations, if desired and if possible. However, it was to be a priority to have those two weeks together.

We had several other clauses: we were supposed to start a retirement fund, which we never did; any major purchases over $500 would be discussed (in reality, the figure became somewhat higher); extra attention was to be paid to either spouse who became ill; a clause concerning religion, how to bring up the children; and in the case of the death of either of us, there was to be a mourning period. Ralph also suggested that a photograph of the deceased always be left around the house so that the children would never forget that parent. It was something I hadn't actually thought about, but once Ralph brought it up I realized what a good idea it was. There are, of course, other matters you might want to include in an agreement. You might consider a clause about getting counseling if any serious problems arise during the marriage, or you might mention other relationships outside of marriage or even about sex within the marriage.

Finally, we agreed that each year amendments to the contract would be made, if necessary. This was to be done on our anniversary each year.

As I recall, the contract was signed the morning of our wedding. Over the first three or four years we were married we did, in fact, make several amendments to the contract. We've always made it a habit to go away for at least a long weekend on our anniversary and, in the beginning at least, we took along our contract and reviewed it. As I've mentioned, we haven't done this recently.

It's also important to understand that we drew up our agreement in a light spirit of good will. Nevertheless, it turned out to be a very positive vehicle for communication, and I think it helped set some of the ground rules for our relationship. Issues we hadn't really articulated or even thought of before were spread out on the table, issues that were best discussed before we got married. I think prenuptial contracts such as ours can be a very useful tool in the first couple of years of marriage. But after a certain number of years of marriage you inevitably begin to accept your spouse for who he or she is, and you find other ways of working out your problems.

There are some things, however, that probably ought not be put in an agreement, and both spouses should be sensitive to these areas of potential conflict. It's important to be flexible and trust the other person. In our agreement, for example, there was that clause about each spouse paying his or her own bills. Well, that's fine, but occasionally it's nice to break that rule. I'm taking horseback riding lessons now. It's only a matter of a small amount of money, but Ralph pays that bill as a gift to me, and I'm very pleased with the idea. I think it's because no matter how liberated women become, there is still that part of us that wants to be taken care of, and Ralph's gesture fills that need.

Friends of mine recently drew up a prenuptial contract, and

theirs was far more comprehensive than Ralph's and mine. Besides including many of the same ideas, they also inserted clauses such as:

- Each party realizes the other is very career-oriented and will regularly work long hours. However, one weekend day and one week night must be set aside— whenever possible—for nurturing the relationship. In addition, a full weekend once every two months shall be set aside for recreation or non-office-related work on projects.

- The husband shall have the option of spending the night of December 24 each year with his family.

- The wife has the option of spending one holiday a year with her family.

- Each realizes that each brings inevitable personality quirks into the relationship. Instead of necessarily accepting these without discussion, each retains the right to express disapproval. Once such disapproval is expressed, the other must decide whether he or she is willing to take steps to change such behavior and, if so, determine what these steps should be.

- Fidelity is expected, and a lapse by either partner is grounds for divorce.

- Each partner has the right to refuse specific sexual requests.

- Each partner is expected to have friendships of both sexes and is expected to exercise appropriate sexual behavior.

I think it's important to realize that these kinds of contracts are not writ in stone. Unlike financial agreements, they breathe a little, and perhaps that's all to the good. They are concerned with the so-called soft issues of marriage, issues that the courts will not and cannot enforce. No court is going to rule on a provision concerning who does the dishes in a marriage, nor is a court likely to enforce a provision like ours concerning the appointment of an arbitration panel to deal with disputed property in the event of a divorce. And yet these provisions do serve a valuable purpose. They are thought-provoking and might even work to avoid future acrimony in a marriage.

Again, although most prenuptial agreements deal with economics, they may also be used on a personal level to promote better communication in the marriage, and for this reason they may be written at any time during the marriage.

FIRST THINGS FIRST

Though our prenuptial agreement dealt primarily with the "soft" issues of marriage, when most people think of these kinds of agreements they think immediately of money and property. In fact, prior to the 1970s, prenuptial agreements were made mostly to protect an inheritance for children from a previous marriage in the event of the parent's death as well as to protect substantial wealth held by one spouse.

The experience of our firm indicates, however, that most of the recent changes in the divorce laws across the country have given rise to a new popularity for prenuptial agreements, not only for those marrying for the second or third time but also for professional couples, those with thriving businesses, and even those getting married for the first time who are aware that nearly one out of two marriages ends in divorce.

Equitable distribution and community property laws, which no longer guarantee a spouse sole ownership of property simply because his or her name is on it, is one reason for the growing prevalence of prenuptial agreements. This has caused some spouses, fearful of losing property they consider theirs alone, to go the route of a prenuptial agreement in order to hold on to what they believe is rightfully theirs.

Some believe that preparing a prenuptial agreement is too pessimistic, almost bordering on being a fatalistic act, presupposing the end of the marriage. But in reality it is in many cases simply a practical way of dealing with a possible eventuality, in much the same way that writing a will simplifies what happens to your estate after your death.

When contemplating a prenuptial agreement it is important to remember that the legal ground rules governing these contracts vary from state to state, and sometimes even within the same state. Thus it is important to find out how the judicial system where you live views these documents. Since prenuptial agreements are relatively new, the law in this area is still changing, which is why it's probably best to get some legal advice.

Until recently there have been few guidelines for prenuptial contracts. In 1979, however, the National Conference of Commissioners on Uniform State Laws appointed a committee to draft a marital property act. In July 1983 the committee issued a report and approved a Uniform Marital Property Act. Though this act has been adopted by no more than a handful of states, it is still a useful tool in predicting how the courts will view prenuptial contracts. In summary, some of the things covered by the act are as follows:

1. Property acquired during marriage is marital property. Both husband and wife have an undivided one-half interest in their marital property.

2. Individual property includes property owned before marriage or acquired at any time by gift or inheritance and appreciation of individual property not resulting from substantial personal effort of the other spouse.

3. Presumptions aid in the identification of marital property, and simple rules, based on a time continuum, are provided for the sorting out of marital and individual property components of life insurance, pensions, and other deferred employee benefits that straddle the date of marriage. In other words, in many cases the court will presume that certain property used by both parties is owned by both parties.

4. Broad scope is granted to husbands and wives to

enter into marital property agreements that may vary
the effect of the Uniform Marital Property Act. Marital property can be held in survivorship form or
transferred to trust without losing its marital property characteristics if this is what the spouses want.

The courts have generally held that prenuptial-type agreements are not against public policy if, when executed, three
basic conditions are met. First, they are entered into freely,
without fraud, duress, coercion, or overreaching; second, there
is full disclosure and a full understanding of the value and extent
of the property in question; and third, the terms of the agreement are not written to promote divorce or profiteering by
divorce.

This last point about the promotion of divorce has been one
of the most compelling arguments against upholding prenuptial
or antenuptial (those made during the marriage) agreements.
Some courts have felt that the drafting of these agreements
in some way anticipates the breakdown of the marriage and
thus tends to encourage divorce, which is a violation of public
policy.

However, lately courts have taken the opposite view; that
is, that such agreements instead of destabilizing the marriage
tend instead to promote marital stability by defining the expectations and responsibilities of each spouse. In a 1985 issue,
the *Journal of Family Law* reported as follows concerning Frey
versus Frey in which Mr. and Mrs. Frey signed an antenuptial
agreement providing that upon divorce or separation each would
retain sole ownership of individual property possessed before
the marriage or thereafter acquired as though the marriage had
never occurred: "Courts have also recognized that the roles of
husband and wife have changed over the years. With more
married women entering the job market, the need for an award
of alimony has decreased. Moreover, the court noted that the
state no longer has an interest in preserving a marriage that is
irretrievably broken. Public policy with respect to divorce has
changed and is reflected in the significant percentages of mar-

riages that end in divorce and the appearance of 'no fault' divorce statutes."

Courts have failed, however, to recognize prenuptial contracts which they consider "unconscionable." In other words, if the agreement appears unfair to either spouse, it will not be upheld by the courts. Furthermore, the courts have even ruled against such an agreement if it appears to be unconscionable twenty years after it was signed. For instance, if at the time of signing the husband's business is worth under $100,000 but twenty years later, at the time of divorce, it has grown to a net worth of several million, the courts are unlikely to feel bound by the original agreement.

In respect to the content of premarital agreements, the Uniform Marital Property Act states that it may contain, among other things,

> the rights and obligations of each of the parties in any of the property of either or both of them whenever and wherever acquired or located; the disposition of property upon separation, marital dissolution, death, or the occurrence or nonoccurrence of any other event; the modification of spousal support; the making of a will, trust, or other arrangement to carry out the provisions of the agreement; the ownership rights in and disposition of the death benefit from a life insurance policy; and any other matter, including personal rights and obligations, not in violation of public policy or a statute imposing a criminal penalty.

The act further states that

> the right of a child to support may *not* be adversely affected by a premarital agreement; that the agreement takes effect upon marriage; that after marriage a premarital agreement may be amended or revoked only by a written agreement signed by the parties.

The reason that the right to child support may not be adversely affected by any prenuptial agreement is that the state has an overwhelming interest in seeing to it that all children are provided for. For this same reason the court will not accept a prenuptial agreement that leaves one spouse destitute and likely to become a public charge. The court has the right to modify any agreement that it feels is unreasonable toward one spouse or toward the children of the marriage.

MONEY TALKS WHEN SOMEBODY WALKS

We've already seen what my prenuptial agreement, primarily concerned with the so-called soft issues of marriage, looks like, but how about one that deals primarily with the nuts-and-bolts financial side of marriage?

In addition to dealing with the soft issues, an example of issues covered in an agreement recently prepared by one of our attorneys included the financial responsibilities each spouse was expected to fulfill. Some of those were as follows:

- Each party is responsible for maintaining and/or developing a credit history.
- Each party is responsible for maintaining his or her own medical plan.
- Each has the option of taking up to one year off for a "project" such as a book or screenplay. If the other contributes financially or in some other tangible way during the time period, he or she will receive a proportionate share of any profits, to be agreed upon on an individual basis.
- Graduate studies: Any support toward one partner's advanced degree entitles the other partner to a percentage of earnings resulting from the degree—the exact amount or percentage to be determined in advance.
- Career moves: Each partner realizes that career moves may put each partner in a different city, and com-

muting is an option up to one year. Then it has to be
renegotiated.

- If the marriage lasts less than five years and if there
  are no children, each partner forgoes maintenance or
  support. (This clause might be considered against
  public policy and therefore unenforceable in some
  states.)
- IRA: Each partner is responsible for maintaining an
  IRA account with yearly contribution goals of $1,000.

We had another agreement that included these traditional
issues but also went as far as noting how the offspring of their
male and female cat would be distributed.

Other prenuptial contracts limit the claims to the amount of
money each spouse is entitled to in the event of a divorce.

By now we're all familiar with the Joan Collins–Peter Holm
divorce case, which was front-page news for weeks during the
summer of 1987. Holm, after being married to Collins for thirteen months, was asking for a settlement worth $2.8 million,
which was an even split of the $5.6 million Collins had earned
during the time of their marriage, and temporary support of
$80,000 a month.

Unfortunately for Holm, however, he had signed a prenuptial agreement with Collins that limited the amount of any
divorce settlement to twenty percent of any income accrued
during the marriage. After a dramatic five-day settlement hearing, followed closely by the news media, the court found that
the premarital contract signed by Collins and Holm was valid,
thus limiting Holm's settlement to twenty percent of that $5.6
million. It's obvious from the court's ruling that Ms. Collins
was wise in getting Holm to sign a prenuptial agreement; it
resulted in saving her almost $2 million, which Holm would
have been entitled to under California's community property
divorce law.

ADVICE TO THE LOVELORN: WRITING THE AGREEMENT

There are a few things to remember if you do decide to enter into a prenuptial or antenuptial agreement. First of all, it's advisable for both parties to be represented independently by an attorney. Although one attorney might draw up the agreement, the other party should still have the document reviewed by his or her own attorney. This will serve to strengthen the document, thus possibly eliminating problems later on. It's also a good idea to familiarize yourself with your rights under your particular state's divorce or inheritance laws before any consideration is given to waiving them in a pre-nuptial agreement.

Make sure you and your partner are willing and able to make full disclosure of *all* your assets. If not, a court is un-likely to accept any agreement that you make.

The courts are particularly interested in the "fairness" of any prenuptial or antenuptial agreement. For this reason it might be best to include modifications into the agreement. For instance, there might be periodic escalations of property ownership or alimony. In other words, the amount of alimony given for three years of marriage might not be considered fair for someone married fifteen years. You also would want to take into consideration the cost-of-living index. An amount that seemed fair in 1970 may be ludicrous in 1988.

If you keep in mind these and some of the other things mentioned in this chapter, the chances are that a court will uphold your agreement if it is in a jurisdiction that accepts the notion of these kinds of contracts.

ALL BETS ARE OFF

The notion of a prenuptial agreement might sound great, but it doesn't always work out that way. Some relationships simply cannot bear the weight of these documents. It wouldn't be fair not to tell the tale of a couple who came into one of our offices to negotiate such an agreement. All issues were covered, but there were several areas that simply could not be agreed upon.

The couple finally went home to discuss the matter further. The main sticking point was financial. The prospective husband wanted his prospective wife to agree to a limit to the amount of money she would receive in the event of a divorce, and she was hesitant to do this. One week later our attorney received a call informing her that the wedding had been called off, in large part due to the impasse concerning the prenuptial agreement. Of course the realists among us might argue that it was better this marriage was called off when it was since it was obviously doomed to failure.

Many women, especially, sign prenuptial agreements that are not in their best interests. If you are going to agree to a prenuptial agreement, however, it's always better to seek a percentage rather than a fixed amount; that is, the amount should be determined by family income.

Prenuptial agreements are not for everyone, and we certainly don't mean to suggest that they are. Over the past several years, however, our attorneys have noticed a growing demand for these agreements. They can be especially useful for second marriages where a spouse wants to protect the inheritance rights of his or her children from a prior marriage.

Although prenuptial agreements are not ironclad, courts across the country are taking them far more seriously. For instance, a New York appellate court recently upheld the validity of a Westchester couple's contract despite the fact that the man failed to disclose his financial status fully. And an appellate court in Kansas upheld a contract signed an hour before the wedding in which the divorced wife of a multimillionaire was to receive only $24,000 a year in spousal support.

For these reasons alone it's wise to involve an attorney when contemplating a prenuptial contract.

CHAPTER 7

Your Rights
and Obligations
in Marriage

A REAL LIFE FAIRY TALE

Once upon a time, in the not so distant past, in a land not so very far from here, where people fell in love and got married, for rich or for poor, in sickness and in health, the marriage vows included the phrase "love, honor, and obey." It was only a generation or two ago, prior to a movement in the land some called women's liberation, that few women would have thought of questioning the notion of obeying their husbands.

In the not so distant past, in this land not far from here, the man was often considered the "king of his castle" and the woman little more than his serf, there to do his bidding by cleaning house, ministering to their children, and seeing to his overall well-being. And perhaps, if she fulfilled all that was expected of her, she might then be "rewarded" with a new dress or a night on the town.

And once upon a time in this land, a mere thirty or forty years ago, there were statutes that set forth an extensive series of rights and obligations that a married couple had to follow, with most of the rights going to benefit the husband and the obligations falling to the wife.

But the people in this land finally saw the light. The word "equality," which had always been in the dictionary of this land, though it was rarely used in regard to marriage, was suddenly discovered. And today, after decades of struggle, more of a balance has been struck between husband and wife.

THE WAY IT IS NOW

Today we have reached a point where we have also begun to achieve a balance, delicate as it may be, in the relationship between men and women. It is a balance that is reflected even in the way we now refer to the married couple. Presently, in many states, instead of using the traditional terms of husband and wife, each member of the married couple is referred to by the unisexual term "spouse."

We have reached the stage where marriage is considered more of an economic partnership than a contract defined by roles. But as in partnerships each member has certain rights as well as certain obligations. What we're alluding to here are not those obligations and rights that any well-intentioned, moral, and sensitive human being offers to anyone he or she is involved with, but rather those marital rights and obligations that are protected by law.

There really aren't too many of these rights and obligations. Nevertheless, many people are not fully aware of what these include until they suddenly find themselves in a position in which something is awry. At this point they might well wonder, "Can my spouse do this to me?" or "Do I have the responsibility to provide this service?" or "If my spouse does have to provide this service but is lacking in performance, is there anything I can do about it?"

TROUBLE SPOTS

It's well known that the majority of problems within a marriage revolve around sex and money, though not necessarily in that order. And, not surprisingly, that's where the rights and obligations within a marriage fall.

The reality is that many of these matters of marital responsibility do not arise until there is already a problem in the marriage, a problem that often leads to divorce. And yet, if both spouses became aware of what they "owe" each other as well as exactly what they are entitled to, perhaps these problems can be straightened out before they reach the stage of consulting a divorce attorney.

WHAT DO YOU MEAN YOU'VE STILL GOT A HEADACHE?

Generally speaking it's the law that one spouse cannot deny sex to the other without good cause. This is one of those laws, however, that is virtually unenforceable, not only by the state but also by either spouse. In fact, if one spouse attempts to force sex on the other, in many states this could be considered rape and, in others, assault and battery.

In some states failure to have sex for more than one year constitutes grounds for divorce. (This does not apply, however, to an inability to have sex, perhaps the result of some disability.) In New York these grounds are called "constructive abandonment." Constructive abandonment in divorce cases offers a far less embarrassing and less potentially painful out than mental or physical cruelty, or adultery, and is used as a convenient and expedient compromise grounds for divorce.

The whole thing may be thought of as something like a well-choreographed dance in which the participants, the husband and wife, both lawyers, and even the judge, are willing to accept these grounds in order to obtain a divorce.

You can't always count on the cooperation of everyone involved, however. We once had a case in one of our New York offices in which the judge refused to believe one spouse was withholding sex from the other. It seems that although the husband wanted the divorce and claimed "constructive abandonment," saying that his wife refused to have sexual relations with him for more than a year, his wife denied his allegations. She didn't want the divorce and argued that she was perfectly willing to have sex with him but that he wasn't interested. The judge in this case believed the woman and refused to grant the divorce.

In cases like these, it may be argued the marriage is so irretrievably broken that the divorce should be granted despite the fact that the grounds may be a convenient charade. Some judges, however, going strictly by the book, refuse to compromise by playing along. In this particular case the husband tried again, at which time his wife, after negotiating a more favorable settlement, chose not to contest.

Prior to 1980 Pennsylvania was a state in which you needed fault to obtain a divorce. As a result, something called "indignities" was the most popular grounds for divorce. "Indignities" included anything from physical abuse to a spouse who ate peanuts in bed and then deliberately threw the shells on his or her partner's side and to problems of sexual relations within the marriage. Consequently, if one spouse totally withheld a sexual relationship from the other, this could be considered an "indignity" to the marriage, thus constituting grounds for a divorce. Now, however, since Pennsylvania has joined the ranks of no-fault divorce states, the matter of withholding sex within the marriage is moot.

In states such as California and Pennsylvania, which recognize no-fault divorce, refusing to have sex with your spouse is not an issue since particular grounds for divorce are not necessary. If a husband or wife is dissatisfied with his or her sex life and the problem cannot be worked out, he or she may simply file for divorce without having to resort to such grounds as "constructive abandonment" or "indignities."

There is, in some states at least, an obligation to have sex in marriage, but this is not to be taken as a license to have *any* kind of sex if it is not agreed to by both spouses. We had a rather strange case in New York in which Katharine came into one of our offices looking for help. She had been married to her husband for some time, and one day he told her that he wanted to do, in her words, "some kinky stuff" in bed. What was this "kinky stuff"? Well, to put it as delicately as possible, he wanted to partake of a certain all-American dessert using a portion of her anatomy as the dining room table.

At first, Katharine objected. Finally, however, after days of prodding and cajoling, she agreed. She wasn't particularly thrilled with the idea, but when her husband then wanted to add two different-flavor desserts to his nocturnal diet, well, that's where she decided to draw the line.

"It was disgusting," she told our attorney. As a result she got turned off completely and refused to have any kind of sex, kinky or not, with her husband. He threatened divorce. Was he, she wondered, entitled to a divorce simply because she refused to have sex with him?

The answer was, in New York State at least, yes. If she continued to refuse to have sex with him for more than a year, he could sue for divorce using the grounds of the aforementioned "constructive abandonment."

It should be pointed out that if things have reached this point in a marriage, the couple might be ready for a divorce or at least counseling. Since Katharine could not bear to have sexual relations with her husband, thus coloring their whole relationship, the marriage was, at a minimum, on the road to breaking down.

MAKING ENDS MEET

There are, of course, other, nonsexual rights in marriage. For instance, a married couple does not relinquish any civil rights that have been granted under the Constitution. You may,

for example, individually own property, obtain credit, negotiate and sign contracts, carry on business activities, and hold
on to your own earnings. If there is a divorce, however, individual property and money may be subject to division.

Marriage also grants each spouse rights to the other's estate
and, depending on the state in which you reside, you are also
entitled to a portion of the assets acquired during the marriage
(subject to the rule of either community property or equitable
distribution).

Generally speaking there is a legal obligation to provide
necessities for one's spouse. These necessities include food,
clothing, and a roof over one's head. This obligation to support
is dependent, of course, on there being the money to do so. If
there is no money, then there is no obligation. For instance,
if the husband loses his job, has trouble finding another, and
runs out of money, the wife would not be able to take him to
court to force him to provide for the family, or vice versa.

This brings up the question of whether either spouse has an
obligation to work. Interestingly enough, the law recognizes
either spouse's right to choose to be financially dependent upon
the other. In this case, the nonworking man or woman is considered a "dependent spouse" and has no obligation to provide
for the family's financial support as long as the other continues
to be the breadwinner.

We had an interesting case in one of our Pennsylvania offices.
Judy came in and said that her husband provided her with the
barest of necessities but stopped there. She said that he didn't
even provide her with enough money to buy proper clothing
for herself or enough money to travel outside the home. In
fact, she had to borrow bus fare from a neighbor in order to
come to our office.

Unfortunately, Judy was stuck. She didn't have enough money
to move out of the house. If she had, she could have gone to
court to receive support, arguing that she was living in an
intolerable position. She was, in short, in a Catch-22 position.
She couldn't get any more money from her husband while she
stayed in the house, and she didn't have enough money to

move out so she could force him to give her financial support beyond the bare necessities.

She wanted to know if our office could do anything to make her husband loosen his grip on the family purse strings. At that time, 1980, in Pennsylvania, there was nothing we could do for Judy. Since then, however, there has been a movement toward helping people who find themselves in Judy's position. Now there is greater leeway. Pennsylvania, along with many other states, does allow the courts to order support within a marriage. It's not easy to get, but it is possible.

The process usually includes going to Family Court, proving that the situation is intolerable, and then persuading the court to give equal management control of the finances, including access to the family bank account.

Thus there is a possibility that a court may order your spouse to maintain you in a style consistent with his or her financial position. More likely than not, however, the courts will steer clear of what might be considered purely a family matter and leave it up to the spouse to set the standard of living for the family. The reason for this is that all the law actually demands is that either spouse prevent the other from becoming a public charge.

MAID SERVICE

In this time of equality among the sexes, another question is raised. If both spouses work and share the financial burden, is the man obligated to share the housekeeping burden with his wife? The answer is that legally there is nothing the woman can do to make sure her husband shares the housekeeping chores with her. This is, rather, something that could be worked out in a prenuptial agreement.

If both spouses work and one earns more than the other, this does not necessarily mean that he or she must contribute more to pay the marital expenses. Again, the law simply says that the couple must support each other, leaving it up to you to figure out how best to do this.

CHAPTER 8

Property Ownership, Debt, and Credit in Marriage

A WOMAN'S PLACE

Historically, marriage has been somewhat paternalistic in structure. In return for the promise of a man's financial support of the family, the woman tacitly agreed to provide a solid home life for her husband, which included certain traditional housewifely duties such as cooking, cleaning, and taking care of the children. If there was a divorce, the courts looked exclusively to title to determine who had rights to any property. If the husband's name was on everything, the wife got nothing except a settlement that generally included alimony. (In some situations the wife might have received an additional settlement based on the theory of constructive trust.)

There was a balancing effect, of course, since years ago it was far more difficult to get a divorce. As a result there were tradeoffs. If the man wanted a divorce badly enough, the woman was often in the position of demanding a higher settlement. However, if it was the woman who wanted the divorce, she was usually without leverage.

This is no longer the case today. The law is gender neutral, and marriage is now looked upon more as an economic partnership between the husband and wife. This economic partnership is even reflected in changes that have occurred in how the law views who owns what within a marriage—no longer is title considered the determining factor. Both equitable distribution and community property laws guarantee, or at least make the attempt to guarantee, that a woman (and in some cases a man) gets her fair share of what are considered to be the marital assets. Simply because one spouse does not work outside the home does not mean he or she has not contributed valuable assets to the marriage. Certain intangibles such as raising children and taking care of the home are factored into the equation, thereby entitling the nonworking spouse to a fair share of property acquired during the marriage.

In order to understand the changes that have occurred during the past twenty-five years or so, it's helpful to turn back the clock to the 1950s. Men returning from the war were getting married in record numbers, and women, who during wartime took jobs outside the home to aid in the war effort, found themselves back inside the home. As a result women who married during this period were thrust into the somewhat unfamiliar traditional role of homemaker.

Nowhere is this more evident than in a report of the daily life of a "typical" housewife that sociologist Mirra Komarovsky published in 1953 and which has been reproduced in Sylvia Ann Hewlett's book, *A Lesser Life: The Myth of Women's Liberation in America* (Warner Books, 1987).

> I get up at 6 A.M. and put up coffee and cereal for breakfast and go down to the basement to put clothes into the washing machine. When I come up I dress Teddy (1 ½) and put him in his chair. Then I dress Jim (3 ½) and serve breakfast to him and to my husband and feed Teddy.
>
> While my husband looks after the children I go down to get the clothes out of the machine and hang them on the line. Then I come up and have my own breakfast

after my husband leaves. From then on the day is as follows: breakfast dishes, clean up the kitchen. Make beds, clean the apartment. Wipe up bathroom and kitchen floor. Get lunch vegetables ready and put potatoes on to bake for lunch. Dress both children in outdoor clothes. Do my food shopping and stay out with the children until 12. Return and undress children, wash them up for lunch, feed Teddy, and put him to nap. Make own lunch, wash dishes, straighten up kitchen. Put Jim to rest. Between 1 and 2:30 depending on the day of the week, ironing, thorough cleaning of one room, weekend cooking and baking, etc.; 3 P.M. give children juice or milk, put outdoor clothes on. Out to park; 4:30 back. Give children their baths. Prepare their supper and help put them to bed. Make dinner for husband and myself. After dinner, dishes and cleaning up. After 8 P.M. often more ironing, especially on the days when I cleaned in the afternoon. There is mending to be done; 9 P.M. fall asleep in the living room over a newspaper or listening to the sound of the radio; 10 P.M. have a snack of something with my husband and go to bed. (pages 324–25)

In the 1950s this daily routine of the American housewife was the rule rather than the exception. In the 1960s, however, individualism, dormant since the 1920s and buried alive, one might say, in the conformist age of the 1950s, began to force its way to the surface. Men and women, especially those whose consciousness was raised by additional educational opportunities, were learning to assert themselves. In comparison to the "gray flannel suit" days of the 1950s, the decade of the sixties was represented by splashes of color as Americans strived to stand out from the crowd rather than become part of it. As a result the sixties became a time of upheaval and rebellion, a time when the youth of this country began questioning both the moral and ethical values that had been presented to them by their parents.

Thus the decade of the sixties, rather than representing traditional values, stood instead for a breakdown of tradition.

Fundamental and sometimes radical changes were afoot. Movements such as Women's Liberation began picking up steam while civil rights activists began to make themselves felt throughout the country. Some years later, near the end of the decade, this activism spilled out onto the streets in sometimes bloody confrontations with authorities as these "children" of the sixties protested bigotry and racism and the war in Vietnam. But whatever the cause, there always seemed to be something to rebel against, some social ill that needed to be redressed, something to march about.

The introduction of the birth control pill also changed the status of women in this country. The pill created "liberated" women, giving them the freedom of choice to go out into the world. By giving them the ability to postpone having children, the pill allowed them the opportunity to solidify their place in the work force and thereby fulfill their ambitions.

The rebellions of the 1960s led to another phenomenon, one that the writer and social commentator Tom Wolfe called the "Me Generation." Perhaps this was nothing more than the inevitable backlash from the seemingly selfless social awareness of those interested in, among other things, the civil rights of women and minorities. But whatever the reason, the term "self-awareness" became de rigueur, as people all over America began a search for happiness through self. This search eventually gave rise to popular self-help groups, such as Werner Erhard's est training, and visits to Eastern gurus in an attempt to reach the "inner psyche," locate the true meaning of life, and thereby find true happiness.

In some ways a result of this upheaval, traditional roles for women began to fall by the wayside. No longer was a woman supposed to be satisfied staying at home and caring for her family. Now she was expected to pursue her hopes and dreams as far as they might take her.

I was certainly not immune to what was going on during this turbulent period. Growing up in the midst of these social changes, early on I internalized the message that I was always going to have to take care of myself. For some reason I never expected to get married, and so I knew I had to become self-sufficient.

For me the answer was to become an attorney since I looked upon the law as a potent vehicle for social change. As it turned out, by co-founding the firm of Jacoby & Meyers I was able to create the perfect balance of trying to remain self-sufficient while at the same time helping to make fundamental changes in the system.

It wasn't always easy. As I recall, only three percent of my law school class was comprised of women, and we weren't always treated seriously. As a matter of fact, the first time I was called on by one of my law professors he announced in front of the class, "Miss Koff, would you please stand up so we can all see the dimensions of this case."

I remember being very confused at the time about what I was feeling. Not only were there very few women in law school, but they were either engaged or married. As for me, marriage was the furthest thing from my mind. I thought I had to create a life for myself first. I needed to define *myself* before I could successfully maintain a relationship with another person.

Looking back, I now realize my life went through certain very distinct periods. In my twenties, like many in my generation, I focused primarily on myself; in my thirties I focused on my marriage and my business; and now, in my forties, I find that I focus on my family and my business.

During this period of change, marriage, too, began to evolve. What had always been something of an unequal partnership now, partially through the prodding of feminists such as Gloria Steinem and Betty Friedan, began to take on the characteristics of a truly equal partnership, economically if not emotionally.

Slowly, this economic partnership began to be reflected in laws that were passed regarding property ownership. This evolution in the law continues as courts struggle to synthesize these changes in the social structure and the emerging relationship between men and women.

Ironically, some women, caught up in this transitional period, have found themselves to be the casualties of changes in the rules of the game that have taken place in the midst of the game itself.

EQUITABLE DISTRIBUTION

The question of who owns what within a marriage is unlikely to become a matter for discussion until the marriage is well on its way to divorce. It's highly unlikely, for instance, for a husband and wife to argue about who owns a stereo or even an automobile when they are in the midst of a harmonious marriage.

To begin with, there are a few general rules concerning property ownership within a marriage. First, whatever you bring into the marriage remains yours unless it is considered a gift to the marriage. In other words, if you get married and already own an automobile, that car remains your property unless you either add your spouse's name to the title, make a gift of the car to your spouse, or otherwise make it clear that the car is now to be considered jointly owned. If you bring a piece of furniture, a valuable antique dining room table, for instance, into the marriage and it's clear that this table is a gift to the marriage, then it is jointly owned. This doesn't mean, however, that because your spouse uses the table it automatically becomes his or hers. Unless you specifically make a gift of the table to the marriage, you still retain ownership, no matter how much your spouse uses it.

This is also the case with money, stocks, and bonds. You "own" everything you bring into the marriage. This can get a little sticky, however, since inevitably cash and other negotiable instruments are often mingled, and the line between whose money is whose is blurred. Consequently, you'd have to prove that you came into the marriage with so much money and such stocks and bonds. In the case of money it's best to keep any that you want to remain yours in a separate account that only you have access to. The same can be said of stocks and bonds. Keep them in your own name. Regarding real property, such as furniture, jewelry, and a car, the best way to ensure that there's no problem later on is to make a list of all your assets before marriage.

The situation becomes somewhat more complicated when property that increases in value during the marriage is to be divided up. When this happens, both spouses might be entitled to share in the appreciation of the property.

This is exactly what happened in a case that we saw in one of our New Jersey offices. Herb, a doctor with a very successful practice, was already divorced from his first wife when he met Marcy. Marcy was much younger than Herb, and he was dazzled by her beauty and vitality. She, in turn, was impressed with his sophistication and life-style. They went out together for several months and then, on the spur of the moment, Herb asked Marcy to marry him. She agreed and they set a date a few months in the future. Before they were actually married, though, Herb purchased a cooperative apartment for $150,000. The apartment was registered in Herb's name.

Three months later Herb and Marcy were married, and they moved into his co-op apartment. Within the first year of marriage Herb realized something was very wrong with his marriage. Marcy began to act indifferently toward him. She began to stay out late at night without him, sometimes not returning until the next morning. When Herb asked about her absences, she refused to offer any explanations. Finally, Herb realized Marcy wasn't going to change and that the marriage was a mistake. He initiated a separation.

Herb came to see one of our attorneys and asked her to handle his divorce. Under normal circumstances the divorce proceedings should have been relatively simple, but in this case Marcy's attorney was insisting that she was entitled to a share of the appreciation of his co-op apartment, which was now valued at close to $300,000. His argument was that since the apartment appreciated in value while Marcy was married to Herb, she was entitled to a share of the $150,000 profit that Herb would get if he sold the apartment.

New Jersey is an equitable distribution state, so unlike in a community property state, Marcy would not be entitled to half the profit. Instead, considering such issues as the length of the marriage, each spouse's contribution, whether children exist, and so forth, she would get what a judge deemed fair and equitable.

Rather than go through lengthy, expensive litigation with an unpredictable settlement, our attorney persuaded Herb that his best course of action was to settle with Marcy. Although he felt he was being taken advantage of by his wife and that she was entitled to no part of the appreciation, especially considering her behavior, he finally took his attorney's advice and offered to settle for a payment of $12,000.

Another case somewhat similar to Herb's came up when Betsy came into one of our Pennsylvania offices and asked us to handle her divorce. The major stumbling block concerned a vacation home that her husband owned before their marriage. He never bothered to add her name to the deed after their marriage. Nevertheless, they both made use of the property. They pooled their money to help fix it up as well as put in their own physical labor, doing things such as paneling the living room and turning part of the basement into a family room. During the course of their marriage the value of the property tripled. Now Betsy wanted to know if she was entitled to any part of this property, even though it was in her husband's name.

We informed Betsy that, yes, she was entitled to a share of the increased value of the vacation home not only because some of her money was used to improve the property, thereby causing it to increase in value, but also because she gave of her own physical efforts to fix up the house. Since Pennsylvania is an equitable distribution state, it would be up to a judge to decide (based on the positions set forth by each person's attorney) just what percentage of the appreciation she was entitled to. In this case the judge agreed with our position and ruled that since both Betsy's money and time went into the vacation home, she was entitled to an equal share of the appreciation value, which amounted to $80,000.

Another one of our cases involving the ownership of a home

concerned Fred, seventy-six, who married Ann, forty-five years his junior. At the time they met, Fred owned a house in the suburbs outside New York City. Once they were married, he and his new wife lived in the house. Unfortunately, a short time after the marriage, Fred discovered that Ann was cheating on him. Her behavior was so brazen that she didn't even bother to go to the trouble of trying to hide her various affairs from her husband. Bitter and looking for some way to get back at his wife, Fred transferred title of the house, which had been in his name alone, to his children. Having done this, he came to us and asked us to file for divorce.

Fred was under the impression that by transferring title of the house to his children, he could keep Ann from making any claim to it. Unfortunately, this was not the case. Although the house was his before the marriage, Ann was entitled to a court-determined share of the appreciation value in the house during the time she was married to Fred. If Fred had wanted to avoid this situation, the only thing he could have done was transfer title of the house to his children *before* his marriage took place.

SHARING THE WEALTH

The home is often not the only property whose ownership is in dispute. We had a case where a couple, Martha and George, both in their mid-fifties, separated and filed for divorce. They had grown children and, according to Martha, who was our client, it had been a miserable situation for some years. Prior to the divorce they sold their home and split the profits right down the middle. When it came time for the terms of the divorce to be negotiated, Martha decided she wanted more money from George.

During the time they'd been married, while Martha did secretarial work in an office to help with the household bills, George had developed an insurance business. He also had invested some money in a Keough retirement plan. Besides her portion of the money from the sale of their house, Martha felt she was also entitled to a little more in order to help her get back on her feet. We agreed, especially since Martha raised the family and took care of the home while George was building up his business.

The figure Martha originally had in mind was a rather modest amount, $20,000, but George adamantly refused to give her as much as an additional dime. As a result we instituted an investigation into his finances, which included having his pension and business valued. Our investigation revealed his business to be worth approximately $150,000 and his Keough plan just under $30,000.

Finally, almost a year later, only a month before the trial was to take place, George's attorney contacted us and offered Martha a settlement in the amount of her original request, $20,000. By this time, however, taking into account the value of George's business and his Keough plan, our attorney felt that this figure was inadequate and advised Martha to turn it down. She did. The day before the trial, George's attorney raised the settlement figure to $50,000; after a bit more negotiating that included a higher figure as well as attorney's fees, on advice of her attorney, Martha decided to accept.

In this instance the courts probably would have found that Martha had a vested interest not only in George's insurance business but also in his pension because during all those years while George was trying to get the business off the ground she worked, contributing financially to the household, and took care of their children. It's likely that a judge would have ruled that Martha's job made it possible for George to start a business, which therefore entitled her to share in the fruits of both their labor.

We had another case handled by an attorney in one of our Pennsylvania offices that concerned Mary, who was married for nearly a dozen years to Richard, now a retired police officer. They decided to divorce. Mary wanted one-half the value of their house, the equity of which amounted to about $50,000. What complicated matters somewhat was the fact that only Richard's name was on the deed, and he refused her request.

As of 1980, Pennsylvania became an equitable distribution state, which means that it is "title blind": The state doesn't care whose name is actually on the deed, but rather the courts will look to the facts of the situation and try to come up with some kind of equitable judgment. Prior to 1980, however, if Richard had been calculating enough to put his name on everything, which he had in the case of the house, he could have walked out of the marriage with everything.

In this case, after an intensive investigation, our attorney found that Richard had a very generous civil service pension worth somewhere in the neighborhood of $200,000. When this fact was brought up, Richard suddenly changed his tune and offered to give Mary the entire house as a settlement. With this information now at his disposal, however, our attorney believed this was not enough. He knew Mary was entitled to a portion of Richard's pension which, it has been ruled, is the property of the marital estate. As a result Mary was able to obtain a very generous settlement, far more than half the value of their home.

COMMUNITY PROPERTY

There are eight states in this country that recognize the concept of community property: Arizona, California, Idaho, Louisiana, Nevada, New Mexico. Texas, and Washington. The concept of community property will be discussed more fully in the section on Breaking Up, but it is important to understand now just what this term means.

Community property consists of all property including earnings that is acquired after the marriage by the work and efforts of both spouses. Each spouse owns what is called an "undivided" half of this property. "Undivided" means neither spouse may individually sell, give away, or otherwise dispose of the property except in the event of a divorce or the death of the other spouse.

The situation regarding property ownership is somewhat different in community property states. Under this theory both spouses would be entitled to an *equal* share in the appreciation of any property such as a house. Thus, in a case such as Richard and Mary's in a community property state, Mary normally would have been entitled to one-half the value of the house as well as one-half the value of Richard's pension (assuming he didn't own the pension before they were married).

In a community property state, if one spouse owns a home but upon marriage adds the other spouse's name to the title of that house, it immediately becomes community property. This means that despite the fact the house may have once been owned solely by the husband, the act of putting his wife's name on the deed results in her becoming a joint tenant. Thus she is entitled to half the value of the house. This doesn't mean, however, that one spouse is not still entitled to reimbursement for any separate contribution he or she makes to improve the property. If community funds are used to make improvements, then the house remains community property.

WINDFALL PROFITS

You're married with two kids. One day you get a phone call from a lawyer who says that your great-aunt Matilda has just passed away, and you have been mentioned in the will. In two weeks you will receive a check in the mail for $5,000. Winter is coming on, your ratty cloth coat has just about had it, and you could sure use a nice, warm fur. Five thousand dollars would just about cover the cost. Isn't this your lucky day?

When your husband comes home, you tell him the good news. That's nice, he says, but we could use that money to fix up the house, for paint and aluminum siding. But I don't want to use it for paint and aluminum siding, you say. It's my money and I want to use it for a coat.

Too bad, your husband says. We're married. What's mine

is yours, and what's yours is mine. That money belongs to both of us, and we have to agree how it's going to be used.

Is your husband right?

No. In the matter of gifts, inheritances, or bequests, these remain the property of the person to whom they are given. This is true even in community property states. Unless you specifically put that money in a joint account, that $5,000 inheritance from your aunt Matilda is yours and yours alone, and your spouse has no right to it. If you do mingle it with marital funds by putting it in a joint account, however, you can generally no longer claim that it is exclusively your property; or if you put it in a bank or invest it, your spouse might be entitled to a portion of the appreciation (interest, dividend payments, and so forth).

Occasionally there are situations that challenge this concept. We once had a case of a woman who was diagnosed as schizophrenic. Ellen inherited $30,000 from her father. During one of her schizophrenic episodes she retained an attorney and transferred this money to her husband. Later, after recovering from this episode, she came to us looking for help in setting aside this gift to him. Unfortunately, in a case such as this, it's very difficult to prove what frame of mind the woman was in when she made the transfer. The case still hasn't been decided; Ellen's only hope is to convince the court that she was incapable of making an informed decision due to her illness. If this can't be proved, then she won't be able to claim the money as hers alone.

A MATTER OF DEGREE

So far we've talked only about tangible property, but recent developments in the law have addressed another, far more controversial area—educational and vocational degrees and licenses.

We're all familiar with the old story of the young married

couple that struggles to make a place for themselves. She works while he completes his education, perhaps attending medical or law school, or even completing courses toward a Ph.D., so he can teach at the university level. He graduates and then the relationship ends. The woman (in some cases the situation is reversed and it's the man) is left with little or nothing while the other spouse has his or her degree and a rosy future filled with high-income years.

With this inequity in mind, in the past few years courts have entertained cases filed by the spouse who's been left behind. In the past the courts generally ruled that a degree or license was not considered property. As a result the spouse without the degree or license was not entitled to any kind of compensation despite the fact that he or she made a major contribution that enabled the other spouse to earn the degree or license.

Lately, however, there has been a trend in the other direction. One recent New York State case illustrating this change is O'Brien versus O'Brien. In 1981, only two months after he earned his medical license, Dr. O'Brien filed for divorce after almost ten years of marriage. When they were first married, Dr. O'Brien was a senior in college. His wife convinced him to finish college and then moved with him to Mexico, where he entered medical school. During the time they were married she gave up her job as a teacher in this country, along with the opportunity to obtain permanent certification which eventually would have meant a substantial increase in her earnings.

Down in Mexico, while he attended medical school, Mrs. O'Brien worked as a teacher, homemaker, and tutor. When they returned to New York, Dr. O'Brien enrolled in post-medical school studies and began his medical internship.

Throughout their marriage Mrs. O'Brien contributed all of her earnings toward meeting their joint expenses. Though both spouses contributed to their living expenses and the doctor's educational costs, having received additional financial help from both their parents, the court established that Mrs. O'Brien's share amounted to seventy-six percent of their finances.

The trial court rejected the idea of mere reimbursement as an equitable remedy. Instead, it awarded Mrs. O'Brien forty percent of the present value of her husband's medical license (which the court evaluated using expert testimony in terms of potential earning power), payable in annual installments over eleven years for a total of $188,000.

Eventually the New York Court of Appeals unanimously upheld the trial court decision which ruled that a professional license was marital property and therefore subject to equitable distribution. In making this judgment the court offered two reasons. It said that a professional license was a valuable property right which was "reflected in the money, effort, and lost opportunity for employment expended in its acquisition, and also in the enhanced earning capacity it affords its holder." The court stated further that marriage was an "economic partnership" and that "the working spouse is entitled to an equitable portion of it [the license], not a return of funds advanced."

Coincidentally, at just about the same time the O'Brien case was still in litigation, we were handling a case with a similar fact pattern, only we were representing the husband. While the O'Brien case was on appeal, our attorney negotiated a settlement in his behalf in the amount of $10,000, which, considering the final O'Brien decision, turned out to be quite a coup. In fact, if the settlement hadn't been made before the O'Brien appeal was decided, our client most likely would have been forced to pay a much higher amount.

This rather new concept of a professional license as marital property is beginning to take hold across the country, although it is far from being universally accepted.

We recently had a case in which Jack, a history professor at a local New York college, obtained his doctorate degree while he was married (for seven years) to Susan, who worked as a legal secretary while he attended school. She not only contributed money toward his education but also paid for most of the household expenses. A few years after Jack earned his degree and found a teaching position, they decided to split up. Susan asked us to handle her divorce. One of the things our attorney wanted included in Susan's settlement was compensation for Jack's educational degree. Jack wasn't making all that much as a professor, somewhere in the neighborhood of $30,000 a year, but our attorney believed that Susan, who was instrumental in helping her husband earn his degree, was entitled to benefit from that degree, which did have a monetary value. In the end she received a settlement in the amount of $25,000.

On the other side of the fence we represented Barry, an accountant who, during his marriage to Jane, also obtained a real estate license. At no time during the marriage, however, did he make use of this license. Jane nevertheless claimed that this license should be considered part of the marital property because Barry obtained it during the time they were married. We believed otherwise. The matter was taken to trial where the court decided in Barry's favor, reasoning that since he never actually used the license during their marriage, it had no value and therefore should not be considered part of the marital property.

Recently, a New Jersey judge took the concept of marital property a step further when he ruled that comedian Joe Piscopo's "celebrity" status should be considered property in his divorce proceeding. The judge, in attempting to place a value on "celebrity good will," ruled that Mr. Piscopo's former wife had made a significant contribution to his becoming a celebrity and was therefore entitled to an award. As a result, the judge ruled that Mrs. Piscopo was entitled to forty-eight percent of her husband's business assets and that celebrity good will was one of those assets.

This case represents only the second national case in which a judge has found a property interest in celebrity status, but it will be interesting to see if this constitutes a trend, or whether it is simply an aberration that will not be upheld by higher courts.

One important fact to remember here, however, is that the courts have ruled that the degree or license, in order to be considered marital property, must have been obtained *during* the marriage. In other words, if you marry someone who is already practicing medicine and subsequently there is a divorce, you may not claim that his or her medical license should be considered part of your marital property.

DEBT AND CREDIT

DEBT

The flip side of marital property or assets is marital debt. On this subject the law is generally quite clear: If you are a partner in the assets of a marriage, you are probably a partner in its debts. If a joint return is filed, for example, any debts incurred to the Internal Revenue Service during the marriage are debts of both partners.

This is also the case with debts incurred for the necessaries of marriage, food, clothing, and shelter; these are also marital debts, and both spouses are held responsible for them. Marital assets, such as a joint checking account, could be attached by a creditor.

In community property states both spouses are responsible for debts accumulated during the marriage. This doesn't mean, however, that every debt incurred by a husband or wife is the responsibility of the other spouse. In fact, debts other than those considered necessaries of the marriage are generally the responsibility of the person who incurred them.

Let's take the example of a man who buys an expensive automobile and then fails to make the payments. Can the creditor go after the marital assets or perhaps even his wife's personal assets? Or how about the case where a woman with her own credit card buys an expensive fur coat and then fails to make the monthly credit card payments—can her husband be held responsible for this debt?

The answer to both these questions is no. Unless the woman

cosigned for the car loan, only her husband is responsible. It is his debt and his alone, and the courts have no right to execute a judgment against marital property. In the case of the fur coat, since the woman made the purchase on her card, she is solely responsible for the debt. If the card happened to be in her husband's name or in both names, however, and she ran up a debt, then it would be the responsibility of both, and marital assets could be attached.

If debts are incurred by one overspending spouse in both spouses' names and the nonspending spouse wants to do something about it, he or she can. The best way is to pay off the outstanding debts and then notify your credit sources that you are no longer responsible for the other spouse's debts, or cancel your credit cards. In some cases local law might require you to publish a notice to this effect in the local newspaper.

CREDIT

As to the matter of credit, the man and the woman in the marriage are both entitled to be looked upon as individuals. Theoretically, then, you cannot deny credit to one spouse simply because the other spouse is a bad credit risk. There can be something of a Catch-22 situation here, however, since in order to get credit you must have a credit history. Many women who have never worked lack this credit history and may not use their husband's credit history to obtain their own credit. Though this may seem unfair, it does make sense from the standpoint of the potential creditor. If the spouse without a credit rating received a bank charge card in his or her own name, for instance, and ran up a bill he or she could not pay, the credit card company could not come after the spouse to make good on the debt.

The fact is that married women who have always used credit in their husband's name and perhaps have never worked outside the home and who find themselves divorced and on their own will have great difficulty obtaining credit. Suddenly, after years of traveling on the credit coattails of their husbands, these women find themselves in the position of being financially anonymous.

What these women must do is establish a credit history for themselves, and it isn't always easy. As any banker will tell you, "You can't get credit without already having credit." It's very much like that old saw about finding a job: You can't get a job without experience, and you can't get experience without a job. The bottom line is that it is extremely important for anyone looking to establish credit to show steady employment.

So how do you do it? Well, first you can try to get a bank to issue you a credit card. If you have a job that pays enough or have alimony payments high enough, the bank might issue you a card. But if you don't have a job and your alimony payments are either nonexistent or not high enough, in all likelihood you will be turned down. The reason for this is simple: Upon application the bank will run a credit check on you; if you've never had credit under your own name, they'll find nothing and will deny you the card.

Don't give up. Try getting a credit card from either a department store or a local shop. These cards are often easier to obtain since the stores sometimes do not run a credit check. Instead they may just verify the income you put down, derived either from a job or from alimony payments.

Once you get the department store card, make purchases and, most important, be sure to pay them off on time. Although it's best when trying to establish credit to pay off each month's bill in the full amount, it will also do to make the minimum payments or a little more. Again, the important thing is to make the payments.

After a while, when you've built up credit at one store, try for another store card. Once you have two or three, try for that bank card again. Since you've now established a line of credit and a credit history, the chances are pretty good the card will be issued.

BREAKING UP

CHAPTER 9
Annulments

NOW YOU SEE IT, NOW YOU DON'T

Fran was a single woman who worked in the public relations division of a large New York City book publishing firm. One of her duties was to drum up publicity for an upcoming book that described the latest medical advances in heart surgery. In her capacity as publicist she had to attend several professional cocktail parties and mingle with guests, many of whom were doctors. At one of these events she met a South American physician named Manuel.

Manuel was forty-two years old, handsome, charming and, having been recently divorced, eligible. Fran was smitten. Manuel, who was visiting New York for several weeks to attend medical conferences and to study city-owned hospitals, wined and dined her. By the end of the first week, Fran found herself in the midst of a very passionate affair.

Unfortunately, after only two and a half weeks Manuel had to return to Brazil. Before he left, however, he professed his love for Fran and, once back in Brazil, phoned her several times a week, sent flowers to her home and office, and wrote letters almost daily telling her how much he missed her and how he wanted to be with her always.

On his return to New York a month or so later, he immediately resumed his affair with Fran. The second time they were together, as they sat having dinner at a fancy French restaurant, he suddenly brought up the idea of marriage.

Fran was surprised and somewhat reluctant. She'd known Manuel only a matter of weeks, and he seemed to be pushing too hard. As a result she began to show signs of stress. She felt tired, rundown, and was plagued by headaches. Manuel, in his capacity as a doctor, offered to give her a medical checkup. Fran agreed.

A few days later Manuel called with the surprising results of Fran's physical: She was pregnant. Now, said Manuel, he *had* to do the right thing, he had to marry her.

Fran was in a quandary. She thought she loved Manuel and, at thirty-six, her biological clock was ticking away. She wanted to have a child before she was too old. So finally, after thinking it over for some time, she accepted Manuel's proposal.

Manuel maintained that they had to do it quickly for propriety's sake. He would give up his practice in Brazil and move to the United States, where he was sure he'd find work.

A week later they were married, and Fran began to watch for further signs of her pregnancy, but they never came. Baffled and growing suspicious, Fran visited her own physician who told her that she was not pregnant at all.

Now Fran realized that she'd been duped, that Manuel had used this ruse of pregnancy to get her to marry him so he could obtain his green card and remain in this country. Feeling both outrage and shame, she visited an attorney in our New York office to see if anything could be done that would not only rid her of Manuel but also erase this terrible nightmare from her mind.

Fortunately, there was something we could do for Fran. Because her marriage fit into one of the appropriate categories, she was entitled to an annulment. As differentiated from a divorce, this meant that in the eyes of the state a legal marriage had never taken place. Not only did this extricate Fran from a marriage she never really wanted, a marriage based on fraud, but it also went a long way in erasing the psychological scar of a divorce that would have haunted her.

Manuel's attempt to marry a United States citizen so he could legally remain in this country is not uncommon, but make no mistake about it, it's against the law. It constitutes fraud, which is a criminal offense, and one of the criteria necessary for obtaining an annulment is that a marriage cannot be based on fraud.

The Immigration and Naturalization Service, in order to protect against this kind of fraud, is ever vigilant. In fact, the green card issued when a noncitizen marries a citizen is good for only two years, after which time the couple must return to the immigration authorities and prove that they are still married. As mentioned earlier, this proof consists of separate in-depth interviews with each spouse in an attempt to make sure the couple is actually living together.

PROMISES, PROMISES

An annulment, which means that there has never been a valid marriage, may be obtained only under certain special circumstances, which include (depending upon the state) fraud, bigamy, incest (in most jurisdictions a marriage with anyone closer than a second cousin), and refusal to have sexual relations with a spouse.

We've all heard stories about people who sought an annulment because one spouse, who originally promised to have a family, reneges on this promise, or a spouse who promises to convert to the other's religion and then does not. But getting an annulment on these grounds, in fact obtaining an annulment under any circumstance, is not an easy matter. Generally speaking the courts are tough on annulments, especially if they are contested by either party.

In the case of promises made before the wedding, the courts insist that a third party bear witness to this promise, someone who will testify that the one who made the promise intentionally deceived the other person. And then, to complete the case, a witness would be needed to testify that the spouse has openly reneged on this promise. It must also be proved that this deception was an integral part of the marriage and that the person would not have gotten married if he or she had not believed this promise was going to be fulfilled.

To give an example, let's say Frank and Beth decide to marry and Frank has agreed to have a family, which is very important to Beth. In fact, it's one of the main reasons she wants to get married. They marry, and some time later Beth says, "Well, how about getting started with our family now?" Frank replies, "I don't want children. I've never wanted children. They're too much trouble, they cost too much, and I don't even like kids." For Beth, marriage to Frank was based on his willingness to have children, and so in most states the courts would find that she is entitled to an annulment.

One must not confuse this kind of situation with a genuine change of heart. Simply because a person changes his or her mind about having a family does not mean this constitutes grounds for an annulment. There must be the *intent* to deceive or an annulment will not be granted and the marriage may be dissolved only by divorce.

CAVEAT EMPTOR

Marriage for immigration purposes is not the only example of a fraud that can qualify for annulment. An attorney in one of our New Jersey offices consulted on a case that, though it involved a different set of circumstances, still amounted to fraud.

Penny met Ralph at a singles bar. They began going out and, after several months, Ralph proposed marriage. Penny accepted, and two months later they were married. The first hint of any problem came one day when Ralph asked his wife to show him how she applied makeup. Seeing nothing wrong with his request, Penny demonstrated her technique. Not long afterward she came home one evening and found Ralph wearing some of her clothing. This, of course, was the tip-off, and after an emotional scene Ralph admitted he was a transvestite.

Penny was appalled. She immediately came to us for help. After telling her story, our attorney told her that in his opinion she was entitled to an annulment on the grounds of fraud. Ralph decided to contest the annulment, and so it went to court. As proof of his transvestism, we had Penny bring in samples of his wardrobe, including his size thirteen high-heeled shoes. The court granted Penny an annulment.

We had another case in New Jersey in which an annulment was granted on the grounds of fraud. June married Sam, and soon after their wedding she found that he was a deadbeat and that he owed money all over town. It wasn't long before she caught him selling many of her possessions in order to get money. He also dipped liberally into her bank account, almost depleting it entirely. Sam didn't work, so he spent all his time with June, making it impossible for her to seek help. Finally, after months of being a virtual prisoner, June made her escape one afternoon while Sam was watching a football game. She came to us for help, and our attorney filed for an annulment on the grounds that Sam had married her only to get her money, and therefore it constituted a fraudulent union. The court agreed, and June was granted her annulment.

ONE AT A TIME, PLEASE

Herb had been married to Janet for nearly twenty-five years when he came into one of our Arizona offices to seek a divorce. During the time they were married they purchased some property together, but the house they lived in remained in Herb's name. The breakup was acrimonious; Janet had been seeing other men, and Herb was hoping to limit any kind of settlement he might have to make.

In the interview with our attorney, Herb mentioned that his wife had been married three times previously. Our attorney decided to investigate and found no record of a divorce from one of her former husbands. Since in a case like this the burden of proof would be on Janet to prove she had been divorced, our attorney informed Herb that he might be entitled to an annulment. If Janet had not been divorced from a previous spouse, she could not legally be married to Herb. She was, in fact, a bigamist. Furthermore, if an annulment was granted, despite the fact that they had lived together for twenty-five years, Janet would not be entitled to any kind of settlement. The reason for this is that in the eyes of the law, the marriage to Herb was never valid, and therefore Janet would not be treated as a spouse.

As it turned out, an annulment was granted, and Janet received only $100,000, which was her share of the property that had been held in both names. Because they were not married, Janet lost out on a settlement of close to $1 million.

In granting the annulment, the court ruled that Janet knew or should have known she was not actually divorced from a previous husband, and therefore the marriage to Herb was illegal. If Janet had been able to prove she actually *thought* she was legally divorced, however, the result might have been different. In that case she would have been what is called the *putative* spouse (reputed or supposed spouse), and despite the fact of an annulment, she would have been entitled to the same settlement she would receive if she had been married to Herb.

One subtlety in this case that aided our client in receiving the favorable decision was his attorney's knowledge of the particular judges in the jurisdiction. What is sometimes not understood by the layman is that certain judges are known to rule in certain ways. Better, more knowledgeable attorneys are acutely aware of a judge's record, a pattern to his rulings, and will, if able, attempt to jockey for a position in a particular judge's court. In this case our attorney maneuvered so that Herb's case was heard by a judge who might be sympathetic to Herb's plight. This is not always possible, but when it is, it can measurably improve the chances of a favorable decision.

Once again, annulments are difficult to win and are quite rare. Still, they are possible. In a situation such as the one described above, there is a very palpable advantage to obtaining an annulment (Herb avoided paying any kind of divorce settlement), but in most cases the only real advantage to an annulment as opposed to a divorce is the psychological effect of being able to block an unpleasant marriage out of your mind. Sometimes that is a very important factor to a client who needs help overcoming what might have been a very unpleasant experience.

CHAPTER 10
Domestic Violence and Marital Rape

THE BATTERED WIFE

Karen and Clifton Straw met in New York City in 1979 when Karen was twenty-one years old. Three years later, in 1981, they were married and within the next few years Karen gave birth to a son and a daughter.

But Karen and Clifton Straw's marriage was not the stuff of Norman Rockwell paintings. There was a dark side to this relationship, a side that included repeated beatings and humiliations of Karen Straw at the hands of her husband. The beatings were at times so violent, in fact, that during the first few years of their marriage Karen wound up in the hospital on at least four occasions as a result of injuries inflicted by her husband.

The abuse, according to Karen, began about five months after they were married. At different times Clifton beat his wife with a steel pipe, threw boiling water underneath the closet door behind which she was hiding, stabbed her, causing superficial wounds, and even beat her with a pistol.

"He would say he was going to kill me," said Karen. "He would put the bullets [in] the gun and click it and put it to my head. He would just threaten me with it. And make me stand up in the corner of the room [for] maybe an hour."

In 1985, four years after their marriage began, Karen finally left her husband and moved into a welfare hotel with her children. But this did not put an end to the abuse; in fact, Karen was forced to call the police at least ten times to complain that her husband had beaten or abused her. She finally obtained an order of protection from the Queens Family Court in 1986, the legal effect of which was supposed to keep her husband away from her. It did not work. The beatings continued, and some time later, after a particularly brutal beating, she even filed assault charges against Clifton. He was arrested and charged with felony assault but was released on bail, and eventually the charge was reduced to a misdemeanor.

On December 18, 1986, Karen returned home from Christmas shopping shortly before midnight to find her husband sitting at the table of her sixth-floor studio apartment in Jamaica, Queens. He was rolling a marijuana cigarette. According to Karen, as soon as she came close enough, her husband grabbed her and threatened her with a knife.

As she sat there, Clifton smoked crack, after which, with a knife pressed to her throat and with her two small children watching, he raped her. The next morning Karen tried to escape. A struggle ensued. Her husband had a knife, and so Karen picked up a knife of her own. "I waved the knife at him and told him to stay away from me," she said. "And he kept coming at me. Then I cursed him—I stabbed him."

Karen, after years of abuse at the hands of her husband, twice plunged a knife into his chest. When a police officer responded to the call, he found Karen in the lobby of her apartment building, hysterical. "I stabbed my husband," she cried. "Please help him."

It was too late.

Karen was arrested and charged with second-degree murder, the most serious charge possible in New York State under the circumstances, and faced a prison term of fifteen years to life. There was a public outcry, with many women's rights groups lining up solidly behind her cause. Perhaps as a result of all this publicity, the prosecutor eventually offered to recommend a prison term of two to six years if she would plead guilty to manslaughter. Karen refused. She insisted that after years of abuse and a final night of rape at knifepoint, she was justified in killing her husband.

The Queens District Attorney, John J. Santucci, said of the case at the time,

> I suppose it is possible for a person to accumulate a certain number of indignities and then fly off the handle. But the battered spouse defense is difficult because the defendant relies on a series of prior acts, none of which may depend on what's occurring at the time of the homicide. Who is to make the determination as to whether she acted as a result of the prior abuse she suffered or that she acted aggressively on her own? It's easy to come out and want to be a champion of women's rights, but a life's been taken.

Fortunately for Karen, a New York jury agreed with her that the killing of Clifton, after years of brutal abuse, was justified, and she was acquitted of all charges.

Karen Straw's case garnered a good deal of attention at the time. It became a symbol of spousal abuse—how pernicious and pervasive it is, how it can destroy so many lives. But perhaps this case is especially noteworthy because, up until the time of the killing, Karen had done everything the law allows in an attempt to protect herself from her husband. Not only had she sought and received an order of protection from the court, which turned out to be useless, but her repeated calls to the police for assistance had brought little response. In fact, Karen told the court at the time of her trial that police response to her frequent complaints seldom went beyond issuing a verbal warning to her husband. "I don't remember nothing ever happening," she said. "They would just write a complaint and leave."

Unfortunately, this kind of failure of the system is not altogether unusual. Tragically, at virtually the same time Karen Straw was on trial for murdering her husband, another New York woman, Wilhemina Virginia Burgos, was in the process of obtaining a second order for protection from the Brooklyn Family Court, a last-ditch attempt to defend herself against repeated brutal assaults by her former husband, Jose A. Burgos. No more than an hour before she was to appear in court to again petition for protection, she was beaten by Jose and then pushed to her death from an eighteenth floor apartment window as her neighbors watched, horrified.

At that time Margaret Klaw, who was the assistant general counsel to the Metropolitan Assistance Corporation, the social service agency that operates New York City's victim services agencies, was quoted in the *New York Times* as stating that attorneys in the Family Court system long have realized that orders of protection "make it a great deal easier to get an arrest made" but are not "a guarantee of safety."

In fact, police do not provide twenty-four-hour protection to victims of domestic violence. Instead the Family Court system allows for a woman to return and file another grievance if the person abusing her does not comply with the first order for protection. It is highly unusual for the courts to send the spouse to jail, however. This, according to a 1986 report from the New York State Task Force on Women in the Courts, relates to the way domestic violence is treated in the court system in general.

WHO AND WHERE

Though statistics in the area of domestic violence are understandably flimsy since many, if not most, spousal abuse goes unreported, it is estimated that at least 4 million women are beaten each year by husbands or boyfriends and that approximately four thousand die each year as a result of this kind of abuse. The problem is so widespread, in fact, that in nearly fifty percent of all the matrimonial work our firm handles (and we are probably involved in more divorce work than any firm in the country), we find there is some kind of spousal abuse, often aggravated by alcohol- or drug-related problems.

I recall observing the managing attorney (something I do periodically) in one of our offices who was handling a case in which a woman's husband had beaten her severely, breaking her arm, and then locked her out of the house. After hearing her story, the managing attorney told her exactly what to do, step by step, including how to file for an order of protection, how to get temporary support for herself and her children, and then the steps to be taken so he could file for divorce on her behalf. She listened carefully and made an appointment to return the next week. When the woman left the office our attorney turned to me and said, "I see so many women who are in similar situations and I never see most of them again." This case was no different. The woman never returned.

Unfortunately, this is not the exception. It happens all the time. Usually the husband, contrite, promises the abuse will never happen again, and the woman, wanting desperately to save her marriage, believes him, and they become temporarily reconciled. The sad fact is that these reconciliations rarely, if ever, last. It is our experience that there is a continuing pattern to abuse, and unless the couple seeks professional help, the problem is almost sure to recur. The frustrating fact is that most women, if they do seek the help of legal authorities, eventually drop the charges against the men who batter them.

Though the public perception might be otherwise, not all victims of spousal abuse are from the lower socioeconomic classes. Domestic violence transcends social strata. In the middle and upper classes, spousal abuse is a dirty little secret that dares not whisper its name. Somehow we tend to accept the fact of violence among the poor and lower classes. It is a daily fact of life. But when it occurs in the so-called higher echelons of society, we flinch and close our eyes, making believe it has not and could not happen. Nothing could be further from the truth.

In fact, only a matter of months after Karen Straw was acquitted, a new, horrible tale of abuse hit the headlines in New York City. Joel Steinberg, a New York City attorney, was accused not only of beating his long-time live-in girlfriend Hedda Nussbaum, an editor and children's book author, but also of beating and murdering their six-year-old adopted daughter Elizabeth. (The issue of child abuse, which is often inextricably connected to spousal abuse, will be handled in the section on Children.) Here was a tragic example of an educated upper-middle-class woman who was the victim of an educated upper-middle-class man—an example of how abuse crosses all social and class definitions.

One case in the news not long ago further illustrates this crossing of class lines. Charlotte Fedders was married to John Fedders, formerly with the Securities and Exchange Commission. Mr. Fedders, who stands six feet ten inches, publicly admitted that he had beaten his wife seven times during their eighteen years of marriage. According to Mrs. Fedders these beatings caused various injuries including a broken eardrum, a wrenched back and neck, cuts, bruises, and blackened eyes. She also stated that her husband had beaten her around the abdomen when she was pregnant with the first of their five children.

As a result of her ordeal, Charlotte Fedders wrote a book with Laura Elliott *Shattered Dreams* (Harper & Row, 1987), concerning her marriage and the domestic violence she endured. Her husband, in the midst of divorce proceedings, sued for a portion of the profits from that book, arguing that his wife should share the blame for his violence because she denied him emotional support during his periods of depression.

Surprisingly, according to a *New York Times* report, "the court official—a domestic relations master who rules on the division of marital assets in divorce cases—found both parties equally at fault for the marital breakup and awarded [John Fedders], among other things, twenty-five percent of the proceeds from the sales of Mrs. Fedders's book."

This decision is being appealed, but no matter what the outcome is, it still does harm to the plight of women who are victims of domestic abuse. "This sends terrible messages to the community," said Ann Pauley, a spokeswoman for the Women's Legal Defense Fund. "It says to men there are some circumstances in which you are justified in physically abusing your wife or girlfriend. It says to women that you are responsible for the domestic violence."

The plight of the abused spouse is not limited to large urban areas such as New York; it is nationwide. Unfortunately, there are simply not enough shelters for battered women and their children, or legal services available to poor women who are looking for either protection or a divorce. In 1985 and 1986 in New York City alone, 3,859 battered women were sheltered by the city while an additional 2,359 were turned away due to lack of space.

Across the country there are many women who were in much the same position as Karen Straw and who, pushed to the limit, struck back. But they were not as fortunate as she. For them, the so-called battered wife defense did not convince the jury and, unlike Karen Straw, they are now serving time for murdering a spouse.

"Nearly all," reported the Committee on Domestic Violence and Incarcerated Women, a panel of women's advocates, public officials, and civic leaders, "are women who had never been convicted of a crime until they committed the crimes to which they were inexorably led: the killing of men who had brutalized them."

In addition, as pointed out by Bonnie Wagner, executive director of the New York State Coalition Against Domestic Violence, most of "their attorneys never raised battering as an issue. In some cases the fact that the woman was battered became a motive for murder as opposed to a woman's right to self-protection."

A HISTORY OF ABUSE

In an enlightened society the idea of a husband beating his wife with impunity is abhorrent, yet it was not always so. In 1768 William Blackstone, in his *Commentaries on the Laws of England,* wrote of the husband's right to moderately chastise his wife in order to enforce obedience to his lawful commands.

Incredibly enough, common law actually went as far as to set a criterion for measuring this so-called moderate chastisement, a literal "rule of thumb" that stipulated a husband could discipline his wife with any reasonable instrument including a rod that was no thicker than his thumb. God help the woman who had a husband with an especially large hand.

It was in 1824 in Mississippi that the first state supreme court case on wife beating referred to this "rule of thumb" when the court held that the husband could chastise his wife according to this standard without being subject to prosecution for assault and battery. Later, in 1854, a North Carolina court decision actually held that inflicting a nonpermanent injury from which the wife could recover did not constitute an assault.

It wasn't until the early 1870s that state courts began to reverse this trend by striking down the marital exception for assault; an Alabama court finally held that wife beating was "a relic of barbarous and unchristian privilege."

Today, of course, there is absolutely no legal marital exception for assault. Still, serious problems remain with the judicial system's handling of domestic violence. Often, both women and men who are victims of such violence are dissuaded by police and other law enforcement officials from proceeding in criminal and family courts "by having their claims trivialized or ignored," according to that 1986 report from the New York Task Force on Women in the Courts. Not only are these complaints often trivialized or ignored, but they are oftimes disbelieved, especially if no outward signs of assault are evident.

But the women's movement of the late 1960s and '70s has helped to cast a spotlight on these problems of abuse, and as a result every state has now passed laws that address the issue of domestic violence. But whether these laws are enforced properly is another question.

In fact, it took a 1982 case concerning a woman named Tracey Thurman to move the law a step further in helping to prevent or at least control spousal abuse. Tracey Thurman, a young Connecticut woman, was repeatedly attacked and threatened by her estranged husband. She duly reported these attacks to the police but was, over a prolonged period of time, ignored by the authorities. Finally she again was viciously attacked by her husband, who this time stabbed her in the chest, neck, and throat thirteen times, leaving her near death.

After a long recovery period, Tracey sued the Torrington, Connecticut, police department for violating her civil rights, citing their failure to protect her adequately. She won the case and was awarded $1.9 million in damages.

After the favorable decision her attorney, Burton Weinstein, said, "The Thurman case is the first time anywhere that a battered woman has been permitted to sue the police for failure to protect her in a domestic situation. It was based on sex discrimination because ninety-five percent of the victims of domestic violence are women. We alleged denial of equal protection under the Fourteenth Amendment as well as violation of Section 1983."

As a result of the Thurman case, Connecticut passed a law that requires police to arrest any perpetrators of domestic violence whether or not the victim wishes to press charges. This case has already had positive ramifications in other jurisdictions although, unfortunately, these laws are not always enforced.

WHY THEY STAY

Perhaps the first question that comes to mind when women tell of domestic violence is: Why do they stay? Why don't they simply pack up and leave the minute their husband or boyfriend raises a hand to them?

It sounds so simple, but is it really? There are, in fact, several psychological and sociological reasons why women tolerate domestic violence. First, there is the obvious—the element of fear. Many women are afraid that if they leave, the man will come after them, most likely resulting in further harm. Some even fear for their lives and, as we've seen in the Burgos case, this fear is sometimes well founded. This fear may translate into an almost overwhelming sense of helplessness, often leading to depression. This depression may, in turn, fuel an attitude of "What's the difference? I'm doomed no matter what I do," which only adds to the futility of the situation. People who find themselves in this predicament, often do nothing. As a result, the intolerable eventually becomes more intolerable.

Oddly enough there is also a related element of guilt. Some women actually believe they are to blame for the abuse, that they asked for or deserved it. They earnestly believe that if only they'd behaved differently, if only they'd obeyed their spouse, they would not have "caused" him to abuse them. This is most certainly due to low self-esteem. If my husband beats me, these women say to themselves, I must deserve it. The other side of this coin is, if I deserve it, I must be doing something wrong. Furthermore, these women truly believe that they are incapable of making it on their own, that they won't be able to support their children, that they will never find any other man who will "love" them. Consequently they settle for what they have.

In our experience we have often met women who are ashamed to admit that they are the victims of abuse. They don't want family or friends to know that the relationship they're involved in isn't working, or perhaps they don't even want to admit it to themselves. As a result they remain with their spouses and continue taking the abuse, sometimes going to extraordinary lengths to hide the physical effects. But the psychological effects, impossible to mask for long, are always there.

Additionally, there are some very practical reasons why women stay with the men who abuse them. Though women have come a long way in working and earning outside the home, a large majority remain economically dependent on their husbands. Few have the financial resources or emotional independence to venture out on their own. If a woman is not working and has no way to support herself, where is she to go? There are shelters for victims of domestic violence but, as we've noted earlier, there are too few of them and usually they are filled and have long waiting lists. Sadly, for these women the only option, as they see it, is to remain where they are.

THE SHOE THAT IS SOMETIMES ON THE OTHER FOOT

Joe, who owned his own men's apparel shop in a suburban area outside New York City, had been married to Helen for nearly ten years. Joe was a meek sort, rather small in stature, and Helen could be overbearing and overly demanding of her husband. It seemed she always found something wrong with Joe—he either did too much or not enough: He didn't make enough money; his hours were too long at the store; he didn't clean up after himself adequately enough; he spent too much time watching movies on TV. The list went on and on.

Helen also had a rather violent temper when aroused. She had a tendency to throw things, often in Joe's direction. On one particular evening, after an argument that began when Joe said he didn't want to visit her parents, she physically assaulted him, grabbing him by the throat and biting off a portion of his earlobe.

This was the final straw. Joe came to us for help. We went to court on his behalf and received an order of protection, the same step we would have taken if it had been a woman who was the victim of this kind of domestic abuse. This case eventually ended in divorce, but while the action was in progress, Joe's wife stopped harassing him due to the order of protection.

In turn this probably allowed the divorce proceeding to run more smoothly than it might otherwise have.

It may be difficult to believe that a man can suffer physical abuse at the hands of a woman, especially if he physically outstrips her, yet it does happen, and though some might smile at the prospect, it is no less horrifying than when a man attacks a woman. The man may be afraid to strike back, or perhaps the attack is unexpected and by the time he realizes what's happened, it's over. Even more often than in the case of women, these attacks go unreported since the man feels embarrassed and ashamed, having to admit that he is the victim of violence at the hands of a woman.

We had another case in Arizona that illustrates just how far out of hand these kinds of situations can get. Frank and Janet had been married for fifteen years and had three children aged ten to fourteen. The couple fought a good deal, and sometimes these arguments escalated to the point where violence was imminent. On one occasion they got into a particularly bitter argument, and Janet called the police. When the police arrived they found Janet nearly hysterical. She claimed she was the victim of spousal abuse and pointed to an open gash on her arm. The police immediately put Frank in handcuffs and led him away.

The next day the police returned to the house to investigate the complaint further. On speaking to Frank and Janet's children they found that it was not Frank who had attacked but Janet. The oldest boy said that his mother had actually taken a piece of broken glass, slit her own forearm with it, and then blamed her husband. As a result the police arrested Janet for spousal abuse.

This case eventually resulted in a divorce action, as many of these cases do. We represented Frank and worked out an arrangement whereby he would live in the house for two weeks with the children, then he would move out and his wife would move in for two weeks, until the final divorce settlement could be worked out.

WHAT TO DO: SPOUSAL ABUSE

If you are a victim of spousal abuse, there are certain steps you can take not only to protect yourself in the future but also to see to it that you get the kind of professional help you need.

The first thing you ought to do is remove yourself from the dangerous situation immediately. Go somewhere your spouse can't find you. If you don't have relatives or friends who can take you in, try one of the battered women shelters. But remember that most of these have long waiting lists, which reflects the seriousness of the problem. One important bit of advice we can give the woman is not to move in with another man. If you do, you risk the loss of custody. The courts might consider this abandonment. At the same time it's not at all a good idea to leave your children with your husband because there is always the chance that he might, in frustration, take his hostility out on them. To avoid this possibility, take them with you when you leave. (It should also be pointed out that leaving your spouse might constitute grounds for abandonment in those states where grounds for divorce are necessary. It is highly unlikely, however, that this charge would stand up under proof of abuse.)

If you have been injured in the assault, get medical attention as soon as possible, either from a hospital emergency room or a private physician. Don't try to protect your spouse. Be honest. Tell the attending physician exactly what happened so that there is a record of the assault. If you fail to do this, your medical record cannot be used against your spouse.

It's also a good idea to get hard evidence of the battery: color photographs, taken and signed by a witness; perhaps even the bloody clothing if there is any. Proper medical records and a police report are necessary to document the battery and will help facilitate any legal assistance you may require.

After you've obtained medical assistance, make sure you notify the police of the incident. You might even want to bring criminal charges against your spouse. Be prepared to visit the local precinct to swear out a complaint since the police may refuse to come to you. Once you're at the precinct, if the police refuse to make out a complaint, be sure to take down the name and badge number of the officer and inform him that you will report him to his commanding officer or a civilian review board if he refuses to take action. The reason you may experience a problem at this point is that the police are sometimes reluctant to get involved in what they consider a "family dispute." They feel that it may be a waste of their time since in many instances charges are eventually dropped. A battery is far more serious than a mere family disagreement, however; it is a crime and should be treated as such.

The next step is to obtain what is called an order of protection or, as it's called in some states, a temporary restraining order from Family Court. Although the terms of this order may differ slightly from state to state, it generally removes the offender from the home and forbids him from having any contact with you.

As we've seen earlier, all too often these orders are not enforced by the courts. There is nothing mysterious about getting these orders. In fact, an order of protection can be obtained relatively quickly and easily, often taking no more than three hours. The order will restrain a spouse from harassment or assault, but it will not order the offending spouse out of the house. Only a court can do this. Most judges are inclined to issue restraining orders that are mutual, keeping each party away from the other.

ORDER OF PROTECTION OR TEMPORARY RESTRAINING ORDER

If you are the victim of domestic violence, your first recourse is to obtain an order of protection or temporary restraining order from Family Court.

It should also be pointed out that this is a difficult area of the law. It is not totally unheard of, for instance, for one spouse to use an order of protection to get back at the other.

Although procedures may differ slightly from state to state, the following is a generalized version of how you can go about getting an order of protection:

1. You may go to an attorney who will prepare a petition for an order of protection, which should take less than an hour. If you do not have an attorney, you may go directly to Family Court where a petition will be prepared for you. We generally recommend that our clients obtain the order on their own rather than pay an attorney to do it. The process is simple enough, and having an attorney gives you no particular advantage. This is not the case in a state such as California, however, where procedural differences along with certain requirements make it advisable to use an attorney. The best thing you can do is go to an attorney in your jurisdiction and determine what the requirements are in your own state.

2. This petition is taken to Family Court where it is presented to a judge that same day. The judge will almost certainly issue a temporary order of protection. This temporary order will not force your spouse out of the home unless the judge decides there are special circumstances; these might include a reasonable fear of more serious danger (in California, for instance, examples of past violence are sufficient to have a spouse ordered out of the home). This might be indicated by the seriousness of the beating. A separate order must be issued to accomplish an eviction of this sort.

3. The order of protection must then be served on your spouse. This may be done by a police officer.

4. Be sure to file the order of protection at your local precinct. This will make it easier to enforce if your spouse decides to disregard the court's order. (See the Appendix for a facsimile of an order of protection.)

Once you have the order of protection it must be served on your spouse. The police will often do this. At the same time you request they serve the order, make sure you register it with the local police precinct. This way, if there is a further problem, you will be on record with the police; consequently they will be more likely to answer any call from you.

A hearing will usually be held anywhere from two to three weeks after the order of protection is obtained. If the order is contested at this time (usually it is not), the hearing will provide an opportunity to make an investigation into the facts of the case. In the meantime, while you wait for this hearing, your spouse must cease from harassing you. At the end of the hearing the court may issue a permanent order of protection or even force the offender out of the house. In some states, California among them, the court can also award custody of the children to the victim of abuse, along with spousal support.

There are cases, of course, where the order of protection is contested, sometimes successfully. We represented a man who had lye thrown in his face by his wife. Her defense was that during an argument her husband "pushed her." Based on the evidence presented at the hearing, the court decided that the "push" was not sufficient to be considered a battering and, as a result, her action was found to be totally inappropriate as a self-defensive measure. Although in this case the woman was not charged with assault, she could have been.

If the order of protection is violated, the best thing to do is call the police. If your order is registered in the local police precinct, they are more likely to be responsive, due in no small part to such lawsuits as the one Tracey Thurman brought against the Torrington, Connecticut, authorities. Your spouse will be taken into custody and, if he has indeed violated the terms of the court order, he will usually be charged with a misdemeanor. He should receive jail time, and each subsequent time he violates this order he should be given a longer sentence.

In the real world it doesn't always work this way. Very rarely will a man receive jail time for violating an order of protection and, if he does, it is usually no more than a slap on the wrist. Women's rights advocates across the country are trying to change this, but it is an uphill battle as they fight against ingrained practices.

Again, it should be pointed out that most cases of spousal abuse never go this far, in large part because the victim, usually the woman, is unwilling to pursue the matter. In many cases this is a result of the same set of reasons she remains with her abusive spouse. In fact, we had a case in one of our New Jersey offices in which our attorney represented a woman who, after being periodically abused by her husband, obtained an order of protection that denied him access to the house. He ignored the order. She called the police. They came and arrested him. In jail, he immediately telephoned his wife and asked her to put up bail. Not so surprisingly, she did.

The sad truth is that most battered women are likely to reconcile with their spouses. Unfortunately, this can often lead to someone getting seriously injured. Sometimes it's the abused spouse, as we saw in the Wilhemina Burgos case, while sometimes the victim is pushed so hard she retaliates, as we saw in the Karen Straw case. And sometimes it's an innocent child, as evidenced in the case of Elizabeth Steinberg.

RAPE IN MARRIAGE

Rape in marriage presents one of the more problematic areas of the law. Although it certainly falls into the category of domestic violence, perhaps an act falling short only of murder, it is clouded by the issue of an obligation to have sex within marriage. Sexual obligation, however, does not mean that there is a license for one spouse to use bodily force on the other in order to have sex.

Though rape within marriage is very difficult to prove, the woman does have another avenue to pursue if force is involved. For instance, in California we had a case that involved Sheila who, after being married to Doug for several years, told him that she had fallen in love with someone else and wanted a divorce. Doug became enraged. He struck her several times, then threw her down on the floor and raped her.

Frightened and angry, she came to us for help. Since there was a battery involved, we filed for an order of protection. At the same time we had Sheila file criminal charges of assault and battery against her husband.

A woman in a position similar to Sheila's would have to do pretty much as she did: file criminal charges against her spouse, not for rape but rather for physical abuse.

CHAPTER 11
Divorce

DIVORCE CRAZY—AN OVERVIEW

If marriage is the beginning of a dream, then divorce can be the end of a nightmare. In fact, we've often wondered at Jacoby & Meyers whether we're in the business of destroying dreams or creating new hope.

Divorce, no matter what the circumstances, whether the parting be amicable or bitter, is an extremely trying and emotionally charged episode in the lives of both spouses. It is a time of collapse and, warranted or not, both spouses can experience a sense of failure. Divorce affects both partners profoundly, but if there are children involved, it has an especially long-lasting effect on their lives as well.

In today's world the old structures that worked to keep married partners together are gone. Whereas in the past married couples seemed to stay together even under sometimes insufferable circumstances, now divorce is an option that people choose freely. Since 1975 there have been more than one million divorces annually, and recent figures tell us that one out of every two marriages in this country will eventually end in divorce, which leaves us with one of the highest divorce rates in the world.

Why is this so? Well, in general, people seem to be less committed to the institution of marriage. It appears that we are always on the lookout for something better, always looking for greener pastures. Perhaps this is an offshoot of the "Me Generation" and the search for "inner happiness." Or perhaps it is simply the result of the apparent need for easy answers and quick remedies in what has become a disposable society. If you can't fix it right away, why not throw it out and get a new one?

Another factor to be added to the equation is that people are living a good deal longer than they used to. In fact, the apocryphal statement made by Margaret Mead that three marriages, not one, might be a more reasonable number for a lifetime that now spans, on the average, well over seventy years may be more in line with the situation as it is today. The first for romance, the second for children (or, in some cases, money), and the third for companionship.

And, finally, there is a far greater number of married women in the work place today. Given these new dynamics of the two-income family, couples cannot have the same historic expectations that they held in the past if the marriage is to survive. Men should understand that they must share in some of the household responsibilities, while women should understand that they must share some of the economic burdens of the marriage. Unfortunately, as a society we are still holding on to many of our old expectations. Though they may deny it, women still expect the prince on the white horse to come along and take care of them, while men are still looking to have their socks matched.

Too often marriage becomes simply a question of time management. It's a matter of trying to create that difficult balance between working and giving quality time to your spouse and children. Most of us lack the economic wherewithal to get this time together by hiring domestic help; as a result we are forced to do the best we can, often forgoing such things as taking vacations or even something as simple as sharing an evening out together. The result can be tension and a feeling of entrapment. Is it any wonder, then, that so many marriages seem to collapse under the weight of these pressures?

TELL ME WHY

Based on the experience of the attorneys in our firm, generally the reasons for divorce fall into four general categories. The first is money. Marriages often break up due to economic pressures. Perhaps the husband feels his wife is spending too much money, while his wife feels her husband is being too tightfisted. For many women the complaint is that the spouse isn't contributing enough to the household. He can't hold a job. The job he has doesn't pay enough. A lack of money can often be directly traced to some extracurricular activity such as gambling, drugs, or alcohol. We hear many times, "My husband is always off in Atlantic City, gambling" and "He spends all his time and money at the local bar. He doesn't even come home at night."

The second reason for divorce is sex: Husbands leave wives for other women, and wives leave husbands for other men. It frequently is a matter of traditional stereotypes such as husbands looking for the excitement that comes in an affair with a younger woman, or the wife feeling ignored by her husband and turning to another man for affection. Either way it takes an unusually strong marriage to withstand these kinds of tensions.

The third reason, one that may well be tied to the first two, is lack of communication. A recent study found the marriages that lasted longest were those in which couples discussed issues that were bothering them. This criticism is primarily leveled by the wife. "My husband never talks to me" or "We never seem to talk about anything important. My husband refuses to confide in me, and he never listens to my problems." Occasionally, however, it's the husband who voices this complaint about a wife who seems to be too busy with the house and kids to take an interest in what has happened to him during the day.

The fourth reason is in-laws. This problem is more likely to crop up when the couple is living with or near the parents of one of the spouses. Perhaps the in-laws pick on one spouse, who then wants to move out of the house or neighborhood while the other wants to remain. We see these problems particularly when the couples are of different nationalities or religions, with pressure coming from one or both sets of in-laws.

IF THE SHOE FITS . . .

Although divorces come in all shapes and sizes, many having unique sets of facts, there are still certain similarities. Generally speaking we see three different kinds of divorces in our offices. The first involves the so-called quickie marriage, one that lasts for a very short period of time, perhaps less than three years. These are normally the least complicated divorces to handle.

The second type is a longer marriage, over ten years, but one in which there are no children and the woman has worked outside the home. Since more marital property has been accumulated, it is somewhat more complicated than the first but certainly not as potentially difficult as the final kind of divorce.

The third and most difficult is a marriage that has lasted ten years or longer, where there are children involved, and the woman has stayed at home to take care of the family.

Whatever the reason for the divorce or the kind of divorce it is, I've always believed that the better people are at separating their emotions from what is admittedly an emotionally charged situation, the better off they will be ultimately. The paramount goal should be for people to educate themselves as to what is involved in both a separation and a divorce. The extent to which they can do this will provide both husband and wife with the tools to deal as reasonably and intelligently with the breakdown of their marriage as possible.

THE TIES THAT BIND

Historically the rights and obligations of husbands and wives were based solely on gender. In return for lifelong support by her husband, a wife agreed to fulfill her part of the bargain by promising to take care of her husband, the home, and their family.

This common-law tradition was brought over from Great Britain and quickly became established as the law throughout this country. The husband was legally responsible for providing for his wife and family, while the wife was legally responsible for tending to the domestic duties, which included companionship and child care. The husband was considered the head of the household, an authority based on the common-law doctrine of coverture, which meant that a husband and wife took on a single legal identity at the time of their marriage. The identity was that of the husband. In effect, then, at the time of the marriage, the woman, now the wife, essentially became a nonperson.

Lenore J. Weitzman points out in her book, *The Divorce Revolution* (Free Press, 1985, page 3),

> The married woman's subordination was reflected in rules permitting women to marry at a younger age (because they were presumably already prepared for their life's work), the wife's loss of an independent identity by assuming her husband's surname, the husband's power to determine the family domicile, the husband's right to his wife's sexual services, and the gender-based standards in grounds for loss of consortium (only the hus-

band was entitled to sue anyone who deprived him of
his wife's love and sexual services).

This union of a man and woman, reflecting the religious
beliefs of marriage as a sacrament, was intended to last forever.
In fact, legal divorce did not exist in England, other than by a
special act of Parliament, until 1857. Prior to that it was intended that the marriage endure until the death of either spouse.
The reason was that marriage was considered of such value to
the society that it had to be preserved by both the Church and
the state. The most efficient if not the only way to preserve
marriage was by severely limiting the ability to divorce.

Gradually, of course, the laws were relaxed and divorce was
permitted, though only under very special circumstances.

In this country the concept of coverture was mercifully eliminated by the Married Women's Property Acts passed in the
nineteenth century. Nevertheless, the notion of the husband
as head of the household has actually remained with us in some
form all the way up to the 1960s, and to some extent it remains
deeply ingrained in our collective unconscious.

THE FAULT LIES NOT IN US . . .

In the last twenty-five years or so there has been nothing
less than a divorce revolution in this country. Prior to 1970 we
had what was known as the "fault" system of divorce, which
is best described by Frances Leonard, an attorney for the national Older Women's League in Oakland, California:

> In the old days women had a marriage contract unless
> it was broken through adultery, abandonment, or cru-
> elty. If the husband wanted out of the marriage, she
> could strike an economic bargain with him—i.e., you
> support me and I'll give you a divorce. The impolite
> word for this is blackmail. Nobody feels that it was a
> good system, but it helped place a value on the marriage

contract. (from *A Lesser Life,* Sylvia Ann Hewlett, page 56)

Hence, marriage was held together by a far more effective glue than we have today. Divorce, which was made very difficult to obtain without the accord of both parties, was predicated on grounds such as adultery, cruel or inhuman treatment (which included both mental and physical cruelty), abandonment, and imprisonment for more than a certain number of years.

The rules of property ownership were different too. You "owned" only what actually bore your name on the title. As a result, if everything was in the husband's name, he owned everything. But the woman's bargaining chip in any marital breakup was her ability to withhold a divorce that had to be agreed to by both parties in the absence of proof of any of the requisite grounds. It became a classic trade-off situation. If the woman permitted the divorce to go through by agreeing to a charade of grounds, such as mental cruelty for instance, she was assured of an appropriate financial settlement as well as a suitable amount of alimony. Historically, if a woman wanted a divorce, she was stuck if he had all the property and didn't want to give her a divorce.

In 1970, in large part as a reaction to the social turmoil of the 1960s, California became the first state to institute what is known as no-fault divorce laws. Since that time almost every state has to some extent followed this lead (with the exception of South Dakota), though some, like New York, maintain a quasi-fault system (which we will describe a bit further on).

The original motive behind no-fault legislation was to improve the woman's situation and, in the beginning at least, no-fault divorce was readily embraced by feminists across the country. This new concept in divorce law meant that women would no longer be publicly humiliated by charges made in open court and that the charade of fictional charges could end. It was also meant to promote equality between men and women by treating them as equal partners rather than as overseer and subordinate. This legislation was viewed as a positive step toward freeing women from the traditional restraints of marriage.

The most important change of all was that the law began to view divorce as the termination of an economic partnership between a husband and wife. No matter who had legal title, everything that had been accumulated during the marriage was to be considered marital property. All property owned prior to the marriage or received as a gift during the marriage remained separate (except in the case of appreciation which came as the result of the marital partnership).

Arguments about whether no-fault divorce has, in reality, helped balance the scales abound. Sylvia Ann Hewlett believes it has not:

> Experience has shown that no-fault is a bad economic bargain for women because it tends to reduce alimony as well as acrimony. For example, in California it has triggered a drop in the "overall frequency of alimony awards" along with a noticeable "decrease in the percentage of open-ended awards" and an increase in "transitional awards."
>
> Many women's groups originally supported equitable-distribution legislation on the grounds that wives would be awarded a more equal share of the property, but at least some feminists are now ruefully admitting that "the [new] law is primarily a device to deny women alimony." True, wives now have a slightly better shot at a fair division of property, but the new laws have eliminated alimony, replacing it with something called maintenance—a temporary award designed to help wives (or, in rare cases, husbands) get back on their feet. (*A Lesser Life,* pages 56–57).

Others might argue, however, that the reason fewer women are receiving alimony is that their need for it has lessened because they are doing far better economically.

SPLITTING IT UP—"THERE IS NO JUSTICE, ONLY LAW"

In the matter of property settlements, forty-two states now have what is commonly known as equitable distribution, while the other eight (Arizona, California, Idaho, Louisiana, Nevada, New Mexico, Texas, and Washington) adhere to community property.

In Chapter 13 we will discuss the consequences of each procedure of property settlement in more detail, but I think it is important at this point to understand what both mean, the differences between them, and the ramifications when each is employed.

EQUITABLE DISTRIBUTION

Under equitable distribution laws, all property acquired during the marriage is deemed "marital property" and is subject to equitable distribution. The exception to this rule is property such as gifts to the individuals from third parties, inheritances, and compensation for personal injuries; these are considered separate property and do not qualify for equitable distribution.

It should be pointed out that *equitable* distribution does not necessarily mean *equal* distribution. What it does mean is that the courts, when allocating marital property, are required to consider a list of factors set forth in the Domestic Relations Law of each state. These factors include the length of the marriage, the respective economic and noneconomic contributions of both spouses, and the relative financial circumstances of the parties during the marriage. The ostensible objective of this consideration is to ensure that each spouse receives a *fair* share of the financial fruits of the marriage.

The goal of equitable distribution is for financially dependent spouses (in most cases the wife) to share in both the money and the property that the partner has accumulated during the marriage. But one of the by-products of equitable distribution is that the dependent spouse is expected to go to work as soon as possible in order to become self-supporting. As a result the old concept of alimony, which could and often did last forever, has been replaced by what is now called spousal support or maintenance. Maintenance is supposed to be awarded for only a short period of time, the average being from three to seven years; the courts feel this is sufficient time for any spouse to get back on his or her feet. There have been a few cases, however, in which the courts have granted unlimited maintenance, when it was believed that due to special circumstances the spouse has little hope of obtaining a job.

The aim of equitable distribution is to distribute the burden of support on both spouses equally. While in theory this might be a fine idea, in reality it doesn't always work out. Ex-wives are often woefully unequipped to bear this *equal* burden, especially if they have not worked during the marriage and have children to raise. They are bound to have a difficult, if not impossible time finding suitable employment.

Lenore J. Weitzman noted in a discussion of the problem at an American Bar Association meeting in August 1986 as follows:

> When the legal system treats men and women equally at the point of divorce, it ignores very real economic inequalities between men and women in our society, inequalities that marriage itself creates. Since a woman's ability to support herself is likely to be impaired during marriage, especially if she has been a homemaker and mother, she may not be equal to her husband. Rules that treat her as if she is simply serve to deprive her of the financial support she needs. A divorce provides an opportunity for society to articulate what it expects of husbands and wives. For example, if a court awards alimony to a fifty-year-old woman who has been a homemaker and mother for twenty-five years, it's

saying that those years count, that she has earned the
right to share the standard of living she helped to build.
If the court denies her alimony and tells her that she
should go get a job and support herself, it is saying that
her years as a homemaker and mother do not count—
as if she too had built her earning capacity during marriage, as if she had not played a special role. (*New York
Times,* August 17, 1986)

Theoretically, then, equitable distribution may be the best
method we have of dividing property after a divorce, but historic perceptions of marriage may well negate the effectiveness
of this theory of recovery. For instance, women almost always
wind up with the responsibility of child care even though this
is not always considered under the theory of equitable distribution. Unfortunately, in many jurisdictions judges are still
dealing with societal mores of thirty or forty years ago, those
mores that had the husband as head of the household and owner
of all property.

We are in a transitional period now, as judges begin to catch
up with changes in our society. Nevertheless, some people,
especially women between the ages of forty and sixty-five,
find themselves caught up in this transition and suffer because
of it.

COMMUNITY PROPERTY

As we mentioned before, there are eight states that mandate
community property distribution for married couples. In short,
community property is property, including earnings, acquired
after marriage by the work and efforts of both spouses. Upon
divorce this property is shared equally according to the law of
the state. In a manner of speaking it is a kind of deferred
compensation. The theory is that a community effort went into
the marriage, therefore property obtained during the marriage
should be divided equally.

In addition there is a formula, much too complicated to go into here, that is used on property that is brought into the marriage and then appreciates due to the efforts of the "community." For instance, take the case of a pension. Let's say the couple has been married for ten years, but the husband had the pension for ten years prior to the marriage. Upon divorce, the wife is entitled to twenty-five percent of the pension because she was married to her husband for only half the life of the pension. She might be able to get more, however, if she can prove that her husband made a larger contribution to the pension during the ten years they were married.

TIME WAITS FOR NO MAN . . . OR WOMAN

One unexpected fallout from equitable distribution is that it seems to be taking longer to divorce—on the average up to one year or more—because of the process of settlement.

As reported in a *New York Times* article on January 5, 1987, some states have taken steps to alleviate this problem:

> California, Oregon, and several other states are adopting what are called summary dissolution laws. Such statutes permit childless couples who have been married less than five years and have acquired little property to complete the necessary forms in the presence of a court clerk and thereby avoid going to trial. . . . Other states, like Connecticut, are using a group of lawyers known as special masters to speed the settlement of divorce cases. A couple, their lawyers, and a special master meet to discuss the disagreement in an informal setting without adhering to the rules of evidence. The master then recommends a possible settlement to both sides that is reviewed and approved by the court. If the couple rejects the recommendation, the case is scheduled for trial at a later date.

CHAPTER 12
Preparation and Separation

To liberally paraphrase Tolstoy, happy marriages are all alike, but every unhappy marriage has its own story.

The 3,288 divorces that occur each day in this country do not come out of the blue. The seeds usually are sown well before the tree bears fruit. This is not to say that those involved are always aware of the telltale signs of an impending breakup, but they are there. The symptoms may take the form of small arguments that escalate into big ones, often about seemingly insignificant things; or, at the other end of the spectrum, the problems may manifest themselves in the form of silence, resulting in an utter lack of communication.

The truth of any situation, especially one as emotionally charged as a marriage breakup, is always elusive. One thing that can be said for certain is that in every divorce there is the *Rashomon* effect or three separate perceptions of the facts: the wife's, the husband's, and the court's.

If you're having problems in your marriage, you should seek, if possible, some kind of professional counseling, especially if there are children involved. But if counseling fails or is inappropriate, and a separation or divorce is inevitable, there are certain steps you can and should take not only to protect yourself but also to ensure that the period of divorce and adjustment is as painless as possible.

IN QUEST OF EXCELLENCE: CHOOSING AN ATTORNEY

Before hiring an attorney I would first advise doing some research on your own. Read as many books and articles on the subject of separation and divorce as possible. This isn't always feasible, of course, either because of time or because people in the midst of this predicament aren't in the proper state of mind to digest all this information. Yet, if you can, reading on the subject can provide you with a good deal of information that will almost certainly come in handy.

Also ask friends about their experiences. Try to imagine how, ideally, you would like to see your own separation and divorce. It's important to remember that on some level you are always married to the person who is the father or mother of your child; certainly a relationship will continue to exist. Consequently you need all the mechanisms available to help set ground rules for the future.

After the decision to end the marriage has become irrevocable and you've educated yourself to some extent as to what you can expect, the next step is to find a suitable attorney. This isn't always an easy task.

In the past when fault divorce was the law, a special breed of attorney was sometimes sought: the tough, no-nonsense, antagonistic, often nasty and hostile, so-called bomber who relished the fight. His or her specialty was getting in there and shaking things up, unearthing the "dirt" on the opposition, and then "sticking it" to the opponent, often using intimidation as a potent weapon. More often than not these attorneys simply exacerbated the problems, sometimes forcing a formidable wedge between the spouses. But just as often they were enormously effective and got the job done for their clients.

Once the rules of divorce changed, however, once fault was no longer an issue and the emphasis shifted from sin to economics, this brand of attorney went the way of the dinosaurs. In today's climate, with marriage viewed as an economic partnership, an attorney who is familiar with the practical aspects of divorce is necessary. For situations that involve the distribution of assets, including property, shares in a business, art collections, pensions, and so forth, this would include possessing a background in business, finance, and real estate as well as a working familiarity with the complexities of property matters. Instead of hiring detectives to raid motel rooms in search of adulterous behavior, today's attorneys must often be prepared to trace monetary transactions, locate and determine the value of certain assets, and work closely with accountants and appraisers.

You wouldn't go to a neurologist if you had stomach pains, and for the same reason it's a good idea to find an attorney who specializes in matrimonial law. The laws pertaining to divorce are quite complicated and getting more so all the time, and thus ideally you'd want someone who was intimately familiar with and experienced in matrimonial law. For this reason it's not always a good idea to retain the attorney who handled the closing on your house, for instance, or the one who drew up the partnership papers when you started your own business.

As a result of the changes in divorce laws and the need for legal assistance for the middle class at affordable rates, there are today more attorneys who are familiar with the problems faced by those in middle-income brackets, people who own modest houses and perhaps are owners of small businesses. These are the people who are often lost in the shuffle. Unlike the poor who own little property, they have accumulated enough so that they need the help of an attorney; but unlike the very wealthy, they can neither afford to spend huge amounts on legal fees nor do they require the variety of experts necessary when large amounts of property and highly complex businesses are involved.

THE RULES OF THE GAME

One important advantage to finding an attorney who specializes in matrimonial law is that he or she is more likely to be familiar with the local court system, how particular judges are likely to rule, and what the prevailing sentiment of the sitting judges are. Although no one can guarantee how an individual judge will rule on a particular case, it's still helpful to know the dimensions of the field before you play on it. You'd be surprised how critical this can be in obtaining a satisfactory outcome. Here are two examples that illustrate this. One went in our favor, the other, due to circumstances beyond our control, did not.

Tom and Merry were high school sweethearts who married as soon as they graduated. Merry wanted to go on to college, but Tom said they couldn't afford it. Tom decided he wanted to become a police officer, and Merry, while taking a few college courses at night, worked during the day as a waitress in order to further Tom's career. After four years of marriage, with Tom now on the local police force, Merry enrolled in college full-time, but she had to repeat some of the earlier courses she took because so much time had elapsed.

After five years of marriage, Tom and Merry, childless, separated. At the time Tom was making $38,000 a year. Merry had a year and a half of college left before she could get her degree as a registered nurse. Tom refused to support Merry during this period.

Merry came to one of our offices in California and asked us to help. After studying her situation one of our attorneys maneuvered it so that her case would be heard in front of a judge he thought would be sympathetic to Merry's case. He was successful. The judge's decision held that Tom had to pay Merry $500 a month in support for two and a half years, reasoning that a five-year marriage had earned Merry the opportunity to obtain a degree and make a salary comparable to Tom's.

In another case, however, the client was not so fortunate. After twenty-two years of marriage Margaret found that her husband Alex was having an affair with her best friend. To make matters worse, five years earlier Margaret had been diagnosed with an ailment that confined her to a wheelchair. Margaret had never worked and had only a tenth-grade education. The three children from the marriage were sixteen, eighteen, and nineteen.

Unfortunately the case was heard in a "one county judge" jurisdiction, and this one judge had been divorced four times. The judge ordered Margaret out of the family residence. As a result, while Alex lived with his girlfriend, Margaret was forced to reside with church friends for a year while the house was being sold. Mortgage payments on the house were listed as a debt, and Margaret was responsible for half. Alex was paying community bills but was giving no support to Margaret.

At the trial Margaret gave up her right to Alex's pension in order to offset her share of the community obligations, that is, bills that were the result of the marriage. She was to receive $500 a month in support payments from Alex, who worked as a policeman and made $40,000 a year.

Less than a year after the divorce Alex fell behind in his support payments, and Margaret came to us for help. Our attorney tried to get her what is called a wage assignment, which meant that her money would be taken directly out of his salary check, and also moved to have her support increased. Alex contested this motion. The judge in this case refused to increase the support and did not rule on the wage assignment.

Our attorney believed that in another jurisdiction, in front of another judge, one more partial to the wife's predicament, his motions on Margaret's behalf would have been ruled on favorably.

So, as you can see from these two cases, it's very important to have an attorney who knows the local court system and can, when possible, use this knowledge to the benefit of his client.

WINDOW SHOPPING

To reiterate, perhaps one of the best ways to find an appropriate attorney, one who will meet your needs and with whom you can work well, is to ask friends and acquaintances who've gone through a divorce for a reference. Or ask them if they had friends who were pleased with theirs. You might even find that a friend will recommend the attorney that represented his or her spouse. Also, by reading as much as you can on the subject, you might come up with some likely candidates. Ask for a consultation and then try to see if you can get an estimate of how much the attorney's services will cost.

In the current environment of consumer awareness, many clients now shop around for good-quality legal services. As a result, since 1972 when Jacoby & Meyers created the niche for accessible, reasonably priced legal services, the marketplace for legal services has burgeoned, which is in the consumer's best interest.

When looking for legal representation it's always a good idea to interview prospective attorneys. Don't be afraid to ask questions. Don't hesitate to ask about fees and expenses. The attorney you choose will be working on your behalf, and you should be absolutely comfortable with him or her.

Following is a sample of the kinds of questions you might ask, subject to the complexities of your case.

1. About the attorney's background: Law school attended? (And find out if it is accredited.) Any background in business or a knowledge of accounting? How long in practice? How long practicing family law? How long with the firm? What kind of law was practiced prior to family law? Membership in the county or state bar association? Served on any bar committees?

2. About recent cases the attorney has been involved in. The outcomes? Pleased with the way the case turned out? Does attorney have a history of settling

cases prior to court appearances or more often goes to trial? This may tell you if the attorney has trial experience and will be willing to take the case as far as you might wish.

3. About the attorney's feelings concerning mediation and negotiation, to see possible willingness to explore alternate methods of resolving disputes. If the attorney believes the only way to settle a divorce case is through the courts and you believe otherwise, that may not be the best choice for you.

4. About the attitudes of local judges. This way you can see how familiar the attorney is with the local court system. A good attorney might be able to give you a good idea of how your case will be decided in a particular jurisdiction.

5. If there are children involved, how does the attorney feel about issues such as joint custody and visitation rights?

6. About fees. Is there an hourly rate? Ask for a breakdown of fees. Ask for a written estimate. Ask how you will be billed.

These are only some of the issues you might discuss with an attorney before reaching a final decision. If the answers seem satisfactory, go ahead and retain the attorney. If not, or even if the attorney's personality doesn't seem to mesh with yours, it's best to look elsewhere. In the end, retaining an attorney who doesn't see things the way you do does no one any good.

HIDE AND SEEK

Once you've chosen an attorney you should be prepared to provide certain essential information. A well-prepared client makes for a well-prepared attorney, which helps to achieve the best possible results. Here are some items you should bring with you:

- A detailed inventory of all property in your home, including such items as antiques, furniture, works of art, jewelry, and even appliances. This will assist your attorney in drawing up an equitable settlement.

- Copies of all pertinent financial records: tax returns, bank account statements, insurance documents, and deeds. You'd be amazed at how many wives don't even know what their husbands earn each year and are totally unaware of the family's economics.

- A diary of any facts pertinent to the divorce proceedings, which may include purchases made by the spouse, business meetings; entertaining you did of a business nature, and, in fault states, any proof of adultery, cruel and inhuman treatment, abandonment, and so forth. Dated entries and names of any witnesses to events might be important.

Once either you or your spouse has retained an attorney, that attorney is likely to offer certain recommendations as to how to proceed. Frankly there are some recommendations that I could not with good conscience endorse, even though they might be in the best interests of the client. Regardless, I think it's best to give here some examples of this advice to prepare you for what might happen.

- Some attorneys advise hiding assets if possible. They also recommend slowly assuming a more modest lifestyle so that evidence of great spending may not be used against their client in court. One example that comes to mind concerns the husband who, after holding two jobs for some time, suddenly quits one. As a result he's bringing home less money, the life-style becomes lower, and he can then claim that his wife ought to receive less than she wants because of this dip in income. If a judge suspects that this sort of thing has been done, the court can disregard this so-called lower standard of living and rule a settlement based on the spouse's previous income. But this adds a complication to an already complicated situation.

- If a spouse is a big spender, many attorneys will recommend efforts to curtail that by closing credit card accounts and ending joint checking privileges.
- With a joint banking account, some attorneys recommend taking half or all of what's in there and putting it in a separate account in order to protect that share.
- Some attorneys recommend that spouses come into the home and remove half (others suggest *all*) the furniture in order to ensure that it's still there when property negotiations begin. Prized possessions have been known to disappear when a divorce action begins.

HEY, BIG SPENDER

It is not unknown for some spouses who see a divorce on the horizon to start spending furiously. This is known to the courts as wasteful dissipation and may consist of running up credit card bills or emptying savings accounts by spending the money on frivolities.

An attorney can prevent this by obtaining a restraining order from the court and then beginning divorce proceedings immediately. Your attorney can also demand a good explanation of just how the money was dissipated and a detailed accounting of any assets purchased with the funds.

Many spouses make attempts to hide assets so that they will be less susceptible to either community property or equitable distribution settlements. They may do this either by opening bank accounts that their spouse is unaware of or by purchasing property unbeknownst to a spouse.

DIGGING FOR GOLD

In the case of states that have adopted equitable distribution, there are at least three major tasks that an attorney faces: identifying all the marital assets, appraising the value of those assets, and then proving the client's right to a fair percentage of those assets by showing sacrifices and contributions made to the marriage.

In most states both spouses must file what is known as a Statement of Net Worth, which lists all income, assets, expenses, and liabilities. Often missing from these statements, however, are items such as fringe benefits, pensions, personal expenses paid for by a business, and tax-exempt investment income. One important task expected of a competent attorney is to make sure these items are reported so that they may be included in any settlement.

SEPARATE BUT EQUAL: THE SEPARATION AGREEMENT

Generally speaking there are three models for resolving custody, property, and support issues that occur upon divorce: adversary litigation in court, settlement through negotiation, and settlement through mediation.

In this section we are most interested in negotiated settlements.

One useful tool in negotiation is the separation agreement, which is simply a blueprint for divorce. The plain fact is that if you can't come to some kind of agreement prior to an appearance in court, then the matter will be taken out of your hands and a judge will force a settlement on you.

A separation agreement may encompass such issues as custody, visitation rights, support, maintenance, insurance, taxes and liabilities, visitation, and even such mundane matters as the support of a pet, or who gets possession of the wedding album. In one of our offices, for instance, we had a case where custody of a pet was given to one spouse and visitation rights to the other. There was a clause included in the agreement, however, which stated that if the pet wasn't happy, custody would then revert to the other spouse. We've had situations where in a separation agreement one spouse was actually given "custody" of certain restaurants while the other spouse was given "custody" of others, so they wouldn't wind up eating at the same places they had frequented as a couple.

There are two primary reasons to get a separation agreement. In some of those states that do *not* recognize no-fault law, New York for example, you can get a divorce solely on the basis of one year's separation; thus a separation agreement is a necessary prerequisite to a divorce action. The second reason to obtain such an agreement is that some people are genuinely uncertain as to whether or not they want a divorce. For these people a separation acts as a kind of trial divorce.

If the divorce is an amicable one, it might be a good idea for the couple to jot down some general areas of agreement and disagreement before visiting an attorney. This will give you an opportunity to decide what you want, what your objectives are, and then work from there. Using this method a couple might even be able to write a first draft of their separation agreement, assuming they can keep their emotions under control.

Once the general issues are hashed out, the couple may choose to go to one attorney whose job it will be to describe what is involved in a divorce and how a separation works, by carefully running through the various issues and alternatives. It's important to note that the attorney can *only* represent one of the two parties (it would be a conflict of interest to do otherwise). He or she can still compose the separation agreement, which should then be reviewed by another attorney representing the other spouse. Obviously, if there are major issues that remain unresolved, this process won't work, and individual counsel should be retained.

Generally speaking if there are any particularly sticky issues, such as down payments on a house or the ownership of certain property, each party should have a separate attorney to negotiate on his or her behalf. It's quite common, for instance, for one spouse to pay the down payment on a house out of his or her own pocket; in other words, out of money that would not be considered part of community property. Let's say this amount comes to $50,000. Subsequently, however, all mortgage payments are paid out of marital funds. At the time of separation the spouse who paid the initial $50,000 might want it written into the agreement that he or she will receive that $50,000 up front, before the final marital split is made (assuming it is a community property state), and any appreciation divided.

When there are situations like these, it's best to find an attorney who will *negotiate* on your behalf, not one who will unreasonably escalate demands.

If you come in with a draft already written, an attorney will take a look at it and make suggestions. Often an experienced attorney will be able to raise matters of importance that might never have occurred to you. He might also be able to help you come to certain compromises over matters that still remain areas of disagreement. For instance, Fred and Sally came to one of our attorneys to draw up a separation agreement. The main area of contention was a house. Our attorney suggested what is a fairly common solution, satisfactory to both parties, which was then written into the agreement: Sally and her two children would live in the house until the children were ready to leave home, at which time the house would be sold and the profits shared equally.

Another benefit of having a qualified attorney examine your document is that he or she can inform you if you've come in with low expectations. This sometimes happens when one party, feeling guilty about the divorce, comes in with the attitude, "You take everything. I don't care." Eventually the party who gives up too much will wake up, regret the decision, and then blame the attorney. In the end it is in the best interests of both parties to have an agreement that is fair to all concerned.

Though you may feel capable of writing your own separation agreement, it is not advisable when children are involved. Questions regarding medical insurance and the education of the children, as well as matters of custody and visitation rights, are best left to an attorney who is fully familiar with such issues. An experienced attorney may also be able to anticipate any problems or issues you may have neglected to address.

It's always best to make the separation agreement detailed, carefully spelling out as much as possible. If you're not sure about some matters, state this in the agreement. For instance, if you want to write in a clause having to do with any change in earning power of one spouse, do so. It's not unheard of to agree to a rise in support payments if the husband's income rises, or lowering it if the wife's income rises. Let's say, for instance, that six months after the agreement is signed the husband gets a raise of $10,000 a year. If there is a clause in the agreement stating that the wife gets a certain percentage when the husband receives a raise, the woman is adequately protected. Since a raise may not be predicted with any certainty, the eventuality can be covered if the separation agreement is properly composed to cover unforeseen but potential circumstances.

Once the agreement is signed you are bound by it unless both spouses agree to renegotiate or when there is child support. The child support issue is always negotiable because it is in the state's best interests to care about the welfare of the child.

Though both parties are bound by the agreement once it is signed, we did have a case in one of our offices concerning such an agreement that was contested by the wife. She maintained that she was on heavy medication when the agreement was struck and therefore failed to fully understand its import. We successfully argued the matter in court on her behalf, and the agreement was set aside.

Though almost anything may be incorporated in such an agreement, certain matters that may not be included: You cannot have an agreement to divorce, you cannot waive the right to child support, and you cannot agree to anything that is unlawful. All these items are deemed against the public interest.

Another matter that can invalidate any separation agreement is the failure to have full disclosure at the time the agreement is composed. Each party is expected to disclose honestly all his or her assets in order that a fair agreement can be reached.

CHAPTER 13

Property Settlements

When Gail met Elliot she was forty-seven years old, living in Arizona, and had been divorced for two years. Elliot, a few years older than she, had worked thirty years for the local utility company and had recently retired. Neither had any children. They fell in love and were married. Two years later Elliot, who had become bored with this newfound free time, returned to work for the utility company and over the next several years bought back his pension before deciding to retire for the second time.

During their marriage Gail experienced several health-related problems including a serious eye condition that necessitated surgery. She still managed to work part-time as a teacher's aide for the local elementary school, earning just under $5 an hour.

Prior to the time they were married, Elliot collected $30,000 from the sale of some real estate he owned, and while he was married to Gail he received an inheritance from an aunt worth close to $60,000. In addition, during their marriage Elliot made a profit when he bought and sold several local apartment buildings as well as some commercial property.

After fifteen years of marriage, Elliot filed for divorce. By this time the property he owned, all registered in his own name, was worth close to $1 million. In an attempt to preserve his interests, during the divorce negotiations he claimed that all this was his separate property and therefore not susceptible to any claim Gail might make as a result of Arizona's community property laws.

Gail visited one of our offices in Arizona and asked us to represent her in the divorce action. One of her attorney's first tasks was to try to evaluate the extent of the marital property. He took the depositions of Elliot and all his business partners, and then hired an accountant to review all of Elliot's business records as well as his personal savings and checking accounts.

With the information concerning the worth of the marital property at his disposal, Gail's attorney entered into negotiations with Elliot and his attorney. Elliot proposed a settlement of $100,000. Our attorney felt this was inadequate, and when Elliot refused to increase his offer, the matter was taken to court.

In this case the result was in Gail's favor: She was awarded thirty-five percent of her husband's monthly pension, $250,000 in cash and real estate, and spousal support for the rest of her life.

In reaching this decision the court found, in effect, that as Elliot's wife Gail was entitled to share in the appreciation of those real estate investments he made during their marriage. Thus, despite the fact that the initial money was his, obtained either prior to the marriage or as a personal gift through inheritance, the appreciation of the investments were demonstrably a result of a marital effort.

But since Arizona is a community property state, why was Gail not entitled to an equal share? The answer lies in the fact that the court was only willing to prorate a share that had appreciated during the marriage. In other words the $30,000 Elliot had received from the sale of property he owned prior to the marriage and the inheritance money were his alone, as was approximately two-thirds of his pension since a good part of it was earned prior to his marriage to Gail. But to the extent that those monies appreciated as a result of the marital partnership, Gail was entitled to benefit.

DIVISION BY SUBTRACTION

This case provides us with a good example of the complications that are involved in determining how marital property is to be divided upon divorce. Although this case took place in a community property state, the theory applied and the outcome would probably have been similar under equitable distribution, though the figures themselves might differ.

In effect, how your assets are divided depends largely on which state you live in and on the particular judge you appear in front of. In an equitable distribution state, for instance, a judge might have concluded that Gail was entitled to only $150,000 in cash because her contribution to the marriage was not worth more. A judge in an equitable distribution state might also have limited her spousal support, even though it seems obvious that due to her age and physical condition she would never be able to support herself totally.

But no matter which jurisdiction it took place in, this case illustrates some of the ways an attorney must operate in this new marital climate, a climate that is a direct result of the changes in the divorce laws—how he must be skilled in ferreting out assets, carefully examining financial records, and generally following a trail of money.

FOLLOWING THE YELLOW BRICK ROAD

As we noted in Chapter 12, one of the first chores an attorney in a divorce case must undertake is to determine precisely what the marital assets are. Sometimes, especially in a case where the financial dealings of one spouse might be very complex, this is neither a simple nor an inexpensive task. The awful truth is that some spouses will attempt to hide assets, either by not reporting them or by making an attempt to transfer title to another party.

We had a case in one of our Philadelphia offices in which we represented an older man, Abe, seventy-two, who married a younger woman, Becky, thirty-four, who four years into their marriage began running around with other men. Our client found out about this, and before filing for a divorce had the title to his house transferred to his children.

This action did him little good, unfortunately, since Pennsylvania, where it occurred, is an equitable distribution state; when the law was changed in 1980, title no longer had any meaning. Regardless of whose name the house was in, his wife was entitled to some equitable portion of it, which would be up to the courts to decide. And so he was not allowed to transfer it without her consent.

Since Abe refused to settle with his wife, they remained living under the same roof. It's a bizarre situation, but Becky brought her boyfriend in to live with them in an attempt to force her husband's hand; in retaliation, Abe brought his children into the home. It became, as Abe described it, "a war of attrition, a battle to see who will give in first." All this simply to avoid a settlement that would give his wife an equitable portion of the proceeds of the house, a share, to be determined, of the property's appreciation during the time they were married.

In order to facilitate the process of determining the marital property, each spouse's attorney has the right to examine the records of the other spouse. This is an extremely important part in the preparation of a divorce proceeding. Although it often constitutes a major expense, you should not skimp on this part of the investigation.

Nevertheless, many clients often cannot afford to hire the appropriate experts to undertake the examination. As a result, in many jurisdictions, spouses who lack adequate funds to embark upon such a search may apply to the court for an order that directs the other spouse to pay for the examination. However, even these fees are sometimes inadequate to pay the cost, especially if a complicated investigation is necessary.

As Sylvia Ann Hewlett points out in *A Lesser Life,* it is usually the woman who suffers as a result of this situation since the burden of proof always falls to the spouse who does not hold title.

> This is almost always the woman. If a wife can't prove the existence of an asset or can't prove she deserves a share in the asset, she doesn't get a share in the asset. Obtaining such proof means hiring accountants, appraisers, tax and pension specialists and, of course, a good lawyer. The cost of contesting a divorce has therefore escalated. . . . In short, the spouse with the "deep pocket"—most often the man—gets to dictate what an equitable division of property looks like. (pages 58–59)

Additionally, as we've seen in the case of Elliot and Gail, identifying marital or separate property is sometimes a tricky business. For instance, Elliot's $60,000 inheritance was his own, but the appreciation of that inheritance that occurred during their marriage through real estate investment was to be shared by Gail. The reasoning is that the purchase of real estate was considered an *active* investment, which meant that Elliot was actively involved in the business effort. Theoretically, then, by acting as a marital partner Gail made it possible, at least in part, for Elliot to tend to his real estate business. On the other hand if Elliot had simply put that inheritance in the bank (or in stocks and bonds) where it earned an interest rate of six percent, Gail would probably not be entitled to that appreciation because it was a result of what the courts consider a *passive* investment.

TAKING STOCK

Once all marital assets have been identified, the next task the attorney faces is to place a monetary value on them. If the property in question is not easily valued, then your attorney will be forced to call upon the appropriate experts, which adds appreciably to the cost of the divorce. This procedure sometimes includes the evaluation of a family business, which itself can turn into a complicated affair.

Following are some of the yardsticks used by attorneys and courts in measuring the value of a business:

> Nature and history of the business
>
> General economic outlook for the particular industry
>
> Financial condition of the business, including the book value of the stock if any
>
> Dividend-paying capability
>
> Earning capability of the company
>
> Tangible assets of the company
>
> Market price of stocks of similar companies
>
> Sales of the company stock and the block of stock that is to be evaluated

But remember, no matter what your experts come up with as to the value of the assets, your spouse's experts are liable to come up with a figure that is significantly lower since it is in your spouse's best interests to do so. As a result, no matter whose side provides the figures, they are likely to be contested, which often serves to prolong the divorce.

TURF WARS

"When you're talking divorce in New York City, you are talking real estate." So said Joseph Hamer, a New York actor, as quoted in a *New York Times* article titled, "In Divorce Wars the Apartment Can Be a Battlefield." Mr. Hamer, having spent three years sleeping on the couch in the living room of his apartment during the time he and his wife went through divorce proceedings, could be considered an expert.

Though this particular problem is most relevant in large urban areas, due in large part to the high cost of real estate and the impractibility of dividing rental property, it is still a good illustration of one of the major problems spouses face during a divorce: who gets custody of the domicile. Many attorneys recommend to their clients that they remain in their homes at any emotional cost simply to maintain their right to the house or apartment. This often creates a very sticky situation because spouses, perhaps not on the friendliest of terms to begin with, wage a silent and sometimes petty war against each other.

I know of a case in which an elderly couple, living on a fixed income in an apartment that was rent controlled, decided to file for divorce after some thirty years of marriage. When the case came before the judge, he was unable to grant the divorce due to the financial plight of the couple. He felt that neither spouse would be able to find another affordable place to live, and so he refused to grant the divorce. Instead he ordered the apartment to be partitioned with a separate entrance for each. In this way they could continue to live under the same roof as a married couple, enjoying the benefit of the low rent, while at the same time rarely having to interact.

Our attorneys use a number of ways to decide the ownership of homes. First of all the house or apartment can be appraised and then sold, with the proceeds split between the spouses. Or one spouse can simply agree to buy the other's share in the home. Another possible solution is to balance the house against the husband's pension. We have negotiated settlements wherein the wife receives full title to the house in return for waiving all rights to her husband's pension.

In most cases, if an agreement cannot be reached between the parties, the courts will order the house sold. As we've seen before, however, certain modifications can be made in these sorts of decisions. We've been able to convince the court that the sale of the house should be delayed when there are children involved until they are old enough to go out on their own. Then the house is sold and the proceeds shared by the spouses.

SLICING UP THE PIE

Once the marital property has been identified and its value ascertained, the next step is to divide it. Emotionally this is not always an easy task. People become attached to such possessions as a favorite chair, an antique, even a record collection. And there are especially strong emotional ties to family homes, places where one's children have grown up. You can divide property, but it's extremely difficult to divide memories, and that is often what happens in a divorce.

But the fact is that it must be done, and as we've pointed out in the preceding chapter, there are two basic rules of property division in this country: community property and equitable distribution.

Briefly here's the difference: Community property is property, including earnings, acquired after marriage by the work and efforts of both spouses; it is shared equally according to the law of the state. Equitable distribution, on the other hand, divides marital property on the bases of spousal contribution, length of marriage, and other factors.

In equitable distribution states, once the marital property has been identified and evaluated, it must then be distributed equitably (not necessarily equally, as we've pointed out earlier). As noted previously, this can be done through amicable negotiation, mediation, or by going to trial.

Amicable negotiation is certainly the preferred method although in some divorces this is not always feasible. In fact, it's an old legal saw that in a fair settlement neither party is happy. But if both spouses are willing to negotiate a fair property settlement, the benefits are obvious. For one thing, they will avoid having a judge make an arbitrary decision, one that might not satisfy the needs or desires of either party.

With all the marital property on the table, negotiation can begin. It might be a simple matter of dividing assets by their declared value (which should be agreed to prior to the negotiation). There are several other elementary methods that might be employed. You might take turns choosing property from the pot, for instance. Or you might try the method parents sometimes use to avoid arguments among their children: "You cut the cake, and your brother can choose the slice he wants."

If negotiation doesn't work, you might want to consider trying mediation, a method that seems to be gaining in popularity. This may be accomplished with the assistance of a professional mediator, often a social worker or attorney trained specifically to help couples negotiate a satisfactory settlement.

Recently private mediation service centers have sprung up around the country. These services, in addition to mediating divorce cases—which includes not only property but custody arrangements—also take on as their clients quarrelling businessmen and feuding neighbors.

Unlike arbitration, in which the participants are forced to abide by the decision of the arbitrator, mediators are there only to facilitate agreement by offering objective, third-party alternatives.

While successful mediation can save both time and money in divorce cases, some detractors believe that mediation often fails to protect the rights of *either* party. Because the mediators may not be trained attorneys, they are sometimes unaware of the legal ramifications of their decisions, and in some cases the "cure" can turn out to be worse than the illness.

The cost of mediation varies. Some services charge a flat fee that falls somewhere between $2,500 and $6,000, often including the cost of preparing and filing the necessary court papers. Others charge by the session, which may run in the neighborhood of $100 an hour.

If neither negotiation nor mediation works, the last resort is to bring the action to trial where a judge will take the matter out of your hands and make the decision as to how the property is to be divided.

In New York, as in other equitable distribution states, there is something called the Domestic Relations Law which sets forth a number of factors that should be considered when deciding how property is to be shared in the event of a divorce. Some of these factors include the duration of the marriage, the age and health of the parties, the contributions that have been made to the acquisition of property by the non-title-holding spouse (and this would include the contributions made as homemaker, parent, and spouse), and the probable future financial circumstances of each spouse. Also written into the law is the leeway for the court to consider any other factor that it deems relevant to an equitable decision. For instance, as Julia Perless, an eminent New York City divorce attorney, has pointed out, "If a woman has been a complete shrew and bouncing from bed to bed or has inherited money of her own or has a healthy independent income, an equitable state judge might award her a smaller than fifty percent cut of the pie."

It's our experience in equitable distribution states that the most a woman can look forward to is a fifty percent share, and the average is closer to thirty percent. We did have a case in which a woman who worked, earned as much as her husband, and took care of the home and family was awarded a sixty percent share of the marital property, which the court felt more adequately reflected her contribution to the marriage. This is the exception rather than the rule, however.

Nevertheless, in negotiating a settlement we would always start arguing for at least fifty percent of the assets, try to justify that claim, and then work from there.

When ruling on the division of a family business, the courts will also take into account the personal efforts that have gone into making that business a success. We had a case in which we represented Phil who, while married to Pamela, established a business that manufactured men's ties. Our attorney argued that the success of the company was not due to market factors or inflation but rather to the unique skills possessed by Phil. He traveled extensively, worked long hours, and generally did much better business than his competitors. We did not argue that Pamela, in her role as wife and mother, failed to do her share in building Phil's business, but we did not believe that her contributions merited a full fifty percent share. After arguing the case the court agreed with our contention and awarded Phil a sixty-five percent share of the business.

The fact is that the longer the marriage, the more likely there will be a fifty-fifty split of assets. Since different jurisdictions have a tendency to rule in different ways, however, there is absolutely no guarantee of what a spouse might expect.

It is our experience that in equitable distribution states women often wind up with the shorter end of the stick once the divorce reaches the courts. Although theoretically men and women should be considered equal when receiving divorce settlements, this is not always the case. Consequently, perhaps due to a societal holdover from the days when the man "owned" everything in the marriage, judges seem reluctant to give the woman a "fair" share of the assets. And the divorce/property laws have effectively leaped ahead—although women have made great strides in the labor force, they are still not on an equal footing with men. In spite of what the laws might anticipate for them, the reality is that they often have a tougher time finding appropriate work for wages that can make them self-supporting in the manner in which they were accustomed in their marriage.

On the other hand, when it's a woman who owns the bulk of the assets, judges are just as unlikely to award the man his "fair" share. This is especially the case as far as spousal support is concerned, a matter that will be discussed in detail in the next chapter.

In the case of community property, the decision is a bit more cut and dry. Once the marital assets have been identified and evaluated, the court will normally split them down the middle, fifty-fifty.

SPLITTING HAIRS

In Chapter 8 we discussed the matter of educational degrees and licenses as property, but it is certainly worth a mention here as well.

Because cases concerning this question are rather recent, it's impossible to state a hard-and-fast rule as to how the courts will decide. For instance, a Massachusetts court recently refused to consider a spouse's professional degree as marital property. The court ruled in the case of Drapek versus Drapek that a doctor's medical degree was not subject to equitable distribution. This is contrary to decisions in other states which have given a spouse an interest in professional degrees or celebrity status.

At the time of the decision, Beverly Anne Groner, a Maryland attorney and chair of the American Bar Association's Family Law Section, said, "This is an area that's fluid—that's far from being firm yet." She also added that the states, most of which have adopted various methods of treating alimony awards in professional-degree cases, "are not going to be uniform for a long time. It's too bad—the location of one's home shouldn't really affect the rights one would have." But it does.

PENSION PLANS

In the last several decades pension plans have become big business. Large companies often use generous pension plans to lure top talent to their ranks, and these pension plans often translate into substantial sums of money upon retirement.

As a result pension plans often constitute the largest share of marital assets; consequently it is important that they be equitably figured into the divorce settlement. Because they are sometimes complicated and so much is at stake, I would advise always using an attorney when there is a pension involved. The attorney will be necessary to appraise and evaluate the pension.

As mentioned previously, the pension can be balanced against real property, with the pension going to the employee spouse. There are, however, some other suggested methods that we use to determine how the pension is divided.

One is that a share of the pension may be allocated to the

nonemployee spouse based upon the ratio of years the employee worked during the marriage and the total years of employment. For example, let's say Hank worked five years prior to marrying Susan and fifteen years while they were married. At this point they are divorced, and Susan would be entitled to one-half of seventy-five percent of Frank's pension. Using this method the spouse without the pension would not be able to collect until the employee spouse actually retires.

The risk with this method is that the employee may either lose the job or die before retirement, thus leaving the surviving ex-spouse without a share. Another risk is that the pension fund might go bankrupt, which would leave *both* parties without benefits. Another potential drawback to this method is that the affairs of both spouses remain entangled. This might be fine if the spouses get along, but if not, it might present further problems.

Another method, which necessitates the use of an actuary, substitutes the present value of the nonemployed spouse's share of the pension with other marital property. By this method, complicated though it is, a present value is placed on the pension, and it can be used to divide the pension equitably between both spouses.

As you can see, the nature of divorce settlements in this country has undergone a radical change in the last two decades as the stress is now placed on the economic partnership of the marriage. As a result, it's important that the consumer become more aware of the economic side not only of divorce but of marriage.

This attitude may best be justified by the following case. Because there are sometimes large sums of money at stake, one spouse may go to great lengths to "hide" or dissipate assets. One of our California attorneys tells of a case in which a husband moved out of the state and then asked his stockbroker to cash in all his stocks, put the proceeds in his name, and send him the money. Using an obscure section of the California rules of court, our attorney was able to obtain an order that was served on the brokerage house, freezing the account. A settlement for our client was then quickly reached.

TAKING YOUR CASE TO COURT

If negotiation fails, you may find yourself in court, which can be arduous, time-consuming, and costly. There's the preparation of expert and other witnesses and testimony by those witnesses. You and your spouse may have to take the stand. Financial records will have to be presented. It is, in short, a confrontational, adversarial situation that can take a heavy emotional toll.

During this process parties can file motions, making all sorts of allegations based on disputed issues. Each of these motions constitutes a kind of mini-litigation. This can be both expensive and emotionally exhausting. And this is prior to coming to trial, which can be an ordeal in itself.

CHAPTER 14

Spousal and Child Support

SPOUSAL SUPPORT: LIFE SUPPORT SYSTEMS

Prior to the adoption of no-fault divorce, one spouse was usually entitled to receive alimony when a marriage ended. Traditionally, depending upon the length of the marriage, alimony could run until either the remarriage of the receiving spouse or the death of either spouse. Marriage was a contract between husband and wife, and it stood until it was broken through adultery, abandonment, or cruelty. As a result, in the absence of provable grounds for divorce, the balance of power was equally distributed. A husband could not simply walk in one evening, announce he was leaving the marriage, and then unilaterally obtain a divorce. Negotiations had to take place. A bargain had to be struck. And if the woman felt she was not getting a fair deal, either in the form of a property settlement and/or alimony, she could simply withhold her permission for a divorce. In short, an arrangement was set up—"You support me," declared the wife, "and I'll give you a divorce." Thus,

191

even though the man might own title to all the property, it was useless unless his spouse agreed to a divorce.

This was a flawed system. For one thing, it smacked of blackmail. For another, it created an unfair situation; a spouse had little motivation to retrain herself to compete in the business world, leaving the burden of support entirely on the man. Also, as more marriages broke down, the old laws created a sham for divorce. Couples cited adultery, cruel and inhuman treatment—conditions that didn't actually exist—and in effect perjured themselves to obtain a divorce. The system also offended the sensitivities of many feminists who felt that the system perpetuated the notion of women as dependent victims who could not exist without a man.

No-fault divorce was supposed to change all this. By disposing of the notion of blame, it presumed to treat both spouses as equal partners in an economic relationship. For starters, the new laws eliminated alimony per se, replacing it with a property settlement (which we discussed in Chapter 13) and with what is now referred to as temporary spousal "maintenance," spousal support, or rehabilitation. In effect, then, with the exception of marriages that have lasted twenty years or more, in which one spouse has no employment skills or is physically or mentally unable to enter the work force, the concept of long-term alimony has generally become a thing of the past.

Instead the courts now more frequently provide dependent spouses with short-term payments that, at most, last from five to seven years and never longer than the duration of the marriage (from our experience, the average is somewhere between three and five years). In some situations, however, the court can extend payments if a reason to do so can be demonstrated. During this period the dependent spouse, who in almost every case is the woman, is expected to acquire skills so that she may enter the work force and eventually earn her own living. In other words the law is now written to avoid placing a permanent responsibility on a divorced spouse to support the other spouse indefinitely. Instead, the dependent spouse is under the obligation to prepare herself to be self-supporting.

Most of us growing up in the sixties and seventies probably found the idea of alimony an anathema, making women dependent on men and making men potential lifetime prisoners of a marriage that hadn't worked. The media often carried horror stories of women obtaining huge amounts of money in alimony payments and living in high style while their husbands slaved away simply to keep their heads above water.

But this was the exception rather than the rule. In fact, most of those receiving spousal support would probably argue that the sums they receive hardly serve to make ends meet. For instance, a study of divorced women in New York State found that when women did receive maintenance, the average payment was only about $4,000 a year.

But there is another fallacy at work here—that even with extensive training someone who has been absent from the work force for twenty years or more (or, even worse, someone who has never been in it) can, at the age of forty or over, go out and find a job that pays enough to support herself and a family.

HEADS YOU WIN, TAILS I LOSE

In her book, *The Divorce Revolution,* Lenore J. Weitzman, a professor of sociology at Stanford University, concludes that women are the clear economic losers in the new system; almost all matrimonial attorneys agree. Her research reveals that in California during the first year after divorce, women living with their minor children experience, on the average, a seventy-three percent decline in their standard of living, while their ex-husbands enjoy a rise of forty-two percent. When our attorneys were polled on the subject, the great majority agreed that, as a general rule, upon divorce the man's standard of living rose significantly while the woman's dipped.

Furthermore a 1986 White House report on the American family found that "the divorce epidemic not only has devastated childhood, it has brought financial ruin to millions of women. Divorce reform was supposed to be a panacea for women trapped in bad marriages. It has trapped many of them in poverty."

Ms. Weitzman offers two major reasons for these inequities. First, there is the forced sale of the family home, a step taken in order to satisfy either community property or equitable distribution laws. Once the wife and her minor children are without a home, other suitable and affordable housing is often difficult if not impossible to find.

Some of our attorneys point out, however, that in many cases the court will, if the circumstances warrant it, allow the wife and children to remain in the home until the kids are grown. In one California case handled by our office, the family residence was to have been sold five years after the divorce. But the husband became disabled and stopped making the child support payments, and our attorney was able to get the house awarded to the ex-wife in place of past *and future* support accruals.

The second reason, according to Ms. Weitzman, is the substitution of short-term maintenance for alimony in the mistaken belief that women would have an easy time reentering the work force and soon become the economic equals of men. The truth is that even when women are able to get a foothold in the work force, they often earn less than men doing the same job.

The result, Ms. Weitzman and others believe, has been the "systematic impoverishment" of divorced women and their children; the result is that they are becoming "the new poor."

Ms. Weitzman's research was done exclusively in California, a community property state, and critics of her findings believe they may not be valid for the rest of the country. In any case many states have taken steps to right these wrongs in recent years.

As the impact of the new divorce laws has been felt, states have taken steps to modify the inequities inherent in the system. Now that no-fault has been in effect for more than fifteen years, legislators have seen the impact it has had on the lives of men and women, and they have begun to adjust accordingly.

Nevertheless it seems that a whole generation of women,

now between the ages of forty and sixty-five, have been caught in the transition. They've been told that they are equal to men and the laws were changed to meet this vision. But in reality, though the laws may have been changed, people's consciousness and society's mores have lagged behind. Unfortunately it is unreasonable to expect that this group of women would be able to slip easily into a new role, a new life.

The problem isn't so much that women can't do the job but rather that the marketplace is prejudiced against women, older women in particular. They are usually offered the lowest paying jobs while at the same time having to pay for child care while they work.

Many of the attorneys in our offices who are most experienced in the matrimonial field feel that rehabilitative maintenance is not the solution it was thought to be, due primarily to the fact that it is unreasonable to expect that women out of the work force for such long periods of time can be "rehabilitated." As a result the women who have taken the brunt of the inequities are those who remained home during the marriage to take care of the family.

And yet it is also our consensus that the old system, which often awarded alimony for life was also patently unfair. Perhaps the answer lies somewhere in the middle. But regardless of how one might feel about it, the system is firmly in place at the moment, and in order to turn it to your best advantage, it's a good idea to be familiar with how it works.

LEAN ON ME

Herb and Mary had been married for twenty-five years and had two grown children. Herb was a successful commercial artist who earned close to $100,000 a year. Mary, on the other hand, had never worked during the marriage and had no marketable skills. Herb met Susan, twenty years his junior, on the job. They fell in love. He filed for divorce.

Mary retained an attorney from one of our Arizona offices to handle her interests. She did not want the divorce and, in hopes of winning Herb back, did not push to have his pension divided in the divorce settlement. Nevertheless our attorney, approaching the situation realistically and knowing best how to protect his client's rights, insisted upon having the court retain jurisdiction over this issue. As a result the court did award Mary forty-five percent of Herb's pension as her community property share.

As is sometimes the case Herb, experiencing some guilt over abandoning his wife of twenty-five years, had the best of intentions and agreed to pay Mary $2,000 a month alimony while maintaining a $350,000 life insurance policy on his life with Mary as beneficiary. He also agreed to pay for his wife's health insurance.

Six months later Herb and Susan were married, and a year after that they had a baby and purchased a new home. Herb decided to stop working and collect his pension. At the same time he also decided he could no longer afford to pay $2,000 a month alimony to Mary, and so, without bothering to petition the court to modify his support obligations, he unilaterally cut back his payments first to $1,500 a month and then to $500 a month. This drastic cut forced Mary to go through her savings rapidly. Only then, spiraling deeper into debt, did she return to our attorney to see if she could have the original judgment enforced.

Fortunately our attorney had ensured that the court retained jurisdiction over the pension issue, which at this point was critical. Upon going back to court our attorney was able to convince the judge that in addition to Mary's original forty-five percent share of the pension she was now entitled to an additional thirty percent share in order to cover the more than $35,000 (which included interest at the rate of ten percent) in Herb's back alimony. In addition Mary was given a lien against any pension benefits payable at Herb's death if he should die before she was paid the money owed her.

At the same time, the court reduced Herb's support payments to $1,000 a month, but because Herb had fallen so far in arrears, he had to return to work in order to support himself, his new family, and Mary.

This case makes several points. First, it shows the importance of going to an attorney experienced in matrimonial law; in this case, someone who knew how important it was to retain the rights to a pension. Second, it illustrates how, despite the fact that a spouse might have the best of intentions, circumstances change. When Herb made his settlement with Mary he could not have predicted that he would have a new family to care for, nor could Mary have known that Herb would retire early and lower his maintenance payments. Third, this case shows the importance of taking your attorney's advice. If Mary had not done this, she would have waived her rights to Herb's pension and then been without recourse. And finally there's the importance of educating yourself as much as possible regarding issues connected with divorce.

Although the judgment in the case may appear particularly harsh on Herb, it provides us with an opportunity to explore the different factors that go into a judge's decision in terms of the amount of alimony or temporary maintenance the court will award.

In general the court will consider several factors when ordering spousal support. These include the following:

Standard of living during the marriage

Earning capacity of both spouses

Ability of the spouse to pay

Duration of the marriage

Work experience, educational level, health, and age of the dependent spouse

Number and ages of the children and the nature of their separate estates

Since Herb made upwards of $100,000 a year, the court obviously felt that Mary—having been married for twenty-five years, almost all her adult life, during which time she took care of the home and raised two children—was entitled to have her standard of living maintained. Since she had never worked, had no marketable skills, and was over fifty years of age, the court also felt that she was entitled to spousal support for the rest of her life.

HOW LONG AND HOW MUCH?

The time span for spousal support is pretty much at the discretion of the judge, which means that it may last as long as either death or remarriage. Although it is impossible to generalize and the determining factor is the facts, in most cases the rule of thumb is that the duration is half the number of years of the marriage if the marriage is less than ten years. If the marriage has survived longer, as in Mary's case, the courts will certainly take that into consideration.

Many states (California is one), make use of a chart that offers a standard spousal and child support figure, which includes the minimum, average, and maximum. The court examines these figures and then decides the amount to be awarded according to the individual case. Our attorneys in California have noted a growing trend toward making these spousal awards simply by the numbers, almost as if a computer is doing it.

In Sacramento County, for instance, the family law judges actually read the figures from computer terminals that are installed on the bench.

EQUAL BUT SEPARATE

As we've said earlier, the system, though it's meant to be as fair as possible, doesn't always treat men and women equally. We had a case in one of our New Jersey offices that illustrates the inequities sometimes demonstrated toward men.

Frank, twenty-three, and Sarah, twenty-one, had been married only one year when they decided to divorce. Frank was making $28,000 a year while Sarah was earning $20,000. The judge offered a settlement of one year's spousal support of $100 a month to Sarah. Frank was represented by one of our attorneys who, though he felt the settlement was unfair to his client, advised against going to trial since the cost would have outweighed any better settlement he might have obtained. (It should be pointed out that this might not have been the case in other states.)

Our attorney felt strongly that if the roles had been reversed, if Frank had been making only $20,000 and Sarah $28,000, the court would not have ordered her to pay him $100 a month spousal support. The fact is that, since Sarah, at age twenty-one, was already making a relatively good salary, she didn't require any maintenance. In this instance we believed that the judge, feeling that traditionally the woman is entitled to something, made his judgment on this basis rather than on the merits of the case.

This theory was borne out by another case of ours. Judy, a teacher making $32,000 a year, and her husband Jim, a laborer making only $18,000 a year, went to court for a divorce, and the judge refused to award him any spousal support. Our attorneys, representing Jim, believed that if the roles had been reversed, Judy certainly would have received some spousal support, but due to societal mores the court refused to award support to the man even though he was making far less than his wife.

Now that some version of no-fault divorce has been on the books in every state for a decade or more, the kinks are beginning to be ironed out. Legislatures across the country are reacting to inequities by modifying local statutes. In New York, for instance, there is a new spousal maintenance law that changes the language of divorce laws so that the dependent spouse's post-divorce "reasonable needs," which in the past had usually been interpreted as "mere subsistence," will now be replaced by the "standard of living" that was in effect prior to the separation.

Still, laws and standards regarding spousal support are not

CFLR GUIDELINER(tm)(Revised 1987) Monthly Support at 20% Time with NCP:July 1985 Santa Clara County, CA - Page 120

CDL NETS		NO CHILDREN	ONE CHILD			TWO CHILDREN				THREE CHILDREN				J	L
NCP	CP	SS-TOTAL	CS	SS+	SS-TOTAL	EACH	CS	SS+	SS-TOTAL	EACH	CS	SS+	SS-TOTAL		
3200	0	1280 D	592	984	1576 D	444	888	836	1724 D	395	1184	688	1872	100	231
3200	50	1255 D	588	965	1554 D	441	883	821	1703 D	392	1177	676	1853	98	231
3200	100	1230	585	947	1532 D	439	877	805	1683 D	390	1170	663	1833 D	97	230
3200	150	1205	582	928	1510 D	436	872	790	1662 D	388	1163	651	1814 D	96	230
3200	200	1180	578	909	1487 D	434	867	774	1641 D	385	1156	639	1795	94	229
3200	250	1155	575	891	1465 D	431	862	758	1620 D	383	1150	626	1776	93	229
3200	300	1130	571	872	1443 D	429	857	743	1600 D	381	1143	613	1756 D	91	229
3200	350	1105	568	853	1421 D	426	852	727	1579 D	379	1136	601	1737	90	228
3200	400	1080	565	834	1399 D	424	847	711	1558 D	377	1130	588	1718	89	228
3200	450	1055	562	815	1377 D	421	843	695	1538 D	374	1123	575	1699 D	88	227
3200	500	1030	558	796	1355 D	419	838	679	1517 D	372	1117	562	1679 D	86	227
3200	550	1005	555	777	1333 D	417	833	663	1496 D	370	1111	549	1660 D	85	227
3200	600	980	552	758	1310 D	414	828	647	1476 D	368	1104	536	1641 D	84	226
3200	650	955	549	739	1288 D	412	824	631	1455 D	366	1098	523	1622 D	83	226
3200	700	930	546	720	1266 D	410	819	615	1434 D	364	1092	510	1602 D	82	226
3200	750	905	543	701	1244	407	815	599	1414 D	362	1086	497	1583 D	81	225
3200	800	880	540	682	1222	405	810	583	1393 D	360	1080	484	1564 D	80	225
3200	850	855	537	663	1200	403	806	567	1372 D	358	1074	471	1545 D	79	225
3200	900	830	534	644	1178	401	801	551	1352 D	356	1068	458	1526 D	78	224
3200	950	805	531	625	1156	398	797	534	1331 D	354	1062	444	1506 D	77	224
3200	1000	780	528	605	1134	396	792	518	1310 D	352	1056	431	1487 D	76	224
3200	1050	755	525	586	1112	394	788	502	1290 D	350	1051	417	1468 D	75	224
3200	1100	730	522	567	1089	392	784	486	1269 D	348	1045	404	1449 D	74	223
3200	1150	705	520	548	1067	390	779	469	1249	346	1039	391	1430 D	74	223
3200	1200	680	517	529	1045	388	775	453	1228	344	1033	377	1411 D	73	223
3200	1250	655	514	509	1023	385	771	436	1207	343	1028	364	1391 D	72	222
3200	1300	630	511	490	1001	383	767	420	1187	341	1022	350	1372 D	71	222
3200	1350	605	508	471	979	381	762	404	1166	339	1017	336	1353 D	70	222
3200	1400	580	506	451	957	379	758	387	1145	337	1011	323	1334 D	70	222
3200	1450	555	503	432	935	377	754	371	1125	335	1006	309	1315 D	69	222
3200	1500	530	500	413	913	375	750	354	1104	333	1000	295	1296 D	68	221
3200	1550	505	497	393	891	373	746	338	1084	332	995	282	1276 D	67	221
3200	1600	480	495	374	869	371	742	321	1063	330	989	268	1257 D	67	221
3200	1650	455	492	355	847	369	738	304	1042	328	984	254	1238	66	222
3200	1700	430	489	335	825	367	734	288	1022	326	979	240	1219	65	220
3200	1750	405	487	316	802	365	730	271	1001	324	973	227	1200	65	220
3200	1800	380	484	296	780	363	726	255	981	323	968	213	1181	64	220
3200	1850	355	480	277	758	360	721	238	959	320	961	199	1160	63	219
3200	1900	330	477	258	735	358	716	222	937	318	954	186	1140	63	219
3200	1950	305	474	238	712	355	710	205	916	316	947	172	1119	62	218
3200	2000	280	470	219	689	353	705	189	894	313	940	158	1099	62	218

NOTE: Orders discretionary, but CS not below county guidelines without reasons or stipulation. Total less than guideline needs to be checked for possible Agnos violation. Total less than current AFDC standards. OK to relabel total nder as deductible family support with or without designating all or part as nondeductible. CODE LETTERS: A – probable Agnos violation (check separate Agnosizer tables using Agnos nets); guideline CS is less than 1987-88 AFDC Standard calculated on same nets. 1987-88 AFDC standards 1 child – $633, 2 children – $511, 3 children – $511.250/mo. D – DRTRA recomputation rules may apply. NO CODE – guideline amounts have no AGNOS violation or DRTRA consequences.

CFLR GUIDELINER(tm)(Revised 1987) Monthly Support at 20% Time with NCP:July 1985 Santa Clara County, CA - Page 121

GDL NETS		NO CHILDREN	ONE CHILD			TWO CHILDREN				THREE CHILDREN					
NCP	CP	SS-TOTAL	CS	+SS-	TOTAL	EACH	CS	+SS-	TOTAL	EACH	CS	+SS-	TOTAL	J	L
3200	2000	280	470	219	689	353	705	189	894	313	940	158	1099	62	218
3200	2050	255	467	200	666	350	700	172	872	311	934	144	1078	61	217
3200	2100	230	464	180	644	348	695	155	851	309	927	130	1057	60	217
3200	2150	205	460	161	621	345	690	139	829	307	920	116	1037	60	216
3200	2200	180	457	141	598	343	685	122	807	305	914	102	1016	59	216
3200	2250	155	454	122	575	340	681	105	786	302	907	88	996	59	215
3200	2300	130	451	102	553	338	676	88	764	300	901	74	975	58	215
3200	2350	105	447	83	530	336	671	71	742	298	895	60	955	58	214
3200	2400	80	444	63	507	333	666	54	721	296	888	46	934	57	214
3200	2450	55	441	43	484	331	662	37	699	294	882	32	914	57	213
3200	2500	30	438	24	462	329	657	20	677	292	876	17	893	56	213
3200	2550	5	435	4	439	326	652	3	656	290	870	3	873	56	212
3200	2600	0	432	0	432	324	648	0	648	288	864	0	864	55	212
3200	2650	0	429	0	429	322	643	0	643	286	858	0	858	55	211
3200	2700	0	426	0	426	319	639	0	639	284	852	0	852	54	211
3200	2750	0	423	0	423	317	634	0	634	282	846	0	846	54	210
3200	2800	0	420	0	420	315	630	0	630	280	840	0	840	53	210
3200	2850	0	417	0	417	313	626	0	626	278	834	0	834	53	210
3200	2900	0	414	0	414	311	621	0	621	276	828	0	828	52	209
3200	2950	0	411	0	411	308	617	0	617	274	823	0	823	52	209
3200	3000	0	408	0	408	306	613	0	613	272	817	0	817	52	208
3200	3050	0	406	0	406	304	608	0	608	270	811	0	811	51	208
3200	3100	0	403	0	403	302	604	0	604	269	806	0	806	51	208
3200	3150	0	400	0	400	300	600	0	600	267	800	0	800	50	207
3200	3200	0	397	0	397	298	596	0	596	265	794	0	794	50	207
3200	3250	0	394	0	394	296	592	0	592	263	789	0	789	50	207
3200	3300	0	392	0	392	294	588	0	588	261	783	0	783	49	206
3200	3350	0	389	0	389	292	583	0	583	259	778	0	778	49	206
3200	3400	0	386	0	386	290	579	0	579	258	773	0	773	48	205
3200	3450	0	384	0	384	288	575	0	575	256	767	0	767	48	205
3200	3500	0	381	0	381	286	571	0	571	254	762	0	762	48	205
3200	3550	0	378	0	378	284	567	0	567	252	756	0	756	47	204
3200	3600	0	376	0	376	282	563	0	563	250	751	0	751	47	204
3200	3650	0	373	0	373	280	559	0	559	249	746	0	746	47	204
3200	3700	0	370	0	370	278	555	0	555	247	741	0	741	46	203
3200	3750	0	368	0	368	276	552	0	552	245	735	0	735	46	203
3200	3800	0	365	0	365	274	548	0	548	243	730	0	730	46	203
3200	3850	0	363	0	363	272	544	0	544	242	725	0	725	45	203
3200	3900	0	360	0	360	270	540	0	540	240	720	0	720	45	202
3200	3950	0	357	0	357	268	536	0	536	238	715	0	715	45	202
3200	4000	-0	355	-0	355	266	532	-0	532	237	710	-0	710	44	202

NOTE: Orders discretionary, but CS not below county guidelines without reasons or stipulation. Total less than guideline needs to be checked for possible Agnos violation only if less than current AFDC standards. OK to related total order as deductible family support... guideline SS + or - exceeds $1,250/mo. DARTRA recomputation rules may apply. NO CODE - guideline amounts have no AGNOS violation or DARTRA consequences. standards. 1 child $311, 2 Children - $311, 3 children - $633. O - DARTRA, guideline SS+ or - exceeds $1,250/mo. DARTRA recomputation rules may apply. NO CODE - guideline amounts have no AGNOS violation or DARTRA consequences.

uniform, and how they are interpreted often depends upon the jurisdiction and the sitting judge. Consequently we often see situations where a client will come in and say something such as, "My friend has three kids. He just got a divorce, and he's only paying $100 a week alimony. I want the same deal." Unfortunately, this might not be possible because there are so many variables involved. Who was the judge who heard his friend's case? What was the jurisdiction? What was the family's standard of living?

For these reasons it's impossible to predict accurately what kind of spousal support you're going to have to give or get, or guarantee specific results. The best an attorney can do is give you an idea of what the courts in your jurisdiction have been doing recently, which might provide you with a ballpark figure of what you can expect.

A SPOUSAL SUPPORT CHECKLIST

Spousal support may come in several different forms, and when negotiating a settlement here are items you might want to discuss with your attorney:

- You should choose between a lump sum and periodic payments. If there are periodic payments, they can be either a fixed amount or fluctuate, perhaps being tied to the cost of living index or even the ability of the spouse to pay, or be in relation to the dependent spouse's change in income.
- You should make clear exactly when the payments are due, either on a particular day each week or perhaps the first or fifteenth of the month.
- You may want to include some kind of penalty for late payments.
- You may want to provide for costs tied to spousal payments such as tax consequences, transferral of real estate, audits, attorney's fees, and so forth.

- You may want to include some kind of security system to ensure that payments are made. This may include the posting of some kind of bond.

- You should make sure it's clear whether cohabitation or remarriage constitutes a reason for termination of support. This is a fuzzy area in many states, so it's best to try and clear it up yourself.

CHILD SUPPORT

The courts are empowered to order either or both parents to provide child support. This support may even be ordered on a temporary basis while the divorce action is proceeding.

Generally there are at least five factors that the courts will consider before deciding how much to award:

1. The financial condition of each parent (and also of the children, if they have money in their own names or a trust account). If, for instance, one parent is better off financially, that parent will probably be asked to contribute a higher share of the support.

2. The health and educational needs of the children. If a child is sickly or has need of special education, then the amount of the support should reflect this.

3. The nonmonetary contributions each parent makes in caring for the child. If the mother tends to the children's daily needs, for instance, and if those children are preschool age, the amount of the support may be adjusted accordingly.

4. The standard of living of the family prior to the divorce. If the standard was high, it's likely the court will want to maintain that standard for the child's sake.

5. The tax consequences to either parent as a result of the support order. A spouse paying alimony and child support, most often the husband, is able to

deduct the alimony but not the child support from
his tax returns. And alimony, but not child support,
is taxable on the wife's return.

I'M SORRY, THAT DIME PHONE CALL WILL NOW COST YOU A QUARTER

Recent Census Bureau figures reveal the startling news that
nearly one-quarter of all American children now live with just
one parent. This contrasts with figures from 1960, which showed
that only one child in ten was living in a single-parent household. The same study estimates that 14.8 million children under
the age of eighteen were living with one parent in 1986, up
from 5.8 million in 1960. Of these children, eighty-nine percent
lived with their mothers and eleven percent with their fathers.
Forty-two percent were children of divorced parents, while
twenty-seven percent were children of parents who had never
married.

With these figures in mind, is it any wonder child support
has become a national concern? In fact, in the last decade or
so individual states, at the prodding of the federal government,
have moved to deal with the problems of children living in
single-parent households.

Across the country child support awards vary widely. A child
support survey in Denver found that two-thirds of the fathers
were ordered by the court to pay less for child support than
their monthly car payments. And in New York anywhere from
$50 to $75 per child a week is the most common award.

Unfortunately it is hardly enough. A New Jersey study reported that most judges "lack accurate information" about the
"costs of feeding and clothing a family, the availability and
costs of child care, and the particular employment problems of
the displaced homemaker." The report furthermore found that
judges rarely gave a wife more than thirty percent of her husband's salary in combined maintenance and child support.

A survey of attorneys in our offices concurs. Almost without exception, child support awards are too low. Our attorneys feel that one of the reasons for this is that child support awards rarely take into account the loss of services from the father. Most support recoveries are based on at least twenty percent practical participation by the father. As you might imagine, this is not always the case. The following case handled by our firm, one of many of its kind, is a perfect example.

Barry and Jane had been married for six years when Ethan was born. Unfortunately the child was brain damaged and would require constant care his entire life. The strain of caring for a handicapped child was too much for Barry and Jane, which eventually took its toll on their marriage. When Ethan was three and a half, they divorced.

We represented Jane in the action and, in addition to a property settlement considered by other attorneys to be quite generous, we were able to get her $800 a month in child support. As for visitation, Barry was supposed to take Ethan every other weekend; however, there were several weekends when Barry failed to take the child.

Having to care for Ethan alone began to seriously affect both Jane's physical and mental health. She had looked forward to those weekends when Barry was supposed to take Ethan. Feeling the strain and looking for some kind of relief, she came back to us to see if we could do something. After listening to her problem, our attorney returned to court and argued that because of Ethan's handicap, the emotional pressure on his mother was far too great. She looked forward to and desperately needed the freedom that came when Barry took Ethan as a time to restore her energies.

Taking this argument into consideration, the judge ruled that for each weekend Barry missed, he would have to pay an additional $100 in child support. The judge reasoned that Jane did indeed need a "break" from caring for her child, and if Barry was not going to live up to his responsibility by participating in the upbringing of his child, then he should at least be responsible for paying for professional care during the weekends he was absent.

Here was a case in which the judge took into account something often forgotten in support cases: the amount of time spent by each parent with the child and the services missing when one parent neglects his or her responsibilities. The judge's decision not only spurred Barry to face up to his obligations, but it also meant that Jane would not be penalized when he did not.

STANDARDS: HOW MUCH IS ENOUGH?

In order to deal with this enormous problem of how much child support is sufficient, the Child Support Enforcement Amendment was passed by Congress in 1984. This amendment mandated that all states have guidelines in place by October 1, 1987, along with formulas to determine child support awards.

In coming up with new guidelines, states have taken various approaches. Some plans are based solely on the income of the noncustodial parent; others take the incomes of both parents into account; still others take a percentage of the gross income or the net income. And others provide for subsistence of each parent before apportioning the remaining resources.

So far three different payment formulas have been advanced. First, there is the Wisconsin formula, which has been used by that state since 1983. Under this method the noncustodial parent pays a percentage of his or her gross income, calculated by how many children are involved: seventeen percent for one child, twenty-five percent for two children, twenty-nine percent for three children, thirty-one percent for four children, and thirty-four percent for five or more.

This method has been criticized by some for its failure to take into account the income of the custodial parent.

Another method is the Delaware Melson formula, named for the Delaware judge who developed it. In use since 1979, it sets aside a specific amount, in most cases $450 a month, for the subsistence of each parent. The combined income of the parents that exceeds the total of $900 is then used for the basic needs of the child in the following amounts: $180 a month for the first child, $135 for the second and third, and $90 for the fourth through sixth, with each parent contributing a share proportionate to his or her net income. After these amounts have been allocated, fifteen percent of the remainder of each parent's net income goes to additional child support for one child. For each of the second and third children, ten percent is added, while five percent is added for each of the fourth, fifth, and sixth children.

A third method is the Income Shares model, developed by the federally financed Child-Support Guidelines Project of the National Center for State Courts. It is based on the theory that the child is entitled to the proportion of parental income that he would have received had the family stayed together. Using this method, child support is computed on the basis of the parents' combined incomes. The specific amount of monthly or weekly support is set according to tables indicating what intact families in equivalent income brackets spend on their children. Each parent's income then determines the proportion of the amount he or she must pay. The problem with this formula is that it is somewhat vague, and it must take into account cost-of-living standards across the country.

Prior to 1983 the average child support order in this country was $2,907 a year, according to the Bush Institute for Child and Family Policy at the University of North Carolina. Applying the Delaware Melson formula, the average child support order would have been $6,980; under the Wisconsin formula, the average would have been $6,650.

Though these guidelines may not solve all the problems, they will inevitably go a long way in establishing some kind of workable standard. As Sally Goldfarb, an attorney with the NOW Legal Defense and Education Fund, has said, "Traditionally, child support awards were set at unrealistically low levels. Census Bureau statistics show that the average child support award is not even adequate to raise children at the poverty level. The guidelines have the potential of ensuring that child support awards will more realistically reflect the costs custodial parents must bear.''

THE WISDOM OF SOLOMON

Child support can be a serious point of disagreement between parents. Occasionally one parent feels he or she is being taken advantage of by the other; the mother may feel the support is inadequate while the father may feel he is being "overcharged" or that the support is not directly benefitting the child and the mother is using it for her own needs.

We had a case in which a divorced couple, Victor and Stephanie, agreed that each would take custody of one of their two children. Due to this arrangement Victor believed that neither should have to pay the other any child support. At the time Victor's business was grossing over $150,000 a year while Stephanie was earning only $6 an hour working as a temporary office worker. But when Stephanie asked for more child support, Victor insisted that the business was actually losing money.

Stephanie came to us to see if we could force Victor to give her child support. Our attorney examined Victor's books and found that he was paying himself over $4,000 a month out of his business in addition to having the business pay for many of his household expenses. This made it look as if the business was actually losing money. As a result of this discovery we took Victor to court and were able to receive a fair child support order.

THE CHECK IS IN THE MAIL

We were fortunate in the case of Victor and Stephanie because once the judgment was made Victor lived up to his responsibilities. This is not always the case. Some experts have even gone as far as calling the failure to make child support payments a national disgrace. No wonder, since estimates of unpaid child support run as high as $4 billion each year.

Many might argue that the so-called deadbeat dad is due simply to the inability of a spouse to pay, but apparently this is not always the case. A *New York Times* op ed piece (August 13, 1986) by Harriet N. Cohen and Adria S. Hillman claims that "men with incomes of $30,000 to $50,000 are as likely to ignore child support orders as those with incomes under $10,000 a year."

Why do they do it? After all, we're talking about children who often have to do without essentials because their mothers can't afford them. Some fathers truly can't afford the payments; others resent having to make payments they feel are not being used for their children but for their ex-wives; still others simply don't care.

Sometimes the reasons for fathers neglecting to pay child support are complex, and they go to the heart of a problem that is inherent in divorce. The problem of the "deadbeat dad" was addressed articulately by Bernard R. Goldberg, a national correspondent for the CBS Evening News, in an op ed piece published in the *New York Times* in answer to the article by Cohen and Hillman (August 20, 1986). Quoting a member of the New York League of Divorced Fathers, Mr. Goldberg wrote: "Fathers are actively discouraged from retaining an interest in their children. Why do we wonder that we have an Everest-sized problem in unpaid child support? Hasn't the obvious dawned on social workers, judges, and politicians: If you don't allow a man to feel like a father, he'll stop acting like one."

Mr. Goldberg makes the point that when fathers are left out of the everyday decision-making process concerning their children, when they are in contact with them for only short periods of time, when they are forced to say good-bye after perhaps only an afternoon or a weekend visit, they inevitably feel less like fathers. Consequently they sometimes react, often without malice, in the only way they feel they can, by withholding child support payments.

"The economic realities of divorce are frightening to many women," wrote Mr. Goldberg. "A psychologist in California told me: 'Typically, if you ask a man and woman what they fear most in a divorce, the man will tell you he's afraid of losing his children. Women are afraid of having to eat dog food.' "

When these two fears clash, the unfortunate result can be a storm so violent that everyone, especially the children, are seriously damaged.

COLLECTION TIME

Collecting child support has always been a major problem, now approaching epidemic proportions. In an effort to cope, many states have instituted means meant to make collection somewhat easier. New York is one of them.

In 1985 the New York State Support Enforcement Act was passed. Designed to reduce some of the difficulties experienced by dependent spouses in trying to obtain child support payments, the law provides for wage deductions of up to sixty-five percent, tax-refund intercepts, and streamlined collection procedures aimed at avoiding court hearings against delinquent parents.

New York has also started an innovative computer system program that will aid in finding fathers who fall behind in their child-support payments. After a computer search has located the delinquent spouse, letters are automatically written and mailed. First, there is a warning letter, and then, if the father does not respond within fifteen days, his employer is ordered to deduct the payment from his wages.

As of 1988 the State of Wisconsin has the right to withhold child support from the paychecks of all noncustodial parents. And most recently, California, Massachusetts, and Texas have joined New York and Wisconsin in this attempt to deal with the problem.

In the past if a delinquent spouse left the state and was eventually found, the dependent spouse would then have to hire an attorney in that other state in order to garnish the ex-spouse's wages or otherwise obtain back child support. This was often a costly affair. Now the federal government has instituted the Uniform Support to Dependent's Law to help alleviate this problem. First, the support papers are sent to the appropriate agency in the state where the errant father is located, and then the local district attorney's office serves those papers on the spouse. As a result it is unnecessary to go through a separate litigation in each state.

Our attorneys note, however, that although this may be an inexpensive way of serving an ex-spouse, it is not always the most efficient. This method can take up to a year, and even after that the dependent spouse will not always get what's due her. Our experience is that the individual state offices are often more ready to compromise on the amount owed so the case can be cleared up. Still, this is a step in the right direction.

Our advice is to get an attorney if you can afford it. It's faster, and more likely you'll get the amount due you.

CHAPTER 15
Custody

WINNING THE BATTLE BUT LOSING THE WAR

The majority of couples are able to work out amicably the details of child custody and visitation. Nevertheless, these difficult issues may result in bad feelings and frustrations on both sides. The fathers sometimes feel like visiting uncles and as a result may lose interest in their children. On the other hand, women, who sometimes end up with the total responsibility for raising their children, often feel put upon and undercompensated for what they're doing.

Even under the best of circumstances a custody battle can be devastating and may result in irreparable harm to the children. For this reason it's almost always in the best interests of the child to avoid these confrontations. Divorce is difficult enough on children without a vicious custody battle between their parents. Parents should make a serious attempt to work out a reasonable agreement before it reaches the point where the matter must be resolved by the court. As we noted in an earlier chapter, this can be accomplished either in a separation agreement or be negotiated at the time of the divorce.

When approaching the matter of custody, the first question both parents ought to ask themselves is what is best for the child.

Too often fathers seek an equal relationship with their children and feel that to earn this they must fight for custody, whether they truly want it or not. If you're considering seeking sole custody, you might ask yourself: Am I a better parent than my spouse? If the honest answer is no, then dig deeper. Ask yourself: Why do I want full custody? Is it pride? Bitterness? Revenge?

If you truly believe it would be harmful for your spouse to have custody, then certainly you have an obligation to do something about it, no matter how arduous the battle might become. The following case we handled is an example of the lengths one father had to go to in order to obtain custody of his children.

George and Ellen met and subsequently married when they were in the service together. A year later, while stationed in Georgia, Ellen gave birth to twin sons. Shortly thereafter they were transferred to New York and then shipped out to Italy, where their marriage began to fall apart. Ellen had an affair and then moved out of the house, leaving George and the children.

George took on the responsibility of caring for the twins, while at the same time he persisted in his efforts to have Ellen visit with their children. He also went through military channels to see to it that Ellen was required to contribute to the children's support.

As their tour of duty was coming to an end, George learned that Ellen had put in a request to extend her stay in Italy. Believing it was in his sons' best interests to have continued access to their mother, George filed a similar request. His request was granted, but oddly enough his wife's was not.

A month before she was to leave the country, Ellen took the boys with her on a visit to her home state of North Carolina, where she filed divorce proceedings, seeking full custody of the twins.

When George learned of this, he immediately flew to his home state, Pennsylvania, on emergency leave. In Philadelphia he visited one of our offices, and our attorney advised him to fly to North Carolina and secure the services of a private investigator to locate his children. He then returned to Philadelphia and began custody proceedings. A hearing was held to determine whether the court there had jurisdiction. The Philadelphia court found that it did and set a custody hearing in thirty days. North Carolina counsel was obtained, and the proceedings filed by Ellen in that state were forestalled. Ellen was then informed of the Philadelphia proceedings, including the upcoming hearing.

At this point George returned to Italy and brought witnesses back with him to Philadelphia. Ellen failed to appear at the hearing. As a result, the court ruled in favor of George, granting him custody.

By this time Ellen was in Kentucky where she was now stationed with the children. George immediately flew to Kentucky with the Philadelphia order, secured Kentucky counsel, and commenced proceedings in that state. The result was that the Philadelphia order was upheld.

Now, finally, after months of legal proceedings and traveling halfway around the world, George was able to take custody of his two sons and return with them overseas.

PRIDE COMETH BEFORE THE FALL

All too frequently child custody battles become a matter of pride. Parents sometimes believe that a custody battle is necessary to prove how much they "love" their child. Or perhaps they do it because they feel it is expected of them. Other times it's a way of demonstrating the bitterness one spouse harbors for the other. What parents blinded by emotions sometimes fail to understand is that those truly hurt are the children.

For this reason, before undertaking any custody battle, it's a good idea to ask yourself: Am I doing this for myself or for my child?

When it comes to the question of custody the courts will always base their decision on "the best interests of the child"; however, "best interests" is a somewhat vague concept, one that can be interpreted in many ways.

To help understand how the courts make these decisions, here are a few things judges take into consideration:

- The age and sex of the child. Younger children are more likely to remain with their mothers; girls are less likely to be given to their fathers.
- The child's needs and each parent's qualifications to fill those needs. If the court feels that a particular child is in need of a full-time mother, the decision will be made with that in mind.
- The number of children in the family and their inter-relationship. Most courts are loathe to split up children unless there is a good reason to do so.
- The potential adjustment the child may have to his new home, community, and school.
- The physical and mental health of all those involved.
- The child's own preference (this criteria usually is used only in the case of children ten years and older).

In most jurisdictions, in an attempt to reach a fair decision, the courts have the right to appoint a social worker or investigator to examine the situation and then report the findings to the court. In some cases the court may even appoint an attorney to represent the best interests of the child.

In California, for instance, there are three steps taken before the matter of custody is resolved:

1. A conciliation court session with a counselor
2. A custody evaluation complete with home visits
3. A custody hearing including psychological evaluations and reports from expert witnesses.

THE MORALS OF THE STORY

Theoretically in most jurisdictions the court is supposed to limit its concern with moral issues, especially those that relate to life-styles and sexual matters, to those that actually affect the parent's relationship with the child. If one parent has a drug or alcohol problem, for instance, the court is unlikely to grant that parent custody because the problem would certainly have an impact on the well-being of the child.

Even though they are not supposed to, however, some courts, acting on built-in prejudices, do take the issue of morality, especially sexual morality, into consideration. For this reason many attorneys advise their female clients to stay close to home and cut down on their social life until the custody matter is resolved.

This situation is, in fact, at the heart of Sue Miller's fine novel, *The Good Mother* (Harper & Row, 1986). Briefly, after a divorce that was not particularly acrimonious, though there was some residual hostility, the mother got custody of her young daughter. She became involved with an artist who was sexually liberated and had a tendency to walk around the house without clothes on. The little girl saw this, of course, and when she visited her father, began making comments about male genitalia. Her father became very exercised over his daughter's behavior and took his ex-wife, a model mother in all respects, to court to try to win custody of his daughter. A trial ensues and, on the basis of her life-style, the mother loses custody. In this fictional case the court reacted prejudicially toward the mother, judging her by standards that would not have been applied to the father. This is an example of how a judge reacted according to his own biases.

Some states do not sanction cohabitation. The Supreme Court of Illinois, for example, recently transferred custody of three girls, ages seven to twelve, to their father as a result of their mother's open cohabitation. Other states that go along with this view include Alabama and Missouri. On the other hand, cases in California, Florida, and Pennsylvania, have reached a different result. A California court noted that there was no evidence that cohabitation was detrimental to the children involved.

THE GAY DIVORCÉE

The matter of gay parents gaining custody has also been in the courts recently. While it is difficult for gay parents who live alone to be awarded custody of a child, it is almost impossible for a gay parent who resides with a live-in lover to win custody. Most courts have assumed that children will be disturbed living in a homosexual environment, even without clear evidence that this is so. Courts across the country have expressed grave concerns that children might be inclined or induced to follow a homosexual life-style if they are residing with a gay parent, with or without a lover present.

In a New York case, for example, the court ruled that although a lesbian mother was free to live any life-style she chose, she could not impose this life-style on her child. Other states, such as New Jersey and Washington, have granted initial custody to lesbian mothers but only on the condition that the mother not share the company of her lover when the children are present. New Jersey courts have gone as far as to award custody to a mother who was in an openly gay relationship.

Nevertheless, in determining custody most courts use the fact of homosexuality as but one factor among others. In other words the mere fact of the homosexuality of a parent is not supposed to automatically deny him custody of a child.

One interesting California case that was decided in 1987 involved a sixteen-year-old youth whose custody was awarded to his late father's homosexual lover. The court ruled that this was what the youth wanted, and it would give him the "stable and wholesome environment" his mother, who at one point had snatched the child, could not provide.

To sum up on the subject of homosexual custody, the standard for the courts remains what is in "the best interests of the child," but some courts still appear to give the fact of homosexuality greater weight in determining its effect on those best interests. On the whole, few courts have held the mere fact of the homosexuality of one parent in itself sufficient to deny that parent custody.

THE FAULT LINE

Courts are also not supposed to allow the question of whose fault the divorce was in their custody decision. Most judges realize that in the majority of cases "fault" does not lie with one spouse. Nevertheless, if one spouse has acted egregiously toward the other, the court is sometimes influenced accordingly and considers the offending spouse an unfit parent, in which case it would be loathe to grant custody to that parent.

FAIR IS FAIR

Recently another important case affecting custody was ruled on in the Michigan Court of Appeals, which recognized what is called the doctrine of the "equitable parent" in the context of divorce. In this case a man who learned during the divorce proceeding that he was not the biological father of a son was still treated as the father and given full visitation privileges. The court wrote: "Notwithstanding the fact that the husband is not the biological father of a child born during the marriage, the husband may acquire rights of paternity under the theory of 'equitable parent.' "

In order to qualify as an "equitable parent" the court offered three criteria:

1. The husband and child must mutually acknowledge such a relationship, or the mother must have "co-

operated in the development of such a relationship"
before a divorce complaint is filed.

2. The husband must want parental rights.

3. The husband must agree to take on the obligation
   of child support.

If these criteria are met, the court ruled the spouse in question must then be treated as a parent and "he may also receive the right of custody or visitation." In New Jersey the courts have even gone as far as to rule that if a stepparent has acted in all ways as a parent and has interfered with the natural parent's rights, then he or she must support that child.

A CUSTODY PRIMER

Generally speaking there are four kinds of custody:

1. Physical custody, which means the one with whom
   the child actually lives.

2. Legal custody, which allows one parent to determine
   how the child is to be brought up. This includes
   important matters such as what school to attend,
   when to go to the doctor, when to have dental work
   done, and permission for any operations that may
   have to be performed.

3. Joint custody, in which both parents are responsible
   for determining how the child is to be brought up,
   sharing decisions on such matters as schooling and
   health. With joint custody the child might also reside
   for a specified period of time with each parent. Joint
   custody is only possible when both parents get along
   well. Some professionals feel that joint custody min-
   imizes the psychological damage of a divorce on a
   child. It does so by keeping the noncustodial parent
   an integral part of the child's life.

   In order for joint custody to work several criteria
   must be met: Both parents must be willing to put

their child's interests first and be deemed "fit" by the court. They must be willing to have frequent and continuing contact with each other. Both must be willing to be actively involved in the life of their child, and, obviously, they should live near each other. There should also be a certain amount of flexibility in both parents' jobs so that if an emergency arises one may deal with it. And, finally, both parents should have adequate financial resources.

There are, of course, certain advantages to joint custody. These include equalizing the burden of raising the child; alleviating the problem of divided loyalties for the child; the flexibility of rearranging custody matters without having to go back to court; and finally, it may ease some of the problems inherent in child support since both parents are actively participating in the upbringing of their child.

There are potential disadvantages as well: A power struggle between parents is possible; it may be stressful for children to be shuffled back and forth between parents; each parent's geographic mobility is somewhat limited since they have to live near each other; and finally, it may perpetuate the hopes some children harbor for the reconciliation of their parents.

4. Psychological joint custody is an offshoot of actual joint custody. From our experience joint custody works well only under ideal circumstances, that is, when the ex-spouses maintain an amicable relationship and when they live in the general area of each other. And yet, when the circumstances are not ideal, there can still be what we like to call psychological joint custody. This means that although the courts may have granted custody to both spouses, one spouse maintains physical custody of the children simply because things work better that way. And yet, with this kind of custody, both spouses can maintain an active say in how the child is brought up.

CHANGING THE RULES IN THE MIDDLE OF THE GAME

Custody decisions are always open to modification by the court if circumstances warrant. Such modifications are usually made only if there is a compelling reason. If the home life of the custodial parent changes radically, for instance, causing great instability to the child, then the court will certainly consider altering the original decree. Again the rule of thumb is what is best for the child.

Here are a few conditions under which the courts might consider modifying custody:

1. If one parent deliberately interferes with the visitation rights of the other parent. In this case courts have even been known to take custody away from the offending spouse.

2. If the court sees evidence of the custodial spouse neglecting the child, they will most certainly modify custody.

3. Any evidence of either psychological or physical abuse.

4. Courts are also wary of a parent who tries to turn a child against the other parent.

5. When children get older, they sometimes choose to live with another parent. Some courts will consider this preference, especially in the case of adolescents and teenagers.

VISITATION

Visitation rights should be included in the divorce decree. It's best to work out a schedule with your spouse and not leave it up to either the court or some vague standard that you make up as you go along. The ages of the children involved should be taken into consideration. With younger children the amount of time spent with the child by a noncustodial parent might be less although it might occur with more frequency. With an older child visitation might consist of two full weekends a month as well as specified school vacations.

It's also a good idea to encourage both telephone and written contact with a noncustodial parent. Many believe that unspecified visitation is best if the parents get along well because it allows the greatest degree of flexibility.

A CUSTODY SAMPLER

Perhaps the best way to approach the various problems that may arise in matters of custody is to present a variety of the thousands of cases on the subject that we handle in our offices over the course of a year.

A LIFE OF HER OWN?

Often people are frustrated about their situation, and they come to us with specific questions that need to be clarified as to the present state of the law. This was the case with Evelyn and Jon who had been married for nineteen years and had two children, a boy fifteen and a girl twelve. Jon was an office supply salesman who made close to $50,000 a year, while Evelyn was a secretary earning $30,000 a year. Their daughter had some serious health problems that required a weekly visit to the doctor.

Evelyn received full custody of both children. After a year, however, Evelyn decided she was tired of doing all the housework and child care chores, and she didn't want to continue bearing sole responsibility for her kids. She felt it was time Jon did his share.

As a result Evelyn came to us. Our attorney successfully negotiated for the children to move in with their father. Unfortunately the little girl lasted only three months. She returned to her mother complaining that her father refused to take her to the doctor and, as a result, her health was deteriorating. Two months later the fifteen-year-old boy returned also, complaining that his father was too strict, that he didn't want him to see his mother at all, and that when he did his father locked him out of the house.

Evelyn now had little choice. Torn between wanting her freedom and her love and responsibility toward her children, she returned to our attorney for advice. She was told that there was little she could do but take the children back. With their welfare in mind, that's just what she did.

This case illustrates that there is nothing the courts can do to either force one parent to see a child more often or to take custody. About the only recourse the custodial parent has is to ask the court to give a higher amount of child support to take the place of the loss of services of the noncustodial parent.

HOT POTATOES

Lisa and Richard, both in their mid-thirties, had been married for ten years and had two children, six and eight. Lisa worked in order that her husband could go to school and get his master's degree. Upon graduation he got a job at a community college teaching history, for which he earned $28,000 a year. After ten years of marriage Richard filed for divorce. The divorce was granted.

Lisa, who was still doing clerical work for an advertising agency, decided she wanted to go back to school. Because she had to continue working part-time as well as attend classes and study, she felt she couldn't afford to keep full custody of the children. She approached Richard and asked him to take the children for fifty percent of the time. He refused. She then visited one of our offices and asked for advice.

Unfortunately there was little we could do for Lisa in this case. As in the previous one, we informed her that the courts will not force Richard to take the children because they are loathe to impose custody on one parent who doesn't wish it. The courts realize that this is not in the best interests of the child.

A MOVING EXPERIENCE

When Phyllis, an actress, divorced Bob, who had his own local construction firm, she won custody of their son Joseph. The divorce was an amicable one, and Bob received generous visitation rights. One day Phyllis informed him that she was moving from California to pursue her career in New York, and she planned to take Joseph with her.

Bob didn't mind Phyllis moving, but he did not want to lose contact with his son. However, she was adamant. Bob came to us and asked for help. We went to court on his behalf and made a motion to prevent Phyllis from moving Joseph out of the court's jurisdiction. We were able to convince the judge that it was in Joseph's best interests that he remain in California near his father. The court reasoned that since Joseph was nearing his teens he would benefit from a strong, ongoing relationship with his father.

Again, in cases like this, the court will always look to the best interests of the child, and with more frequency they are limiting the movements of one spouse in order that the child may be near both parents. In this case the judge was convinced that Joseph would benefit most by having his father close by, and so the court ruled that although Phyllis could leave the state, she could not take Joseph with her.

POISONING THE WELL

Simon and Lois had a very bitter divorce. So bitter, in fact, that Simon had to file a paternity action to prove that he was the father of their little girl Vanessa.

Upon proving paternity Simon was granted visitation rights

by the court. However, Lois had made Vanessa very dependent on her. At eight years old she was still sleeping with her mother, and she was told repeatedly that her father never wanted her, that he had wanted her mother to have an abortion rather than give birth to her, that he didn't love her and would hurt her.

As a result of what really amounted to "brainwashing," Vanessa was convinced she shouldn't spend much time with her father, and so, whenever she was with him, she insisted upon calling her mother. Lois then cried and told Vanessa how lonely she was. As a result Vanessa always ended up pleading to go home.

Simon was totally frustrated. Everything he did with Vanessa was carefully scrutinized, and often the child became hysterical because she wanted to be returned to her mother. Simon realized his ex-wife had almost total control over the quality of his relationship with his child, and he came to see an attorney in one of our New York offices to see if he had any recourse.

Our attorney advised him that he didn't have very many alternatives. If he stopped seeing Vanessa, she would feel rejected. If he tried to see her more often, she might end up hating him. The best he could do would be to continue seeing her when he wanted and hope, with patience, he might be able to undo the damage Lois was causing.

This is a good example of how custody issues often reflect the basic problems that divorced parents are having. The children are caught in the middle. They become, in effect, a sponge for all the issues the parents have on the table. Unfortunately the courts cannot play a role in subtle issues like these. At best an attorney can try to educate a spouse as to the psychological nature of the problem. Here, the best advice we could give was for both spouses to seek counseling.

But sometimes events taking place in a parent's life can have a beneficial effect on the other parent's relationship with a child. One of our attorneys tells of a client whose ex-wife had a boyfriend, and as a result his time with his son expanded, with little interference from his ex-wife.

We had a case similar to Simon and Lois's in which one

parent was trying to sabotage the relationship of the other parent with a child, but this one had a happier ending.

ALL'S WELL THAT ENDS WELL . . .

Kim and Gerald were divorced after thirteen years. They had a son Eric who was nine years old. Gerald had visitation rights every other weekend and for several school holidays. Kim insisted, however, that Eric hated his father and so, over the period of a year and a half, Gerald saw his son only two or three times. This made him very unhappy, and he came to us for help.

We took the matter to Family Court, and a judge ordered both parents and the child to undergo counseling. We also told Kim that if Eric didn't want to see his father he could just say so and we wouldn't push the matter.

Several months later our attorney called Gerald to find out how things were progressing. He was told that Gerald and Eric were seeing each other regularly and that Eric even wanted to spend more time with his father.

If a wife refuses to allow her ex-husband the right to see his children, he is not without recourse. Here, with the aid of an attorney, are some strategies available to him:

- He may obtain a court order enforcing his visitation rights.
- If there is still a problem, after obtaining such an order, he can visit the local police station, show them the order, and they will send an officer with him to his ex-wife's house to ensure that the mother complies with the order. (It should be noted that although this is the ideal, it's probably not a realistic expectation due, in part, to police priorities.)

- The court also has the right to stop child support or tie it into visitation rights if the order is ignored.

- In the case of a child who says he does not want to see the noncustodial parent, a judge will speak with the child and then make a judgment. Before rendering his decision he might also ask for a mental health study.

In some custody cases the issue of child abuse or molestation will be raised by one parent against the other. This is a very difficult area, one that we will discuss in Chapter 18. Although these charges may be warranted, it is not unheard of for one parent to falsely accuse the other. The courts are aware of this, but if there is even a hint of child abuse or molestation, a thorough investigation of the charges will be ordered.

While this investigation is under way, to ensure the welfare of the child the court will often order supervised visitation (this is also used when one parent is deemed potentially dangerous). Under supervised visitation a relative or friend of the custodial spouse must be present at all times (you may also hire someone to be present).

KIDNAPPING

In the past ten years or so the problem of one parent kidnapping a child from another parent and taking him or her to another state has made headlines. It is a serious matter that has received a good deal of attention, and rightly so.

The causes of this problem vary. In most cases, however, you will find a parent who feels custody or visitation rights have been unjustly denied. Perhaps he has tried to have the custody decision modified and failed. The fact is that parents who go to this extreme have been pushed to the limits. They feel frustrated and powerless. Unfortunately most do not realize how much harm they are causing, not only to the other parent but to the child as well.

In the past many jurisdictions were willing to reopen custody matters that were originally decided in other states. Unfortunately this sometimes encouraged child-snatching. Lately, aware of this problem, most courts have become reluctant to involve themselves in out-of-state custody matters unless there is an emergency.

In addition, nearly all states have adopted the Uniform Child Custody Jurisdiction Act which was designed to discourage child snatching. There is now also a federal law that makes child abduction by a spouse a criminal offense. It's hoped that these measures will put an end to this problem.

Recently, to add a bizarre twist to this situation, a ten-year-old Long Island, New York, boy who had been kidnapped by his mother and taken to Florida filed an unprecedented $1.5 million damage suit against her. This first-of-its-kind suit against a parent was for assault (he was allegedly chased through the woods, thrown to the ground, and dragged to a waiting car), abduction, false imprisonment, and emotional distress. The boy filed the suit after winning an order from the state supreme court changing temporary custody from both parents to his father.

As of now the suit, which has ramifications in the area of children's rights, has not yet been ruled upon.

TO GRANDMA'S HOUSE WE GO

There are those rare occasions when grandparents will seek custody of children. Though courts prefer to grant custody to a parent, if the grandparents can prove that both parents are incompetent and if there are exceptional circumstances, the courts may determine that it is in the best interests of the child to reside with the grandparents. The court will do a careful examination of those seeking custody, and the grandparents will have to be deemed in good health.

Under normal circumstances grandparents also have inherent visitation rights. As the following case illustrates, however, these rights may be terminated if the court feels that they are not in the best interests of the child.

After fourteen years of marriage Sam and Georgia were divorced. Because Georgia had suffered severe psychological difficulties, which the court determined had a severe impact on the children, Sam was granted full custody, and the decree specifically denied his wife visitation privileges.

Sam moved to Mexico where he met a woman, married her, and had another child. He then moved back to New Jersey. At this point the maternal grandparents, who had little previous contact with the children, now twelve and fifteen, sought him out in an effort to secure visits with their grandchildren.

Sam denied their request. He believed their visits would be disruptive to his children. He was particularly concerned about his twelve-year-old daughter who had received professional help as a result of the treatment she'd been subjected to at the hands of her mother. He also felt that the grandparents would not be a good influence because they were separated and the grandmother was an alcoholic.

The grandparents commenced Family Court proceedings to obtain visitation rights. Sam retained an attorney from one of our New Jersey offices to represent him. Our attorney presented a psychologist who felt the grandparents' visits would be harmful to the children. The judge also spoke directly with the children. As a result he denied the grandparents' petition.

A rather bizarre case concerning grandparents' custody occurred in Florida in 1987. The grandmother, who had custody of a child, lost that custody to a couple she hired as babysitters when the child was an infant. In this case the judge did not rule that the grandmother was unfit but rather that the couple could provide better for the child's welfare.

Briefly, the child was born to a woman who suffered from schizophrenia and had been in and out of institutions. She could not care for the child, and so the child was declared a dependent of the state and custody was awarded to the grandmother. She hired the couple to look after the girl while she worked. The child formed a parental bond with the sitters, calling them "mommy" and "daddy." The couple, in turn, became quite attached to the child, and they sued for custody.

Using the standard of "the best interests" of the child, the court ruled in favor of the couple, though the grandmother was granted visitation rights. The court did not find the grandmother an unfit parent but rather came to the conclusion that the child's best interests would be served by awarding custody to the younger couple.

These cases represent the extreme. In the majority of cases, if the matter does get as far as a courtroom, judges will usually bend over backward to see to it that grandparents receive either visitation rights or custody because the relationship established by grandparents with their grandchildren can offer a unique and valuable experience.

WHATEVER HAPPENED TO THE WICKED STEPMOTHER?

Recent figures tell us that one out of every five American children is living in a stepfamily. As a result the courts are now beginning to see a number of cases in which stepparents are asserting claims not only for visitation but also for custody.

Though the cases are somewhat isolated, more attorneys are drafting divorce agreements that provide for visits between stepparents and children. Although admittedly rare, we are also seeing situations in which natural parents are agreeing to relinquish child custody to stepparents, as well as stepparents agreeing to pay for support of children who are no longer living with them.

In the case of a second divorce between a maternal parent and a stepparent, a clause may even be written into *that* agreement stating that natural parents will in no way block a relationship that has been built up between the child and stepparent.

Prior to 1982 no stepparent in any state had the legal standing to make such a claim on a stepchild, but since then at least a dozen states have passed statutes that can be interpreted as giving stepparents the right to seek visitation or custody after a divorce. California is one state whose laws specifically spell out visitation rights for stepparents, and several other states are in the process of doing the same.

The reasoning behind laws such as these harkens back to "the best interests of the child." A growing number of family law experts now believe that significant relationships in a child's life should be preserved, if possible, after divorce.

In the large majority of jurisdictions, however, the notion of blood being thicker than water still prevails. In addition, almost all of the victorious stepparents were stepmothers who challenged biological fathers, which obviously reflects the traditional mores of the court.

Another question that may arise on this subject is the obligation of stepparents to provide support for stepchildren. Under the common law there was no such obligation, but now there is a growing trend of charging stepparents with child support after a divorce if the court rules that they have, over an extended period of time, acted in loco parentis (in place of a parent) in such ways as providing financial support and assuming custodial duties.

CHILDREN

CHAPTER 16

Birth Rights: Abortion, Fathers' Rights, Adoption, and Birth Control

ABORTION

Abortion has been a subject of passionate and sometimes even violent debate in this country. On one side we have so-called Right-to-Lifers who believe that to perform an abortion is tantamount to murder. On the other side there are the proponents of abortion who cite a woman's right to do what she likes with her own body, which includes the right to abort the fetus of an unwanted child.

Due to recent changes in the law few of these cases now find themselves going through the court system, but our firm often sees clients coming in for consultations concerning their rights in obtaining abortions. Because the laws concerning the right to abortion have changed so radically in the last decade or so, they are confused as to what their rights are. A question we often hear is, "My daughter is pregnant. She wants to have an abortion. Is there any way we can stop her?" (The answer is that if she is of the age of consent, no; if she is under age, you must check your own state's laws pertaining to abortions by minors.) Also, "My daughter is pregnant. She wants to have the child. Is there any way we can force her to give it up for adoption?" (Again the answer is generally no.)

In order to know just what your rights are concerning abortion, it's important to understand the state of the law today.

CHANGE OF HEART

Prior to the early 1970s abortion was illegal in most states, and if a woman wished to undergo the procedure, she was forced either to journey to a state or even a foreign country where abortion was permitted or to visit an illegal abortionist. The latter could be a dangerous, even life-threatening choice since there was always the possibility that the abortionist was not a qualified physician, which presented the prospect of infection or various other serious complications.

This situation changed in 1973, however, with the historic case of Roe v. Wade. Here the Supreme Court ruled that a woman's right to have an abortion during the first trimester of her pregnancy was superior to the state's interest in the potential life residing within her body, as well as to the moral views of a substantial portion of the population.

Though there have been many attempts to overturn or at least limit the court's landmark ruling, as of today this case remains the law of the land. Consequently it is now legal for a woman to obtain an abortion as long as it falls within the first three months of the pregnancy.

END RUNS

The Court's ruling in Roe v. Wade has not dampened the fight waged by the antiabortionists. Recently the Reagan administration fired a salvo in the fight against abortion by attempting to limit federal funds made to family planning clinics that suggested abortions. This move was eventually blocked by a federal district judge in Colorado, and the Reagan administration eventually backed down.

Other moves to limit the scope of abortions have been attempted by individual states. For instance, as this book was being written the Pennsylvania legislature passed a bill that would require women to notify sexual partners before having abortions and girls under the age of eighteen would be required to get parental consent or a court order before being allowed to undergo the procedure. This bill also required physicians to inform women awaiting abortions the nature of the procedure, its risks and alternatives. And before giving her consent to an abortion, in most cases the woman would have to certify in writing that she had received the information.

There have been other attempts to limit the law, especially concerning minors. At least twenty-three states have passed laws requiring either parental notification or parental consent before minors can obtain abortions. As an example, California passed a law that would require women under the age of eighteen to get parental consent before obtaining an abortion. This was not unlike a law that the State of Illinois passed, the aim of which was to restrict minors' abortion rights for the purpose of promoting consultation with their parents.

The Illinois case was eventually brought before the Supreme Court. The state law would generally have required girls under the age of eighteen who wanted an abortion to wait twenty-four hours after both parents had been formally notified or to go to a state court and persuade a judge to bypass the requirement for notification and the waiting period. A federal district court struck down the law before it took effect on the ground that it placed too heavy a burden on minors seeking abortions because it could result in longer delays (the time it would take to go to court in order to bypass the notification requirement) and increase both costs and any medical risks inherent in the procedure. A federal appeals court came to the same conclusion, though for somewhat different reasons. When the case reached the Supreme Court the justices deadlocked 4–4 (Anthony Kennedy, the ninth justice, had not yet been confirmed); consequently the lower court decision was affirmed.

As recently as the summer of 1988 a federal judge struck down a Georgia law that required minors to tell their parents of their intentions to get an abortion. A similar result just occurred in Ohio. On the other hand, the Appellate Court in Minnesota upheld a Minnesota law that requires women under the age of eighteen who want an abortion to notify both parents or get special approval from a state judge.

These decisions basically follow a trend that had been set in six previous decisions involving minors' abortion rights. For instance, the Court has struck down laws that give parents an absolute veto over their daughters' decisions, holding that a prompt and expeditious judicial bypass procedure must be made available for both mature minors and for those emotionally immature or psychologically impaired minors who can show that their best interests would be served by having an abortion without obtaining their parents' consent.

FATHERS' RIGHTS

Women have long argued that they have the right to control their own bodies, which means that they have the right to abortion. Recently, however, some men have argued that they, too, have rights concerning the unborn and that they should be consulted before any decision to abort is made.

In a Long Island case still before the courts, Dr. David S. Ostreicher, an orthodontist, filed suit against his wife, seeking both a divorce and monetary damages because she had an abortion without his knowledge or consent. He maintained that his wife had the abortion to spite him because he refused her pleas to tear up the prenuptial agreement signed prior to their 1985 marriage. She argued that not only was the abortion done with his knowledge but also his consent, primarily because he refused to support the child. Dr. Ostreicher also filed suit against the doctors who performed the abortion and the hospital where it was performed, on the grounds that they had a moral obligation to give him advance notice of the procedure. The courts recently dismissed the case.

After the landmark Roe v. Wade decision, the matter of whether fathers have the right to stop abortions has been the subject of legislation in several states. Many states tried to enforce laws that required a woman who chose to have an abortion to notify her husband or, in some cases, get his consent. In 1976, however, the Supreme Court struck down a Missouri law that required the husband's consent for a woman to get an abortion.

Other cases on this issue have made their way into the judicial system. In Utah, which has a notification law, a state judge issued a temporary order forbidding a pregnant eighteen-year-old to have an abortion. The order was based on arguments by her estranged husband. At a later hearing the judge found no basis for a permanent order, and the woman was allowed to have the abortion.

In Indiana an eighteen-year-old woman whose boyfriend had won a court order forbidding her to have an abortion violated that order and underwent the procedure. The order was obtained as a result of an unusual paternity action in behalf of the fetus. Despite the order, the woman had the abortion and the matter is now in the lower courts.

The likelihood is that we will see other cases as men begin to test the courts concerning their right to fatherhood.

A NEW WRINKLE

Recently a very interesting case with potentially startling ramifications hit the news. The result of this New York case was that a woman was granted the right to sue her physician for damages that came as a result of her submitting to an abortion on what turned out to be erroneous advice of that physician.

Carmen Martinez was a homemaker who became pregnant while under medication prescribed for a glandular problem. On the advice of her doctor she underwent an abortion even though, due to her religious beliefs, she strongly resisted the idea. She finally agreed when her obstetrician was informed by specialists that her medication could produce severe birth defects, resulting in the child being born with an abnormally small brain or no brain at all. As it turned out, two days after the abortion was performed it was discovered that the dosage used to compute the potential danger was more than two thousand times larger than Mrs. Martinez actually took, making the risk of birth defects far smaller than originally thought.

Mrs. Martinez, believing that she had murdered a healthy baby, required five years of psychotherapy to recover from the depression and guilt caused by her decision, which was arrived at as a result of misinformation provided by a doctor.

The ensuing ruling by New York's highest court granted Carmen Martinez the legal right to sue because the "breach of duty" that resulted in the abortion had indirectly harmed her emotionally. In other words it gave her the right to sue for recovery based on emotional trauma, not simply the fact that she had an abortion. It also established a new exception to the prevailing legal concept that damages for emotional trauma may not be recovered by one person for injuries that are sustained by another.

In coming to its decision the court wrote, "The emotional distress for which she seeks recovery does not derive from what happened to the fetus; it derives from the psychological injury directly caused by her agreeing to an act which, as the jury found, was contrary to her firmly held beliefs."

As a result of the court's decision, the case was returned to New York's Appellate Division to reconsider the facts.

BIRTH CONTROL

In this country we have the right to pursue various methods of birth control. There have been cases, however, where birth control methods were suspected of causing serious health-related problems.

One example of this concerns the Dalkon Shield, an intrauterine contraceptive device that was removed from the market as a result of suspicions that it caused injury to as many as two hundred thousand women in this country, who have filed claims against the A. H. Robins Company. (The company has now filed for bankruptcy in an attempt to protect itself from the potentially huge liability it faces.) The company proposed a compensatory fund of $1.75 billion for those women who claim to have been injured by the shield, the use of which allegedly resulted in pelvic inflammatory disease. The plaintiffs in the case argued that this fund is not nearly large enough.

At the time this book is being written, the case is still in the courts. But no matter what the final decision, this case does point out that if damages can be proved to be the result of a birth control device, compensation through the courts can be obtained.

ADOPTION

According to recent estimates there are forty couples waiting an average of five years to adopt every available infant, and that ratio seems to be widening all the time.

The situation has become so desperate for some that prospective parents are placing advertisements in college and urban newspapers, seeking unwed mothers willing to give their children up for adoption. On the shadier side, there has been a noticeable proliferation of organized rings that smuggle infants, some of whom have been kidnapped, across the Mexican border and then sell them to the highest bidder.

According to the National Committee for Adoption, which is an association of some one hundred and forty or so private adoption agencies, the number of adoptions that took place between unrelated people in this country declined to just under fifty-one thousand from just under eighty-three thousand from 1971 through 1982. This decline is attributed mainly to a diminishing pool of children available for adoption, which is the result of a higher number of abortions, the greater use of contraceptives, and a change in social mores that has lifted the stigma historically associated with a single parent.

Connected to these statistics is the fact that the number of foreign-born children adopted in the United States rose from just under five thousand in 1981 to close to ten thousand in 1986. Of those, almost two-thirds of the children came from Korea.

Why the increasing demand for adoptive infants? Some say the reason is that many members of the postwar baby boom generation who postponed parenthood, often for the sake of their career, have discovered that they are infertile, and so they turn to adoption.

It should be no surprise that the most sought after infant is one who is white with no physical or mental handicap. Naturally, this is just the child who is the most difficult to find.

As of yet there are no federal adoption laws per se, only those passed by the individual states. As a result it's difficult to give hard-and-fast rules concerning adoption. If you are considering such a move, it's best to check the laws in your own state, but certain procedures are similar no matter what state you reside in. You can expect to find the following.

There are two legal ways to adopt a child: through an adoption agency or by private adoption. For the most part, adoptions are regulated by the individual state's Social Service Laws. Generally it is illegal for anyone other than a licensed agency or the natural parent to "place" a child. If someone else brings the two parties together—in New York, for instance—that person is required to file an intermediary affidavit with the court.

There are two kinds of agencies: in-state and intrastate. The agency is supposed to screen the biological mother and prospective parents. This screening would include intensive studies of the home environment.

Out-of-state agency adoptions are regulated by the Interstate Compact. Under this compact an authorized agency in one state may place a child in another state.

The cost for an agency adoption can run anywhere from $15,000 to $20,000, and these agencies are more likely to place restrictions on the prospective parents. They may require, for instance, that the prospective parents be married couples with a stable homelife and that they be economically sufficient families; often there are age requirements as well.

Private adoption is recognized in all but five states. In a private adoption the biological mother and prospective parents locate each other, either through friends, relatives, doctors, lawyers, or even advertisements. The adoptive parents may pay expenses for the biological mother, but no other sums may change hands; otherwise it would be considered baby selling or brokering, which is against the law. The cost of private adoption can run anywhere from $3,000 to $30,000.

In most states a home study must be conducted even in a private adoption before the court will approve. In this case, however, the home study, usually performed by the appropriate social services agency, is conducted after the child is in the home.

In every adoption case there must be a proper "surrender" of the child by the birth mother. In most cases the biological mother appears in court to confirm her written surrender. In certain situations the mother may not be required to appear, though the court will require an explanation for her absence.

Though the law does not insist upon each party being represented by counsel, it is almost always a good idea since it's in the best interests of both parties to be properly represented.

Many states have provisions that allow the biological mother to revoke her consent (usually between thirty and forty-five days after the adoption has taken place). This revocation is not automatic, however. It is usually left up to the court to decide whether it should be allowed.

As noted before, "baby selling," which is prohibited in every state, is the placement of children for value. Four states— Delaware, Massachusetts, Michigan, and Minnesota—ban non-agency or independent adoptions by attorneys or other intermediaries. The reasoning set forward by these states is that in their experience licensed adoption agencies best protect the child's interests by limiting fees, requiring psychological counseling of pregnant women, and screening of the prospective adoptive parents by objective social workers and attorneys.

In those jurisdictions where independent adoptions are legal, there are few guidelines as to what intermediaries may do and what amounts of money may change hands. Only a few states have set maximum adoption fees. Instead, most of these states allow adoptive parents to pay for the natural mother's "reasonable and necessary" legal and medical expenses, without defining what these costs may include.

GAY ADOPTIONS

It was only a half-dozen years ago that a California man became the first openly gay adoptive parent. This adoption cannot be said to have opened the floodgates for other gays who wish to adopt, but some have been successful in Alaska, California, and Oregon.

Other states have not been quick to pick up on this trend. In fact, several roadblocks have been set up to make it difficult, if not impossible, for gay parents to adopt. These efforts include Florida and New Hampshire laws that ban adoptions by homosexuals (gay foster parents are also banned in New Hampshire); a Massachusetts policy that prohibits the placement of foster children with homosexuals (this policy does not deal with adoptions); and Arizona, the only state with case law on the subject, has denied a bisexual man's petition to adopt.

STEPPARENT ADOPTIONS

When Richard and Jennifer were divorced, Richard gained custody of their two children. A year later he remarried and his wife Susan took over the role of caring for and mothering his two children. Three years passed, during which time Jennifer remained totally out of touch with her children. She didn't call, she didn't even bother to send birthday cards.

At this point Susan wished to legally adopt Richard's children, and so they came to us. Our attorney informed them that, under law, they would first have to give Jennifer notice of the adoption hearing in order for her to involuntarily terminate her rights as a parent.

Jennifer attended the hearing and sat there stone-faced throughout the entire proceedings. When she was called to testify she said, with no regrets and no tears, that she wanted to continue being the children's mother simply because she *was* their mother.

The court, noting that Jennifer had abandoned her children and further believing that she showed absolutely no remorse, ruled that it would be in the best interests of the children to be adopted by Susan. Hence the court held that Jennifer no longer had any legal rights regarding her children, and the adoption petition was granted.

This case is typical of the kinds of cases our offices across the country have handled. Often, estranged parents will, in the best interests of their children, allow a stepparent to adopt. Other times, as in the case of Richard and Jennifer, the matter must be taken to court.

The most significant thing to remember is that once this adoption has occurred, the natural parent loses all legal rights in connection with that child. This includes visitation privileges, which may now be made only upon consent, as well as the right to make any decisions that have an impact on the child, such as those regarding education or health.

CHAPTER 17

The New Technologies

If you think the legal system has a tough time keeping up with the changes in societal mores, just think about the lopsided race it runs with the scientific community. Hardly a week passes without the announcement of some medical or scientific breakthrough that not only affects the quality of our lives but also may cast into serious conflict basic questions of ethics and morality.

In the last several years few topics have aroused more passionate debate than those concerning reproductive technologies, specifically surrogate parenting. This practice, in use in this country for little more than a decade, has been branded everything from a miracle for those who previously could not conceive their own child, to nothing less than slavery and baby selling by those who vociferously condemn it.

According to the latest statistics one American couple in six is infertile (or is having extreme difficulty conceiving a child). With this number growing, is it any wonder that those affected are desperately searching for some kind of solution to the problem?

One of the solutions available to a couple whose problem involves the inability of the woman to conceive is for her husband to artificially inseminate a surrogate mother. Sometimes this mother is a volunteer, perhaps a close friend or even a relative. Other times a woman is paid to act as the surrogate.

Nearly a decade ago the first birth under a surrogate contract was recorded in the United States, and since that time it is estimated that more than six hundred children have been conceived using this method.

The usual arrangements are for a husband and wife to find a woman who is willing, for certain financial remunerations (usually anywhere from $10,000 to $25,000 plus expenses), to bear a child and then, when it is born, give it up to the natural father and his wife.

But surrogate parenting is not without its critics who claim that not only does it exploit the surrogate mother and is morally reprehensible but it also treats children as mere chattels to be bought and sold.

The United States is not the only country grappling with these difficult issues. In 1986, for instance, Britain outlawed commercial surrogacy contracts, although private agreements are still allowed.

SETTING A PRECEDENT

In this country the arguments both pro and con came to a head with the so-called Baby M affair. Here's a synopsis of this case, which will undoubtedly have long-lasting effects on the issue of surrogate parenting.

William and Elizabeth Stern, a New Jersey couple, both forty-one years old, wanted to have a child. Unfortunately Mrs. Stern, a pediatrician, suffers from a relatively mild case of multiple sclerosis, and it was thought that pregnancy might aggravate the condition. As a result the Sterns decided to hire a surrogate mother who would be artificially inseminated with William Stern's sperm. They approached an agency that screens potential surrogate mothers, and eventually Mary Beth White-head, a twenty-nine-year-old local housewife and mother of two, was chosen.

On February 6, 1985, Mrs. Whitehead agreed to a contract that stipulated she would relinquish all rights to the child in return for $10,000. On March 27 of the next year Mrs. White-head gave birth to a girl whom she named Sara. The Sterns, however, called the child Melissa.

On April 12, 1986, Mrs. Whitehead informed the Sterns that her maternal instincts had taken over, and she would not give up the baby. She also refused the $10,000 payment. Mrs. White-head later testified that she had every intention of fulfilling her contract but that she had "no control" over her behavior: "At the end, something took over. I guess it was just being a mother."

Upon learning of this change of heart, the Sterns sued for custody. They went to court and obtained an order granting temporary custody and, with this in hand, police officers arrived at the Whitehead house. Rather than comply with the court order, Mrs. Whitehead passed the baby through a window to her husband, and the family fled to Florida.

A private detective tracked down the Whiteheads and forced them to return the baby to the Sterns. In August, Judge Harvey R. Sorkow of Superior Court in Hackensack, New Jersey, named an attorney as Baby M's (as she was now to be known) legal guardian, and on January 5, 1987, a trial began to establish who would retain custody of Baby M.

Attorneys for Mrs. Whitehead maintained that a surrogate parent contract was unenforceable, while the counsel for the Sterns argued that the contract was valid.

THE FIRST ROUND

The case, which took nearly three months to try, was the nation's first custody dispute over a child born of a surrogate parenting agreement, and as such it received an enormous amount of publicity.

Prior to this case the highest court to rule directly on the question of surrogacy had been the Kentucky Supreme Court. That case involved the state attorney general's efforts to close down a clinic that brokered surrogacy agreements, on the ground that it was involved in the illegal sale of babies. The court found, however, that nothing in state law prohibited surrogate-parent agreements. In the majority opinion the court wrote, "The advances of biomedical science have carried us forward, willingly or otherwise, into a new era of genetics. If there are social and ethical problems in the solutions science offers, these are problems of public policy that belong in the legislative domain, not in the judicial, under our constitutional doctrine of separation of powers."

But the Baby M case offered a far more direct assault on the notion of surrogacy. And for that reason all eyes were on New Jersey, the chosen battlefield. On one level, the trial was nothing more than a custody case fought between a natural mother and the child's natural father, but on another, deeper level, it was also a test of the legality of surrogate parenting in this country. Critics took advantage of the opportunity to assault surrogacy and other new reproductive technologies in which sperm and ova are manipulated in various ways inside and outside the womb to increase the efficiency of fertilization as being an unnatural assault on human reproduction.

The trial itself, instead of focusing on what most believed was the basic issue—whether a contract for a woman bearing an artificially inseminated infant for money violated New Jersey's public policies and adoption laws against baby selling—hinged on the emotional stability and mothering abilities of Mary Beth Whitehead. In other words a custody battle developed from what had seemed to be a contract dispute.

During the trial it was established by the Sterns' attorney that Mrs. Whitehead's husband, Richard, a sanitation worker, was a recovering alcoholic; that the couple had filed for bankruptcy in 1983; that they had been separated for approximately six months in 1978, during which time Mrs. Whitehead supplemented her income by working as a dancer at a local bar; that one of her other two children resided with her parents for a year in 1985; and that Mrs. Whitehead, in a telephone conversation taped by the Sterns, appeared to threaten to kill herself and the baby if she were forced to give her up.

All this evidence was introduced in an attempt to prove that Mrs. Whitehead was not a fit mother and that, for the "best interests" of the child, custody of Baby M should be awarded to her natural father, William Stern.

After almost three months of hearing evidence the trial ended and Judge Sorkow rendered his decision in favor of the Sterns. In effect, Judge Sorkow found:

- Surrogate parentage does not change the equal rights both mother and father have to a child.

- The right to privacy includes the right to achieve parenthood. A state cannot arbitrarily refuse to enforce surrogate-parent contracts.

- Since all states allow men to sell their sperm, a woman cannot be barred from, in effect, "renting" her womb.

- A would-be surrogate mother can disavow an agreement before conception; however, she cannot tear up the agreement after the child is born, although the decision whether or not to abort the pregnancy is solely hers.

- Enforcement of the contract must be based solely on the "best interests" of the child. Factors include the parents' desire to have a child, emotional stability, and attitudes toward education.

- The New Jersey law that allows a mother to give up her rights to a child only after birth does not apply to surrogate motherhood because it contemplates the mother giving the child to a third person as in an adoption, not to the father.

The judge awarded custody to the Sterns not because he found Mrs. Whitehead to be an unfit mother but rather because in his estimation it was in the best interests of the child.

Immediately after Judge Sorkow's decision the debate raged even more furiously. Many applauded the decision, but others, such as scholar Harold S. H. Edgar of the Columbia University Law School, were appalled: "The judge ignored the pattern of laws controlling adoption and termination of parental rights. This seems an inappropriate way of fitting new technologies— and surrogate mothering is not, in fact, so new—to the preexisting pattern of legal regulation."

IT AIN'T OVER TILL IT'S OVER

Naturally Mary Beth Whitehead appealed the decision, and although New Jersey's highest court affirmed the ultimate outcome of the case by awarding custody of Baby M to the Sterns, it sharply disagreed with the conclusions reached by Judge Sorkow and thereby set some interesting precedents regarding surrogate parenting in this country.

The New Jersey Supreme Court found that in this case surrogacy was nothing more than "the sale of a child, or at the very least, the sale of a mother's right to her child, the only mitigating factor being that one of the purchasers is the father." Furthermore, wrote Chief Justice Wilentz, "the surrogacy contract creates, it is based upon, principles that are directly contrary to the objectives of our laws. It guarantees separation of a child from its mother; it looks to adoption regardless of suitability; it totally ignores the child; it takes the child from the mother regardless of her wishes and her maternal fitness; and it does all of this, it accomplishes all of its goals, through use of money."

The decision of the New Jersey court did not prohibit women from freely becoming surrogates as volunteers, just as long as no money is paid directly to the surrogate mother and she is allowed to revoke her decision to give up the baby.

The court said, in effect, that a mother's parental rights can be terminated only if she voluntarily gives up her child to an approved adoption agency or if she is proved an unfit mother due either to abandonment or to substantial neglect of the child. In short, the Baby M contract violated New Jersey public policy by guaranteeing that the baby would be permanently separated from one of the natural parents without benefit of a custody hearing to determine the best interests of the child. As a result Mr. Stern, through this arrangement, was assured greater rights than Mrs. Whitehead. It also rejected Judge Sorkow's argument that the surrogate contract provided Mr. Stern a constitutionally protected right under the privacy provisions of the Fourteenth Amendment to procreate and retain custody of the baby.

The Supreme Court nevertheless agreed with the lower court's decision to award custody of Baby M to her father, Mr. Stern, since it appeared to be in the child's best interests to do so. "The Sterns," the court stated, "promise a secure home with an understanding relationship that allows nurturing and independent growth to develop together. Mary Beth Whitehead's family life, into which Baby M would be placed, was anything but secure—the quality Melissa needs most. And today," added the court, alluding to the fact that since the trial Mrs. Whitehead had divorced her husband, become impregnated by another man, and then married him, "it may even be less so." The court did allow Mrs. Whitehead visitation rights to her child, which were to be worked out either by the parties or, if they could come to no agreement, by the court.

THE AFTERMATH: THE EXPERTS SPEAK

The decision, along with one in Michigan in which a trial judge ruled that surrogacy contracts are "contrary to public policy" and are therefore unenforceable in that state, will no doubt have a chilling effect on the future of surrogacy in this country. James Boskey, a professor at Seton Hall University Law School and an expert on parental rights, believes the decision "does away with a large part of surrogacy."

Other experts agree and believe that the New Jersey decision will have far-reaching effects. "It was a full and complete consideration of the issues," said Thomas A. Eaton, associate professor of law at the University of Georgia. "It's going to spur legislative action. . . . I expect it will be relied on by other courts. I think it will be persuasive, unless [the other courts are] strongly inclined to rule the other way."

As a result of the Baby M case a shadow has been cast over surrogacy, and yet the chances are there will always be people willing to work out an arrangement with the hopes that the woman doesn't change her mind.

PASSING THE BUCK

Most feel that the fate of surrogacy in this country is now in the hands of state legislatures, where even at the time of the Baby M decision numerous bills, both pro- and antisurrogacy, were pending.

As of today the state of Louisiana has banned surrogate contracts as null, unenforceable, and contrary to public policy; and the Arkansas state legislature approved surrogacy, though the governor vetoed the measure because its regulations failed to provide court reviews of the contracts. Of the states that have entertained bills concerning surrogacy prior to the Baby M decision, the sentiment seems to have been evenly divided.

Recently, a law intended to ban commercial contracts for women to bear children for infertile couples was upheld as constitutional by a Michigan state judge. This will permit surrogacy, but only so long as the surrogate does not give up her rights as a parent

As of now, then, anyone considering the use of surrogate parenting with money changing hands would be well advised to proceed with extreme caution since the likelihood of any such contract being enforced by the courts in this country is in doubt.

A PANDORA'S BOX

The Baby M case is just the tip of the iceberg. There are all kinds of new birth technologies, and all of them raise new legal doubts that must be grappled with by courts and by the legislatures. What about the child who is conceived in a glass dish using the father's sperm and the mother's egg but has been carried by someone other than the biological mother? (This in vitro fertilization has already taken place at least once, in Cleveland, where a woman gave birth to a seven-pound three-ounce girl that is the genetic offspring of the donor parents.) And already some states have passed laws regulating research done on embryos produced through test-tube fertilization.

As more children are being born through the use of various new medical techniques, more legislatures appear to be on the verge of proposing laws to either control, restrict, or expand the availability of new reproductive technology. California has adopted regulations that require physicians to inform pregnant women of the availability of a blood test that may show the presence of a deformed fetus. Other states are certain to follow suit.

All this new technology also raises serious issues of morality and ethics in addition to religious concerns. As a result we can look forward to a long period of examination and public debate as these concerns translate themselves into law.

CHAPTER 18

Child Abuse and Neglect

A TRAGIC CHILD'S TALE

In the fall of 1987, New York City authorities were called in to investigate a report of domestic violence at the house of Joel Steinberg, an attorney, and his live-in lover, Hedda Nussbaum, a former children's book editor. Steinberg and Nussbaum had two adopted children (later it was questioned whether these children were ever legally adopted), the oldest of whom was six-year-old Elizabeth. When the police gained entry to the apartment they found a horrifying scene: Ms. Nussbaum, her face swollen and bruised, obviously had been recently severely beaten, Elizabeth was beaten so badly that she was unconscious, near death, and their young son was tethered and roaming around in his own excrement.

Subsequently, Elizabeth died at the hospital, and Joel Steinberg and Hedda Nussbaum were arrested and charged with murder. As the story unfolded, it was found that Steinberg had systematically abused both his lover and his child over an extended period of time. Several reports had been filed with police and social services, but evidently little was done to stop the abuse.

Perhaps because it involved a professional, well-educated couple, this case was not buried on the back pages of the tabloids but received an enormous amount of publicity. For weeks after the case broke, newspapers carried banner headlines detailing not only the physical abuse Steinberg had heaped upon his family but also sociological stories concerning the growing national trend toward domestic violence, especially against children. Local news shows across the country picked up the story as a springboard for a series of stories on domestic abuse. *Nightline,* ABC-TV's late-night news program, allocated an entire show to the Steinberg case and the problem of child abuse, which seems to be reaching epidemic proportions.

Though the media treated this story as if it were new, the truth is that the problem has been with us for some time. Yet it appears that the silent victims of domestic violence have found a voice only now. Consider the following facts:

- There has been a two hundred percent increase nationally in reports of child abuse in the last decade; this includes an increase of nearly fifty-five percent from 1981 to 1985 alone.

- According to a 1985 study of six thousand American homes, conducted by Dr. Murray Strauss of the University of New Hampshire Family Research Laboratory, spouse abuse, which is often tied in with child abuse, occurs in about thirty-two percent of the nation's homes. Parents abuse about twenty-two percent of the children in those homes.

- Experts estimate that from two thousand to five thousand children nationwide die each year as a result of abuse, and that there was a twenty-three percent increase in child abuse deaths from 1985 to 1986.

- There were 2.2 million abuse and neglect cases reported nationally in 1986.

• The American Association for Protecting Children
estimates that reports of sexual abuse of children rose
from six thousand in 1976 to one hundred and thirteen
thousand in 1985, with twenty-six percent resulting in
court action.

Taken alone, each of these statistics is shocking enough, but
together they form a startling pattern of the growing problem
of physical, emotional, and sexual child abuse.

The *New York Times* of November 16, 1987, presented four
case studies of abused children, including one about a five-
year-old girl who was repeatedly whipped with an electric cord,
forced to overeat until she vomited, and poisoned. Another
four-year-old boy was beaten with a broomstick until he died.
Unfortunately cases like these are not all that rare. It is not
uncommon to see these cases come into our offices across the
country. Yet no matter how many times we see them we are
still horrified that adults can treat children this way.

In the past courts and social welfare programs went out of
their way to keep families together, sometimes at the expense
of the abused child. This is no longer the case. In fact, states
such as Washington are in the process of reversing past laws
and making the protection of a child of paramount concern.
At a result, in Washington as in many states, social workers
no longer need to wait for substantiated proof of harm before
removing a child from the home. They can now intervene simply on the basis of the potential risk of abuse. Going a step
further, Washington has passed a law that makes child abuse
resulting in death the equivalent of first-degree murder. This
law is now under consideration by a host of other states.

As it stands, every state now has some sort of mandatory
reporting law, requiring doctors, teachers, and health or day
care workers who come in contact with an abused child to report
it to the authorities. In addition most states offer a hot line
number to be used by those reporting suspected cases of child
abuse who wish to remain anonymous. As a result of these

steps taken by the various states since the early 1980s, there has been a sharp rise in reported cases of child abuse.

CHILD ABUSE: A DEFINITION

According to the Child Advocate Association of Chicago, Illinois, child abuse and neglect consists of nonaccidental situations in which a child suffers physical trauma, deprivation of basic physical and developmental needs, or mental injury *as the result of an act or omission* by a parent, caretaker, or legal guardian.

The elements of child abuse include serious physical injury; a situation where the child is at risk of serious physical injury, which could be threatened harm; and sexual abuse or exploitation.

Types of neglect or maltreatment, which is a somewhat lesser charge than child abuse, include the following:

- Abandonment
- Failure to provide adequate food, clothing or shelter
- Improper supervision
- Emotional deprivation
- Failure to provide the child with a proper education (this might include not sending the child to school)
- Failure to provide adequate medical care (a parent who neglected to take a child to the hospital or a doctor when it was deemed necessary)
- Failure to provide adequate parental guidance

SIGNS OF ABUSE

Experts in the field of child abuse have compiled a list of obvious indications of child abuse:

- Physical injuries, which include bruises, black eyes, cuts or broken bones
- Lack of alertness on the part of a child
- Chronic hunger or drowsiness
- Loss of appetite
- Repeated absences from school
- Signs of alcohol or drug abuse or wife beating in a household that includes children (as we mentioned before, the correlation between spousal abuse and child abuse is quite high). It is also the experience of the attorneys in our offices that alcohol or drug abuse plays a role in child abuse in up to fifty percent of the cases we see.

In addition to the above there are also a number of other, more subtle indications that child abuse may be taking place. These include how the parent and child relate to each other, whether the child seems terrified of a parent, and whether there seems to be a loving relationship between parent and child.

SEXUAL ABUSE

In addition to physical abuse, recent studies estimate that one in four girls and at least one in seven boys have been sexually abused one or more times before reaching the age of eighteen. And even more startling is the fact that in seventy-five to eighty-five percent of these cases a relative or someone the child knows and trusts is involved.

One case that came through our office in Philadelphia illustrates the difficulty of such a situation. A sixteen-year-old girl who was living with her grandmother was raped by her cousin, who lived two blocks away. When she informed her grandmother of this, the grandmother said she was lying. The girl then reported the sexual abuse to the authorities, and as a result her grandmother was charged with neglect because, although she knew of the abuse, she did nothing to stop it.

Unfortunately the age of a child is not a bar to sexual abuse. We've had many cases similar to that of three- and seven-year-old sisters who were infected with oral gonorrhea. Another typical case we had, with a somewhat bizarre twist, concerned a man charged with the sexual molestation of his seven-year-old stepdaughter. His story was that he was masturbating with molasses. When he had to leave the apartment to move his car he left the molasses on the table. When he returned he found his stepdaughter with syrup in her hair and on her face, indicating that she had played with the syrup on her own. His story didn't quite hold up because authorities also found the telltale syrup in his underwear. He was found guilty of criminal sexual abuse.

The signs of sexual abuse usually are far more subtle than physical abuse since often force is not a factor. Some potential signs of sexual abuse can be found in children's behavior. Sexually abused children may

- Show signs of depression
- Regress to infantile behavior such as thumb sucking or bed-wetting
- Become belligerent and aggressive
- Exhibit sexual behavior or knowledge that is inappropriate to their ages
- Fear a particular adult or place
- Experience an unreasonable fear of separation
- Exhibit unwarranted withdrawal or clinging
- Experience drastic mood swings
- Experience nightmares or difficulty sleeping
- Have physical complaints such as headaches or stomach aches
- Display physical signs such as rashes or pain in the genital area

THE PROCESS

In the close to twenty years that Jacoby & Meyers has been in business, we've been consulted on thousands of cases of physical and sexual child abuse. It is a very difficult area for an attorney to deal with. Society abhors those who abuse children, and rightfully so. And yet, under our system of jurisprudence everyone, guilty or innocent, is entitled to fair representation.

In cases of child abuse the state represents the welfare of the children, and so it falls upon private attorneys to represent the rights of the accused. The delicate balance between the rights of the accused and the best interests of the child present a moral dilemma that is often perplexing both to society and to those who must represent the judicial system.

In cases of abuse and neglect the courts are concerned with the welfare and interests of the children. As noted by the court in a 1968 New York case (Lincoln v. Lincoln) that has become a linchpin on the subject, "Their interests are paramount. The rights of their parents must, in the case of conflict, yield to the superior demand."

But perhaps nowhere is the state's view of child abuse made more clear than in the words from the Law Guardian Reporter of 1987 on child abuse, "Changing Evidentiary Standards under Article 10 of the Family Court Act."

> The state has evinced a strong *parens patrine* doctrine toward children who are allegedly abused. New laws and rulings have strongly and consistently revised the method by which abuse can be proven to provide further protection for children. A mere preponderance of the evidence is sufficient to establish abuse. Abuse may be shown by illegally seized evidence and illegally obtained statement. It may be proven by unsworn out-of-court statements of the allegedly abused child with only the most minimal corroboration and without benefit of cross

examination. Whether all these standards will be upheld
remains to be seen. However, the current attitudes of
the Appellate Court suggest that the standards will not
only be maintained but expanded in favor of children.

In order to examine and understand the judicial process as
it concerns child abuse, it may be helpful to see how the system
works in the State of New York. Although your state might
differ somewhat procedurally, chances are the system is basically similar.

First, the proper authorities must get a report of child abuse.
The majority of these reports are received anonymously, often
through a hot line set up by the city or state. The reports may
come from neighbors, friends, even relatives. When the proper
agency (usually the child welfare agency of your state or city)
receives the report, it will automatically investigate. Most states
require this investigation to be under way no more than twenty-
four hours after the report is filed. If in the act of conducting
their investigation the agents are refused entry to the home by
a parent, they have the right to get the police and obtain entry.

Once the suspicion of child abuse is substantiated, the child
may be removed from the home; proceedings are initiated by
filing a petition in Family Court. A summons or warrant is then
issued for a parent or parents, or other legally responsible
person or persons charged. At the same time a law guardian
is appointed for the child.

A hearing to determine if abuse exists is required to legally
keep the child away from the home. The parent or other person
charged may request an initial hearing within three days. Whether
this three-day hearing is held or waived, another hearing is
required later on, wherein the child welfare agency must prove
the facts of the case by a preponderance of the credible evidence. Hearsay is inadmissible, but there are some exceptions
such as a child's statements to a caseworker relating to the
abuse or neglect.

If a finding of abuse is made, a dispositional hearing is held.

The disposition alternatives include placement of the child (whether the child is to be taken away from the home and put in foster care, for instance, for a period of up to eighteen months with yearly renewals possible); the entry of a suspended judgment; the release of the child under agency supervision, which might mean that a social worker is assigned to investigate the matter periodically and work with the family, possibly providing necessary services to make sure the child is safe; an order of protection (as in the case of an abused wife, this court order is supposed to protect the child from any further abuse; how successful it is is another matter); adjournment in contemplation of dismissal, which means that the case is adjourned for a time and if there is no further problem during that period, the case is then dismissed; or a placement of the accused under supervision.

The brief summary of a case we handled will give you an illustration of how the system works.

Our client was Vinnie who married Connie and became the stepfather of her two girls, aged eight and fourteen. They also had a child of their own, Edward, who was three. The two girls were sent away to boarding school in New Jersey and came home only on holidays. One day they both admitted to teachers that they had been sexually molested by their stepfather. The authorities in New Jersey were informed, and they in turn reported the case to the New York authorities who immediately brought a sexual abuse case against Vinnie.

The allegations against Vinnie were quite severe, enough to warrant a first-degree rape charge in criminal court if the district attorney chose to press the case.

The steps described above were put in motion, and when it came time for the family to appear in court the judge brought the eight-year-old into his chambers and questioned her. She was quite lucid and described what her stepfather had done to her. She did so well as a witness, in fact, that the judge swore her in and her testimony was taken on the record. As a result no other corroboration was necessary.

The fourteen-year-old girl, on the other hand, was unable to testify; she broke down in tears every time the subject was broached. As a result the judge found insufficient corroboration for the sexual abuse of the fourteen-year-old but did find abuse against the eight-year-old.

The disposition of the case was that Vinnie was barred from going near either of his stepdaughters until they were eighteen, and he was not allowed a visit with his three-year-old son until he entered a sex offender program. Even then the visits were to be supervised for eighteen months, after which time the state could choose to extend the period of supervised visits.

This case not only illustrates how the system works but it also points out that the court will act to protect all the children in the family even if the charges are proved against only one member of that family. Again, of ultimate concern is the "best interests"of the children.

In this case our attorney made sure that Vinnie not only enrolled in the sex offenders' program but also attended all the meetings so that after eighteen months, if he successfully completed the program, he could be allowed to pick up normal relations with his son.

PROTECTIVE CUSTODY

In some cases the welfare agency investigating the case might see the need for the immediate removal of the child or children and placement in protective custody to keep them from harm. In New York the law states this may be done if "the child is in such circumstances that his continuing in said place of residence or in the care and custody of the parent, or person legally responsible for the child's care, presents an imminent danger to the child's life or health and there is not time enough to apply for an order."

One of the many cases we've handled in which the state found this step necessary occurred when a father was accused of repeatedly burning the eldest of his three daughters with a cigarette. She was terrified of her father. The two other girls, eight and six, were found to have vaginal infections. In this situation the agency involved wanted the children out of the home immediately, and so all three were placed in foster care. The father was charged with abuse and the mother, who the court felt should have done something about the abuse, was charged with neglect.

As a rule the situation is handled in this way: The court will charge the person or persons accused of the abuse, in this case the father. If the court feels that the other parent, in this case the mother, should have known about the abuse and did something to stop it, he or she will be charged with neglect, a lesser but not insignificant charge.

In New York the following persons may take a child into protective custody:

1. Peace officers
2. Agents of a duly incorporated society for prevention of cruelty to children
3. Designated employees of a city or county department of social services (social worker, for instance)
4. Law enforcement officials
5. Physicians treating children
6. Persons in charge of hospitals or similar institutions

At the time the charge is made, those charged should obtain the services of an attorney. It is our experience that both the husband and the wife will come in to see us. The first thing we tell them is that we can represent only one of them. In most cases it's the father because he's the one who is in the most trouble. We then inform them that in such cases they face the prospect of losing their child (or children) for up to eighteen months and perhaps longer. The father might also face criminal charges. This is relatively rare, however, since, as we discussed earlier, the burden of proof is heavier in a criminal proceeding than it is in a civil case.

The proceeding begins with the filing of a petition by the city or state agency, which alleges facts that are sufficient to establish that a child has been abused. This same petition may also allege both neglect and abuse, and it may contain allegations as to all children who are the legal responsibility of a parent. We had a case, for instance, in which our client's husband, an alcoholic, was accused of repeatedly raping his thirteen-year-old daughter. The district attorney's office, realizing how difficult it would be to prove rape, convinced him to admit to child abuse. Although it appeared that our client was out of the house when the rapes took place, she was still charged with neglect. The father pleaded guilty to abuse; she pleaded guilty to neglect. Besides the thirteen-year-old girl, there were also two other children in the house, a nine-year-old boy and a six-year-old boy. There was no evidence that either had been abused; nevertheless, all three were placed in care for the limit of eighteen months because the court felt they were at risk if they remained in the home.

Parents often come into our offices and deny any and all accusations of abuse. Unfortunately in many situations they are not telling the truth. The following case is a good example. A mother and father came in with their five-year-old son whose hand was severely burned. The mother insisted that the burn was accidental, occurring when her son placed his hand in a sink of hot water, but our attorney did not believe the mother's story was consistent with the injury, which covered the entire hand and required plastic surgery. According to both parents the "accident" occurred sometime between 4:30 and 5 P.M. The father had returned home from work at five but the child was not taken to the hospital until eight o'clock. Consequently he was being charged with neglect. We represented the father. Although he believed the time between the father's arrival home and the taking of the child to the hospital was far too long, the judge still ruled that it was not long enough to constitute neglect on the part of the father. In the meantime, the mother was held guilty of abuse. The child was therefore placed in foster care for eighteen months, and the case against the father was adjourned in contemplation of dismissal.

It's important to note the difference between abuse and neglect. Abuse is the more serious charge, while neglect may consist solely of an act of omission. Take the following example of a case that came into our office recently. Frank and Mary had been divorced for several years. Joan, sixteen, was living with her father. She came to her mother and accused her father of sexual abuse. Mary said, "You're living with your father now, so I don't want anything to do with this." Joan went back to her father and was raped again. She told her mother again, and this time Mary took action, reporting the abuse to the proper authorities. The authorities then charged Frank with sexual abuse and Mary with neglect for her failure to do anything the first time her daughter told her what her father had done. We represented Mary, and fortunately we were able to work out a satisfactory conclusion. The state agreed to drop the neglect charges against Mary if she agreed to take custody of her daughter.

At the time of the proceeding, the child is entitled to the appointment of a law guardian. In New York City, for instance, the Legal Aid Society is under contract to represent all children in child protective proceedings, except the rare case where a conflict of interest exists.

At a hearing an application to return a child who has been temporarily removed from the home may be made by the parent or other person legally responsible for the care of the child. It should be pointed out, however, that in the wake of publicity generated by cases such as that of Joel Steinberg, the courts are under a good deal of pressure not to release the child before the case has been adjudicated.

The next step is a trial. The first thing an attorney will do is obtain the records of any private or public agency that had contact with the child or parent. This includes police reports, hospital records, photographs, Xrays, Board of Education files, and the like. Next, the attorney will want to interview any available witnesses.

In sexual abuse hearings there is rarely any direct evidence, either eyewitness testimony or physical/medical evidence. Unlike rape, force is not necessarily used, nor is there likely to be medical trauma created by the child's resistance. When the accused is a parent or family member, the child is usually induced to participate by threats of force, bribery, misrepresentation of moral standards, seductive flattery, or even intoxication.

When fondling, indecent acts, indecent liberties, or sexual conduct is alleged to have occurred, there is not likely to be any physical evidence. The child victim is usually the only witness.

In the majority of cases, especially if the victim is very young, the child does not testify in open court. This is because the experience will be unjustifiably traumatic, the child is too young to participate in a trial, or the child may refuse to testify in front of the offending parent. As a result the child's testimony is usually taken by the judge in chambers.

Certain basic elements must be proved in any child abuse case:

- That the child is under eighteen
- That the accused committed or allowed to be committed some type of abuse or neglect
- That there is a relationship between the accused and the victim

CORROBORATION

Once the case comes to trial there must be corroboration of the abuse. All children's statements must be corroborated. An accepted standard for corroboration of a child's out-of-court statements is that it must be from an independent source (such as a caseworker or validator whose job it is to evaluate the charges made against the parents); that it must connect those charged to the acts committed; and that it must strengthen the statements made by the child.

For instance, in the case of a four-year-old child said to be the victim of sexual abuse at the hands of her father, the testimony of a psychologist who used play therapy with anatomically correct dolls, along with a taped conversation of the child with a caseworker, was accepted by the court as sufficient corroboration.

As we noted before, the sworn statement of a child is usually considered enough corroboration in itself.

Other corroboration may consist of a medical report; for instance, the fact that two children suffered from oral gonorrhea is prima facie evidence that sexual abuse took place. And if there is sexual abuse, the assumption is that the parent did it, an assumption that is very difficult to rebut.

According to the experience of our attorneys, judges are becoming far more lenient in what they will accept as corroborating evidence, due in large part to the public outcry against child abuse. Certain sources of corroboration are acceptable in combination with one another:

1. Medical evidence
2. Child's testimony in front of a judge
3. Statements made repeatedly by a child
4. Validation by an expert in the area of intrafamilial child sexual abuse
5. Sworn testimony
6. Any admissions made by the defendant or defendants

At the end of the trial the court will make an adjudication. The usual practice is for the court to adjourn the proceedings so that an investigation can be made into the current surroundings, conditions, and capacities of the persons involved before a final disposition is made. A home study is then conducted, usually by a caseworker who was not involved in the case up to this point. Very often mental health studies of the parties are also ordered. These consist of psychiatric examinations by court-affiliated doctors.

POSSIBLE DISPOSITIONS

There may be an adjournment in contemplation of dismissal, which usually comes only in cases of neglect that can be easily corrected. We had a case, for instance, in which we represented a father who had a difficult fourteen-year-old son who refused to go to school, stayed out late, and generally disobeyed his parents. At first they tried talking to him. When that didn't work they resorted to locking him in his room and then corporal punishment, which got out of hand. The court's decision was to adjourn in contemplation of dismissal, under the proviso that this treatment stop.

Other situations in which contemplation of dismissal might be used are those in which defendants agree to correct the situation, as in sending a child to school when they hadn't done so before or guaranteeing that the child will receive proper medical attention or making sure there is a reliable babysitter or even suspending corporal punishment. In all these cases the offenses obviously were not too severe.

In short, adjournment in contemplation of dismissal is directed when the nature of the problem brought before the court is recognized; all parties are in agreement regarding the problems; there is a reasonable basis for belief that the problem can be resolved quickly or become manageable; and a treatment process is in place and functioning.

Another option is the removal of the child or children from the home for a period of up to eighteen months. The child may be placed either with a relative or a social service agency (which would include foster care). This period of eighteen months can be extended or terminated upon proper application. For such placement to be terminated parents must be able to show that they are going to counseling, or are receiving alcohol or drug treatment or are attending parental skill seminars.

FATHERS AS SEXUAL ABUSERS: TRUE OR FALSE?

Recently the media has been filled with stories of fathers involved in divorce disputes who are being accused, sometimes wrongly, of sexually molesting their children. Some experts estimate that thirty percent of all contested-custody cases today involve charges of sexual abuse and that sixty percent of these allegations are unfounded.

There is little doubt that many fathers are guilty of sexual abuse, and yet it is also true that some mothers, either out of bitterness, frustration, or simply due to an honest misunderstanding, are accusing their ex-spouse of sexual molestation.

The situation has become so emotionally charged that mothers have kidnapped their own children in an attempt to keep their ex-husbands from having visitation rights. Many of these women, refusing to yield to court orders to make their children available to their ex-spouses, have even gone to jail on contempt charges. And an underground network of people who will take in the children of accused abusers kidnapped by their mothers has been established.

As Dr. Melvin Guyer, a child psychologist and attorney in Ann Arbor, Michigan, stated in a report in the *New York Times* (January 19, 1987), "Sexual abuse is on everybody's mind and everybody's pointing fingers. We never saw this sort of thing two, three years ago. Before it was, he drinks, she runs around—the usual stuff. This is a new song and everybody's singing it."

According to experts in the field, charges sometimes stem from a mother's misinterpretation of what a child reports after visiting with the father. Perhaps the father bathed the child, touching the genital area a little too roughly, and this is misconstrued by the mother. When this is taken along with the fact that the mother may still have some lingering bitterness concerning the divorce, it can translate into unsubstantiated and untrue charges.

Other experts point out that children often have vivid imaginations, have trouble separating truth from fantasy, and are quite susceptible to suggestion. They want to please, and if they believe that one parent wants to hear a certain story told a certain way, they might acquiesce.

These charges are often difficult to refute, especially since the subject is so sensitive. Not helping the matter much is the fact that sexual molestation by a parent certainly does take place. As you can imagine, the courts must be particularly vigilant in order to at least make the attempt to differentiate between actual and imagined abuse.

Courts take a dim view of trumped-up sexual abuse charges. The courts in at least three states—California, Illinois, and Michigan—have penalized parents because they considered the motives behind the charges vengeful.

WHAT TO DO

If you suspect either physical or sexual abuse of a child, the best thing to do is report it immediately to the local Child Protection Service or to a law enforcement agency. You may even do this anonymously. We've found in our experience that nearly ninety-nine percent of the reports made to the proper agencies are made anonymously.

If your child has been the victim of sexual abuse, you might want to look for a public or private agency that is experienced in the problem and that offers counseling for the child. Counseling for the adults involved might also be called for.

CHAPTER 19

Responsibilities of Parents and Children

NO ONE SAID IT WAS EASY BEING A PARENT

When parents give birth to a child they immediately take on duties and responsibilities that remain in force until the child reaches the age of majority. These duties are not only moral in nature but also include basic rights that are protected under the law.

In short, upon the birth of a child a parent becomes responsible to the state for the well-being of that child, which includes not only a duty to support the child (in the form of providing appropriate food and shelter) and to provide for an education but also to see to it that the child receives proper medical care. Parents also have a duty to control, rear, and discipline their children, all of which may be exercised in the context of the parent-child relationship.

Although parents may have wide discretion in the control they exercise over their children, that discretion is far from absolute: The state has the right to intervene between the parent and child if at any time it is believed that the discretion used by the parent is extremely lacking.

As we mentioned before, when you have a child you become legally responsible for that child's growth and welfare. Following is a general list of the duties and responsibilities that are protected by law.

- Education: Generally a parent has the right to educate his child in any way he deems fit. Nevertheless, this discretion is subject to any state regulations, including compulsory school attendance for minor children. There have been scattered cases around the country where children have successfully sued financially well-off parents who refused to provide for their children's college education.

- Discipline: Parents have the duty to rear and discipline their children, and they are allowed a certain amount of discretion while exercising this authority. A parent may even commit such acts as spanking a child or confining that child to his or her room, acts that might, if directed at someone else, be against the law. This doesn't mean, however, that a parent has the right to either willfully or negligently inflict injury on a child beyond what the courts might accept as reasonable parental discipline (see Chapter 18 to learn more about this).

  Consequently it has been held that a minor may bring suit against a parent for willful, malicious, or negligent behavior. The test as to whether the parent is guilty of such action is whether an ordinarily reasonable and prudent parent would have committed such an act under similar circumstances.

  It is also criminal for a parent to cause or permit a child to suffer unjustifiable mental or physical pain, to allow the health of a child to be injured, or to place a child in a situation where his or her health is endangered.

- Medical care: Every parent has the authority to make

decisions concerning the medical treatment his or her child is to receive. This authority is not unlimited, however, since parents also have the duty to see to it that their child receives proper medical attention. In cases where parents willfully fail to provide such care for their children, they are guilty of a misdemeanor.

In most instances, however, parents cannot be criminally prosecuted for child abuse in cases where, in lieu of medical treatment, a minor child is treated by spiritual means through prayer alone in accordance with the practices of a recognized church or religious denomination. Nevertheless, the state may have the authority to order certain medical care or treatment of a minor over the religious objections of parents; for example, vaccinations may be ordered (often for the protection of the general public), as might blood transfusions, where it is believed that without them the child's life might be endangered.

Failure to provide for the welfare of a child through willfulness, neglect, or abuse, either physical or mental, may result in criminal or civil charges (sometimes both) brought against a parent and the loss of that child for some period of time (see Chapter 18 on Child Abuse).

FREE AT LAST, FREE AT LAST!

In this country a minor can be emancipated, which means that the parent relinquishes control and authority over the child. When a child is emancipated he enjoys the same independence he would have had he reached the age of majority.

A minor can be emancipated by marriage, by express agreement of both the parents and child, or by implication from the conduct of parents and child that has the effect of cutting the parental ties. This might include a child of, let's say, seventeen, moving out of the family home and becoming self-supporting. In most cases a minor automatically becomes emancipated when he or she enters into a valid marriage or is on active duty in the armed forces.

An emancipated child is entitled to be treated as an adult, which means that he or she can receive medical treatment without parental consent, can enter into a binding contract, and can sue or be sued. At the same time, the emancipated child no longer has the right to be supported by his parents (though this does not mean that a parent cannot still support an emancipated child if he chooses to do so).

As a footnote, an emancipated child may petition the court to rescind the emancipation.

A COUNTRY'S SHAME

In many societies the aged are highly esteemed and highly sought after for their experience and wisdom. This is not necessarily the case in this country. Here youth is celebrated. Simply by watching television or reading magazines you can see how youth-oriented a nation we are. As a result, too often the elderly are treated as pariahs, sent off to old-age homes to live out their days, or treated as excess baggage. Sometimes this treatment goes beyond benign neglect.

The House subcommittee on health and long-term care estimated in 1968 that the number of assaults on the elderly was 1.1 million annually. In Texas alone reports of abuse increased five times in the period between 1982 and 1987. But perhaps what's most shocking is that surveys indicate that nearly six in seven of the abused aged in this country are mistreated by their own families. And we can't even be sure that these statistics are accurate since it's further estimated that only one out of fourteen cases of abuse against the elderly is actually reported. This may be the result of confusion, embarrassment, or the shame of admitting that a loved one either beat them or perhaps locked them in a room, causing them to miss meals.

According to the office of Representative Claude Pepper

(D.-Fla.), who has specialized in the problems confronting the elderly and who is himself well into his eighties, mistreatment takes many forms. As an example, a report issued in 1987 tells of a Nevada woman who repeatedly beat her incontinent mother and rubbed feces in her face as a punishment.

Neglect is also rampant among the elderly. Representative Pepper, during one of his many investigations, was also told of an eighty-year-old woman, crippled with arthritis and dependent upon her son for care, who was left in ninety-degree heat tied to her bed, with just a few saltine crackers and a jug of water to nourish her.

Abuse may also include mental cruelty. One New York case involved a malnourished eighty-year-old man who was afraid to eat because his daughter had threatened to poison his food. This case points out how difficult it can be to prove abuse. Many charges are virtually impossible to substantiate. Sometimes it is even possible that the elderly person is imagining the abuse.

Other, more extreme cases may even involve sexual abuse. According to Representative Pepper, elderly women have been beaten and raped by their relatives. A seventy-four-year-old woman was raped by her son-in-law and then told after the attack by her daughter that she'd better keep quiet or "you won't have a home to sleep in."

The reasons for abuse of the elderly are many: The abuser may have been the victim of abuse as a child, drug or alcohol problems, stress, or emotional instability.

THE CHILD AS FATHER OF THE MAN?

The question arises whether a child should be responsible for the well-being of a parent if that parent becomes unable to care for himself or herself. Although the moral and ethical answer may be yes, in general states provide no such obligation. In fact, courts have often found that although there may be a moral obligation to care for a parent, there is no legal obligation.

Most states have what are called adult-protection-services laws. These laws are intended to protect vulnerable adults, including the emotionally disturbed as well as the elderly. The truth is, however, that enforcement is uneven, and when these laws are enforced, the penalties are slight.

The elderly can be a potentially fertile resource for this country, and for that reason they should be protected. Oddly enough, there is hope for change. With the maturing of the baby boom generation, more people will reach the age of retirement at the same time than ever before. With the median age of the population rising, problems of the elderly will undoubtedly be addressed.

THE FUTURE

THE FUTURE

CHAPTER 20

New Frontiers

In the last twenty years or so, due in large part to scientific advances and changes in social mores and behavior, the law has been forced to deal with a whole new set of issues. These contemporary matters, many of them rather controversial, include the right to die, organ transplants, date rape, and sexually transmitted diseases. Because these issues are so current, there is very little case law to use as precedent. Nevertheless, these issues have found their way into our legal system, and as a result state legislatures now have to consider various statutes in order to deal with these emerging issues.

Following is a brief description of one of the most pressing issues and the state of the law as it stands today. Remember that legislatures across the country are only now grappling with these matters. It's best to check your own locality to see what the law is at present.

SEXUALLY TRANSMITTED DISEASES
AND THE LAW

Five years ago it would have been unthought of to have the law interacting with the social sphere in terms of the transmitting of sexual diseases. But today, due in large part to the overwhelming concern caused by the spread of AIDS, the law is now inextricably interweaved with these issues. People are reaching out to the law not only for protection but also for relief. One has only to consider the following recent issues to see some of the changes the legal system is now forced to deal with.

- An army private at Fort Huachuca in Arizona was court-martialed on charges that included aggravated assault because he was accused of having sexual relations twice with a female soldier and once with a male soldier without disclosing that a blood test had shown him to be infected with the AIDS virus.

- Marc Christian, who claimed to be a lover of the actor Rock Hudson who died of an AIDS-related illness in 1985, filed a civil suit seeking $10 million in damages from Hudson's estate because, although he tested negative for the virus, he "lives in constant fear" of getting the disease.

- A divorced Texas man who claimed he got genital herpes from his wife sued her lover for $1.3 million, alleging that the defendant "willfully" infected his wife, who then unwittingly passed the incurable disease on to him.

- A Washington jury awarded a Seattle woman $40,000 in a suit she brought against her husband after she was infected with the incurable herpes virus. The woman claimed she caught the disease when she and her husband renewed sexual relations after being estranged for a period of time.

- A New York court ruled that a woman could proceed

with a $1.5 million suit against her ex-husband who she claimed infected her with a case of herpes he'd caught from a prostitute.

- A San Francisco woman sued a lover over his alleged claim that he was sterile. The woman became pregnant. The pregnancy was ectopic (the embryo was implanted in a fallopian tube rather than the uterus), and it required an expensive operation to correct. The woman claimed the defendant had endangered her life. The case ended in an out-of-court settlement.

- In 1987 the Texas Supreme Court gave a Dallas woman the right to sue her husband for the alleged transmission of a venereal disease during their marriage. Although the woman recovered fully from the disease, chlamydia trachomatis, she maintained that her reproductive system was permanently damaged.

- A Brooklyn woman sued her husband for giving her "AIDS phobia," claiming she was left paralyzed with fear after learning of her husband's homosexual activity. The case was thrown out of court because the judge ruled that if such suits were allowed, separate damage claims for "AIDS phobia" could be filed by any spouse who alleged adultery.

- A homeless New York man was charged with murdering a male friend who told him, immediately after they'd finished having sex, that he had the AIDS virus.

- A bill was introduced into the New York State Legislature in 1988 that would permit doctors to warn sexual partners of AIDS patients that they may have been infected—even if the patients object to the disclosure.

- A Chicago woman filed a $12 million suit for damages against American Airlines after a scuffle in which she was allegedly bitten by a ticket agent who later tested positive for the AIDS virus. Although the woman tested negative for the disease, she sought compensation for "infliction of emotional damages."

- When a twenty-eight-year-old Los Angeles man infected with the AIDS virus left half his assets to a church run by his homosexual lover, his family moved to set aside the will, claiming that the lover had exposed the man to the virus.

• The rights of homosexual fathers to visit their children have been contested using the argument that the men are in high risk of contracting the AIDS virus and then passing it on to their children.

These are just a few examples of the many problems that have arisen over the past few years as a result of the rapid spread of various sexual diseases. Without doubt the seriousness of the AIDS epidemic has propelled the courts and state legislatures into action.

Experts estimate that there are from 5 to 20 million cases of herpes in this country, and six hundred thousand new cases are reported each year. In addition, the number of cases of AIDS is expected to increase markedly during the next few years. As a result, increasing numbers of people who suffer from these sexually transmitted diseases are instituting lawsuits against those they believe knowingly exposed them to the viruses. These lawsuits constitute an attempt for legal relief for both the physical and the emotional harm created by the diseases.

As of the writing of this book at least four states, California, Iowa, New York, and Washington, have issued rules that permit herpes victims to sue or have actually awarded damages after jury trials. Florida and Idaho have made it a crime to willfully or knowingly expose another person to the HIV virus that causes AIDS. Similar statutes are under consideration in other states, and there is even a movement to criminalize the transmission of AIDS.

The precedents for these kinds of decisions, based on the theory of recovery due to negligence, began with an 1896 Wisconsin case in which the court held a householder liable for failing to warn a servant that a family member's typhoid fever was contagious. Twenty-four years later a Missouri court issued a similar decision concerning a smallpox case. In 1979 the Wyoming Supreme Court recognized the possibility of bringing a lawsuit against someone for negligently exposing another person to gonorrhea.

In addition to using negligence to recover damages, the notion of battery has also been tried. The theory here is that the victim would not have allowed the person infected with the disease to touch him if he'd had informed consent. Hence, an unlawful battery was committed.

But no matter which theory is used, it must be proved that the transmitter of the disease knew he or she had the disease at the time of transmission; and to maximize any recovery, it must also be proved that the plaintiff suffered both physically and emotionally.

Because of the nature of these diseases, their gravity, and the environment of fear that has been created by them, it is likely that many more of these kinds of cases will find their way into the legal system. Consequently we look for further legislation to be passed in this area.

DATE RAPE

A study financed by the National Institute of Mental Health was conducted by Mary P. Koss, a psychology professor at Kent State University. Professor Koss questioned seven thousand university students on the question of "date rape." Some of the conclusions are not only enlightening but rather startling:

- One woman student in eight had been raped.
- Ninety percent of the women knew their assailant, and forty-seven percent of these rapes were by either romantic acquaintances or first dates.
- Over ninety percent of these rapes were unreported.
- One out of twelve men admitted to fulfilling the definition of rape or attempted rape, and yet none of these men considered himself a rapist.

Until recently the crime of date rape was largely ignored and undocumented. Few were reported and when they were, they were extremely difficult to prove. The question that most often arose was, "When a woman says no, does she really mean no?" Or, put otherwise, "Is date rape a crime?"

It is a complicated question with a complicated answer. As Peter Westen, a professor of law at the University of Michigan, has said, "Rape law is really in an in-between state right now. It's been changing rapidly over the past two decades. There's general agreement that rape means 'sexual intercourse against the will of the victim.' But there's no general consensus on what 'against the will' means and no consensus on what constitutes illicit force on the man's part and when a woman has really denied her consent to sex."

Date rape often does not include serious violence, as does rape by a stranger, and so it is somewhat less clear-cut. As a result, when the matter is taken to court, juries have had trouble coming to a decision. And even when they did decide to convict, higher courts were likely to overturn the conviction.

This was the case in 1973 when the Wyoming Supreme Court reversed the conviction of a man who had sexual intercourse with a woman he picked up in a bar and offered a ride home. The woman said she did not consent to have sex but did not offer any resistance. Similarly, in a North Carolina ruling in 1984, the Supreme Court refused to uphold the conviction of a man who had earlier had a six-month sexual relationship with the woman.

Some states, however, have amended their rape laws to differentiate between full-fledged aggravated rape, in which there is clear evidence of force and resistance, and less serious cases in which consent and aggression are somewhat more ambiguous. In these states convictions for date rape are more likely to be sustained.

This is what happened in a 1984 Michigan case in which the Court of Appeals upheld a conviction for the relatively mild crime of "third-degree sexual assault" when a man took a woman he had just met to his office to have sex with her against her will. The defendant argued that the woman's lack of resistance implied consent, but the court stated that evidence of resistance was unnecessary to support a conviction for this milder version of rape.

Lately there has been a rather novel solution offered to fight date rape. Negligence suits allow victims to sue and collect damages from men who commit this offense. Such suits have been brought—in small numbers—in California. As Peter Westen has pointed out, "Negligence liability seems a reasonable way to deal with date rape. It's not so much a blaming mechanism as a compensatory system, a good way to handle cases of forced sex where the aggravating factors like violence are at a minimum."

But as to whether these suits will be sustained, only the future will tell.

ORGAN TRANSPLANTS

In the past two decades organ transplants have become an effective way to save lives. On an average day in this country, one heart, twenty kidneys, and sixty-five eyes are transplanted, with some procedures reaching an incredible success rate of ninety percent. Transplant recipients range in age from the very young to the very old; there is, and probably always will be, a shortage of available transplantable organs.

Until 1986 no states had laws requiring hospitals to solicit organ donations from families of dead or dying patients. But today, in order to increase the supply of adult donors, twenty-seven states have passed laws requiring hospital officials to remind the relatives of brain dead individuals that organs are badly needed. In addition, the National Organ Transplant Act of 1984 called for extensive efforts to increase the general supply of donor organs as well as to make an attempt to coordinate their distribution.

These measures seem to be working. California, New York, and Oregon were the first three states to pass these routine inquiry laws, and transplant officials say donations increased almost immediately.

In order for an organ to be donated, it is required that the donor be brain dead. Brain death, according to a uniform legal definition used in almost all states, requires "irreversible cessation of all functions of the entire brain, including the brain stem." Though this definition may seem clear enough, there has been controversy, including cases of anencephalic children whose brains have simply failed to develop completely.

It is estimated that approximately twenty percent of all Americans now carry a signed organ donor card. In practice, however, the large majority of hospitals will not take an organ without the additional approval of the next of kin.

RIGHT TO DIE

According to a 1986 poll sponsored by the Pacific Presbyterian Medical Center in San Francisco, ninety percent of Americans now believe that mentally competent adults should have the right to refuse life-sustaining medical treatment and that a patient's potential quality of life should be considered when a decision is to be made by a doctor as to whether extraordinary technological measures should be used in order to prolong life.

The public's opinion on the issue of the right of a patient to die has begun to be reflected in changes in the law. Prior to the last twenty years or so, the legal system of this country operated on the presumption that there was a strong societal interest in preserving life at any cost, whether the patient involved liked it or not. This no longer seems to be the case. Today the trend seems to be in the opposite direction; that is, under certain circumstances people have the right to choose when they are to die in relation to the quality of life they might have if they continued living.

As of 1987 thirty-eight states as well as the District of Columbia had variations on what are commonly known as "living will" statutes; these permit people to specify, within limits, the sort of treatment or care they would like to forego should they ever become irreversibly comatose. Some states even allow for the choosing of proxies to make medical decisions for those who cannot do so for themselves.

Recent court cases have tended to endorse the right of a patient to die. In June 1987, for instance, the New Jersey Supreme Court ruled that the husband of Kathleen Ann Farrell, who had been completely paralyzed for four years as a result of Lou Gehrig's disease but was mentally fully competent, could honor her request to turn off a respirator that kept her breathing. Interestingly enough, the court's ruling came one year after Mrs. Farrell died, still connected to the respirator, but the court felt the issue was important enough to address and came to a decision to provide guidance for future cases.

In the same month the Arizona Supreme Court in the case of a seventy-year-old stroke victim, Mildred Rasmussen, who had no living relatives to testify as to what she might have wanted, simply bypassed the question of intent and decided it would be in Mrs. Rasmussen's best interests to withdraw all forms of life support including food.

In California the court ruling in the case of Elizabeth Bouvia, a cerebral palsy victim, backed Ms. Bouvia's decision to refuse a life-sustaining feeding tube as part of her right to privacy under the U.S. and California constitutions. As Justice Edwin Beach wrote, "A desire to terminate one's life is probably the ultimate exercise of one's right to privacy."

The issue is a controversial one. Some opponents to the right to die cite these cases simply as "assisted suicide" or, in the extreme, "murder."

Nevertheless, the trend in this country is clearly to allow a person to choose when he or she wishes to end treatment that is sustaining life. In fact, few jurisdictions are countervening this trend. (Oklahoma is the only state where there is a law forbidding the withdrawal of nutrition and hydration for incompetent patients who are not terminally ill, although other states are considering similar legislation.)

THE ULTIMATE PROXY

More problematical, perhaps, is the matter of third persons making life-and-death decisions. Often there is an incompetent person involved, one who is in a coma or whose mental capacities have been severely limited. In these cases a third party, who can be a close relative, may sue on behalf of the patient. Acting on a theory called "substituted judgment," the third party may claim to exercise the incompetent patient's right to die by asking the court to order some action, perhaps the disconnection of a feeding tube or respirator, that will hasten the patient's death.

Occasionally a hospital or nursing home will refuse to take this action. Several cases have addressed this issue recently. In June 1987 the New Jersey Supreme Court ruled that the family of Nancy Ellen Jobes, a surgical accident victim, could have a feeding tube removed over the protests of the nursing home where she resided. This decision triggered dozens of lawsuits across the country by relatives who were seeking to withdraw tube feeding for incompetent family members.

To some critics this action had ominous overtones of euthanasia. As writer Nat Hentoff remarked, "It shows the danger of giving the power of life and death to a surrogate. The best people in the world would understandably have a desire for relief from their emotional burden."

To others, the right to die, or perhaps more precisely the right to choose when it is no longer satisfying to exist under the conditions one is forced to live under, is one of the more fundamental rights we have.

Appendix

COHABITATION AGREEMENT

AGREEMENT, between <u>AB</u>   presently residing at
_____ Street, New York, New York, hereinafter called
"<u>AB</u>"; and <u>CD</u>, presently residing at _____ Street, New
York, New York; hereinafter called "<u>CD</u>"; together hereinafter
called the Parties.

WHEREAS the Parties intend to cohabit with each other and
reside at _____ Street, Apt. ____ in the City of New York,
and desire, in anticipation of this arrangement, to settle certain financial questions which might possibly arise as a consequence of this
arrangement; and

WHEREAS the Parties each desire to maintain his or her financial
independence from the other, except as the Parties shall otherwise
mutually agree;

NOW, THEREFORE, in consideration of the terms specified
herein, the Parties agree as follows:

291

Basic Understanding of Parties:

1. It is the understanding of the Parties that the upcoming or existing living arrangements do not create any legal or other obligations or rights between the Parties. Neither Party shall acquire any property or other interest from the other Party as a result of their living arrangement. The sole obligation arising from this relationship is as set forth herein and no other obligations may be construed or inferred from any conduct or action by an individual unless such conduct or action is confirmed in writing. Neither Party shall acquire any interest or right therefrom as a spouse, either statutory or common law in nature.

Future Financial Obligations:

2. Neither Party shall incur any obligation or responsibility for the support or maintenance of the other Party as a consequence of the subject living arrangement. Each Party shall be obligated to the other solely as provided for in this Agreement. Where the Parties orally or informally modify a specified arrangement or understanding, such modification shall apply only during such time as both agree for it to continue and only written modifications shall have lasting effect.

3. Should one Party support the other, such support shall cease upon the separation of the Parties and shall not obligate the payor to continue such support unless agreed to in writing.

Property to be separately owned:

4. Each Party shall keep and retain sole ownership, control and enjoyment of all separate property, real and personal, now owned by him or by her in any manner whatsoever, and each shall have the absolute and unrestricted right to dispose of such separate property, free from any claim that may be made by the other by reason of their living arrangement.

5. Wherever separate property is a source of income or generates other assets, any such income shall remain the sole separate property of the Party holding it, unless such money or asset derived therefrom shall be placed in the joint names of the Parties or in the name of the other, in which case title shall determine the Parties' rights thereto as provided for herein.

6. In the event that the nature or character of any separate property of either Party shall change, the legal title, as evidenced by an instrument of writing, shall reflect the intent of the Parties as to whether the new property shall be considered as separate property or as joint property.

7. In the event that either Party shall purchase an item which shall be jointly used, the person actually purchasing it, as evidenced by a receipt, shall be entitled to retain such item in the event that the Parties separate. Should the Parties jointly acquire property and separate, they shall divide such property in accordance with its value as of the date of separation, such distribution to be based solely on actual financial contribution to its acquisition.

Debts:

8. Each Party represents and warrants to the other that he or she has not heretofore incurred any debt or obligation for which the other may be liable, and each Party agrees that he or she shall not hereafter, without the consent of the other, incur any such debt or obligation for which the other may be liable. Each Party agrees to indemnify the other against any loss, expense (including reasonable attorney's fees) and damage in connection with or arising out of a breach of the foregoing mutual representation and covenants.

Shared Expenses:

9. The Parties shall equally share the following expenses: (specify).

10. AB shall be solely responsible for the following expenses: (specify).

11. CD shall be solely responsible for the following expenses: (specify).

Estate Rights:

12. This arrangement shall not create a right of one Party to inherit property from the other. Either Party is free to execute a Will of his or her own choice wherein each may or may not include the other as a beneficiary. Should a Party die intestate, such estate shall be distributed in accordance with the laws of intestacy and the other Party herein shall only be entitled to property of the other in accordance with any instrument of writing admissible in determining such distribution.

Representation:

13. Each Party has been represented by separate counsel who has advised him or her of their respective rights. AB has been represented by   , of New York City; and CD has been represented by   , of New York City.

14. This Agreement constitutes the entire understanding of the Parties, who hereby acknowledge that there are no representations, promises or undertakings other than those expressly set forth herein.

15. This Agreement has been made with reference to the laws of the State of New York, by which the validity, interpretation and construction of its provisions shall be governed. If any provision of this Agreement shall be held to be illegal or invalid under the laws of the State of New York or of any other jurisdiction, the other provisions hereof shall continue, nevertheless, in full force and effect, and the provision which shall be so held to be illegal or invalid shall, nevertheless, remain in full force and effect in any state or jurisdiction under the laws of which such provision shall be legal and valid.

16. This Agreement shall inure to the benefit of, and shall be binding upon, the respective heirs, executors and administrators of the Parties.

17. No modification of the terms of this Agreement shall be effective unless it shall be in writing and executed by the Parties hereto with the same formalities as this Agreement.

PRENUPTIAL AGREEMENT

AGREEMENT, between _____ presently residing at 1 West 64th Street, New York, New York, hereinafter called _____; and _____ presently residing at 160 East 91st Street, New York, New York; hereinafter called_____; together hereinafter called the Parties.

WHEREAS the Parties intend to marry each other in the State of New York and reside in the City of New York, and desire, in anticipation of their marriage, to settle certain financial questions which might otherwise arise as a consequence of their marriage; and

WHEREAS the Parties each desire to maintain his or her financial independence from the other, except as the Parties shall otherwise mutually agree; and accordingly, make the following representations:

(A) The Parties have made full and complete disclosure to each other of their respective financial positions, including net worth and income of each of them and their expectancies, including, but not limited to future inheritances.

(B) Each of the Parties represent that they presently, prior to the date of their marriage, own, possess, or have title to certain property or estate of significant value which is to remain his or her sole, separate property in the future as evidenced either by title to such property or ownership.

(C) JOSEPH represents an interest in the property specified in Schedule A annexed hereto. Said property constitutes the total assets of JOSEPH which shall remain his separate property as designated in this Agreement, unless changed in accordance with the terms specified herein.

(D) LESLIE represents an interest in the property specified in Schedule B annexed hereto. Said property constitutes the total assets of LESLIE which shall remain her separate property as designated in this Agreement, unless changed in accordance with the terms specified herein.

(E) Each of the Parties acknowledges that he or she is fully acquainted with the business and resources of the other, that the other has answered any and all questions that he or she may have asked of the other concerning his or her business and resources; each Party acknowledges and understands that by the execution of this Agreement, he or she is waiving any and all rights to any payment of any kind at the death of the other or upon dissolution of the marriage, and that he or she might be entitled to receive a substantial portion of the estate of the other in the absence of this Agreement. Each Party further acknowledges that they have been advised of the right to obtain individual counsel and that each either has received such counsel as expressed below.

(F) Each Party represents that he or she has weighed all of the facts and circumstances herein, that each believes the Agreement to be fair and reasonable in the light of all of the facts and the situation and each acknowledges that he or she has entered into this Agreement freely, voluntarily, and with full knowledge.

NOW, THEREFORE, in consideration of the terms specified herein, the Parties agree as follows:

Property to be separately owned:

1. Each Party shall keep and retain sole ownership and control and enjoyment of all separate property, real and personal, now owned by him or by her in any manner whatsoever as if they had remained unmarried, and each shall have the absolute and unrestricted right

to dispose of such separate property, free from any claim that may be made by the other by reason of their marriage.

2. Wherever separate property is a source of income or generates other assets, any such income shall remain the sole separate property of the Party holding it, unless such money or asset derived therefrom shall be placed in the joint names of the Parties or in the name of the other, in which case title shall determine the Parties rights thereto as provided for herein.

3. In the event that the nature or character of any separate property of either Party shall change, the legal title, as evidenced by an instrument of writing, shall reflect the intent of the parties as to whether the new property shall be considered as separate property or as joint property.

4. The Parties anticipate that they will be purchasing a cooperative apartment in the future, such apartment to be their marital residence. It is the plan of the Parties that the down payment for such purchase shall come from the sale of JOSEPH'S Apartment, 11G at 1 West 64th Street. In such event, JOSEPH shall be credited, in the event of a sale or other disposition, for the full amount of such down payment in the new acquisition. However, title shall reflect joint ownership and each Party shall be entitled to full rights as equal owners, once JOSEPH is credited as above. This shall be the case regardless of the respective contributions of either Party to the payment of mortgage, maintenance or other expense relative thereto.

Debts:

5. Each Party represents and warrants to the other that he or she has not heretofore incurred any debt or obligation for which the other may be liable, and each Party agrees that he or she shall not hereafter, without the consent of the other, incur any such debt or obligation for which the other may be liable. Each Party agrees to indemnify the other against any loss, expense (including reasonable attorney's fees) and damage in connection with or arising out of a breach of the foregoing mutual representation and covenants.

Waiver of equitable distribution and maintenance:

6. In the event of the separation of the Parties or the dissolution of the marriage, each Party waives any right he or she might otherwise have to equitable distribution, to a distributive award or to maintenance or alimony under the laws of the State of New York or of the laws of any other jurisdiction which may be applicable. This provision

is intended to constitute a waiver of any right to equitable distribution or maintenance, as authorized by the provisions of Paragraph 3 of Part B of Section 236 of the Domestic Relations Law of the State of New York or of the same or similar law of any jurisdiction which may be applicable. This provision, however, is not intended to be, and shall not be construed as, a waiver of the right of either Party to claim payments of child support, if the Parties shall hereafter become parents.

Waiver of rights in each other's estate:

7. Except as provided in Paragraph 8 below, each of the Parties (A) waives and releases any rights as surviving spouse to elect to take against the other's will, whether heretofore or hereafter made; (B) waives and releases any and all interest, right or claim of distributive shares of intestate succession, of community property, of dower, curtesy, or homestead rights or any other interest in the estate or property of the other (real or personal) under or by virtue of the laws of any state or country; (C) releases any right or claim to statutory exemptions in the property of the other; (D) waives and releases any right or claim to receive any benefit under Sections 401(a)(11)(A) of the Internal Revenue Code from a qualified plan (or any similarly substituted law), it being intended that this provision shall constitute a waiver of all such benefits under Section 417(a)(2) of the Internal Revenue Code; and (E) waives and releases any right he or she may have to serve as administrator of the estate of the other.

8. Each Party represents that they shall shortly hereafter execute their Last Will and Testament wherein each reserves the right to dispose of their respective separate property by Will as each chooses.

9. Nothing contained in this Agreement shall be deemed to constitute a waiver by either Party of any bequest or fiduciary appointment that the other Party may choose to make to him or her by Will, nor of any transfer by either Party to the other, either by gift or by placing property in joint names or in both Parties' names as tenants by the entirety. The Parties acknowledge, however, that no promises of any kind have been made by either of them to the other with respect to any such bequest, appointment, or transfer.

10. Each Party shall, upon the other's request, take any and all steps to execute, acknowledge, and deliver to the other Party any and all future instruments necessary or expedient to effectuate the purposes of this Agreement.

Representation:

11. Each Party has been represented by separate counsel who has advised him or her of their respective rights. JOSEPH has been represented by _____, of New York City; and LESLIE has been represented by Jacoby & Meyers, of New York City.

12. This Agreement constitutes the entire understanding of the Parties, who hereby acknowledge that there are no representations, promises, or undertakings other than those expressly set forth herein.

13. This Agreement has been made with reference to the laws of the State of New York, by which the validity, interpretation and construction of its provisions shall be governed. If any provision of this Agreement shall be held to be illegal or invalid under the laws of the State of New York or of any other jurisdiction, the other provisions hereof shall continue, nevertheless, in full force and effect, and the provision which shall be so held to be illegal or invalid shall, nevertheless, remain in full force and effect in any state or jurisdiction under the laws of which such provision shall be legal and valid.

14. This Agreement shall inure to the benefit of, and shall be binding upon, the respective heirs, executors, and administrators of the Parties.

15. No modification of the terms of this Agreement shall be effective unless it shall be in writing and executed by the Parties hereto with the same formalities as this Agreement.

IN WITNESS WHEREOF, the Parties hereto have hereunto set their hands and seals as of the date specified below and acknowledges and states that he or she has signed this Agreement on such date at a time prior to their actual marriage.

Dated: , 1988   _____
New York, NY   JOSEPH MIDDLETON

Dated: , 1988   _____
New York, NY   LESLIE VIAMANI

STATE OF NEW YORK
COUNTY OF NEW YORK
On the   Day of   , 1988, before me personally came, JOSEPH MIDDLETON, to me known to be the individual

described in and who executed the foregoing instrument and he duly acknowledged to me that he executed the same.

_____

notary public

STATE OF
COUNTY OF
On the   Day of   , 1988, before me personally came, LESLIE VIAMANI, to me known to be the individual described in and who executed the foregoing instrument and she did duly acknowledge to me that she executed the same.

_____

notary public

PROTECTIVE ORDER

Secs. 430, 550, 740, 828, 1027, 1029 F.C.A.   Gen. Form

At a Term of the Family Court of the
State of New York, City of New York
held in and for the County of
ADAMS STREET, BROOKLYN, NEW YORK

on_____

PRESDNT:

HON._____
            Judge

_____

In the Matter of   DOCKET NO._____

_____   TEMPORARY ORDER OF PROTECTION
            Petitioner

        v.

_____
            Respondent
_____

NOTICE: YOUR WILLFUL FAILURE TO OBEY
THIS ORDER MAY, AFTER COURT
HEARING, RESULT IN YOUR COM-
MITMENT TO JAIL FOR A TERM
NOT TO EXCEED SIX MONTHS FOR
CONTEMPT OF COURT

300   Appendix

A petition under Article _____ of the Family Court Act, sworn to on _____
19 ____ , having been filed in this Court in the above-entitled proceeding alleging that the

above-named Respondent did _____

and it appearing, upon good cause shown, that a temporary order of protection would serve
the purpose of this Act,

       NOW therefore, it is hereby

       ORDERED, THAT _____ shall observe the following conditions
of behavior:

1. Respondent not to assault, menace, harass or recklessly endanger Petitioner.

2. Respondent not to drink alcoholic beverages in the home. Respondent to remain
   away from the home while under the influence of alcohol.

3. Respondent not to exclude Petitioner and children from mutual occupancy of home.

4. _____
   _____
   _____
   _____ , and it is further

      ORDERED, that the above conditions of behavior shall remain in force and effect
until _____

_____
                        J.F.C.

_____ Order extended to _____

_____
                        J.F.C.

_____ Order extended to _____

_____
                        J.F.C.

_____ Order extended to _____

_____
                        J.F.C.

National Directory

Jacoby & Meyers has more than 300 attorneys and 25 partners working in 150 firm-owned offices in Arizona, California, Connecticut, New Jersey, New York, and Pennsylvania.

WEST COAST OFFICES
Office Listing

OFFICE	CODE	ADDRESS	TELEPHONE #
CA ADMINISTRATIVE	1098	11835 W. Olympic Blvd, LA, CA 90064	(213) 478-5900
JAMKO SERVICE, CA		11835 W. Olympic Blvd, LA, CA 90064	(213) 478-7833
ANAHEIM	1009	505 S Euclid Ave, Anaheim, CA 92802	(714) 991-0501
AZ PROBATE		525 W Southern Ave, Mesa, AZ 85202	(602) 969-8940
BAY AREA CRIMINAL		3805 Broadway, Oakland, CA 94611	(415) 547-7301
BAY AREA PROBATE		3805 Broadway, Oakland, CA 94611	(415) 547-7201
CANOGA PARK WARDS	1054	6601 Owensmouth St, Canoga Park, CA 91303	(818) 716-1811
CARSON	1073	509 Carson Mall, Carson, CA 90745	(213) 538-8453

OFFICE	CODE	ADDRESS	TELEPHONE #
CERRITOS, BANKRUPTCY	1031	11444 South St, Cerritos, CA 90701	(213) 860-7322
CHULA VISTA	1079	310 Third Ave, Chula Vista, CA 92010	(619) 426-0163
CITRUS HEIGHTS PROBATE	1023	7331 Greenback Lane, Citrus Heights, CA 95621	
CLAIREMONT	1080	3860 Convoy St, San Diego, CA 92111	(916) 726-4426
COSTA MESA	1019	2960 Harbor Blvd, Costa Mesa, CA 92626	(619) 277-1472
COUNTRY CLUB WARDS	1033	3460 El Camino Ave, Sacramento, CA 95821	(714) 556-8150
COVINA WARDS	1040	848 S Barranca St, Covina, CA 91723	(916) 484-1601
CULVER CITY	1074	11475 Jefferson Blvd, Culver City, CA 90230	(818) 967-5142
DALY CITY	1113	197 87th St, Daly City, CA 94015	(213) 390-4074
DEER VALLEY, GLENDALE AZ	1507	4342 W Thunderbird Rd, Glendale, AZ 85306	(415) 991-2922
DOWNEY	1005	7407 Florence Ave, Downey, CA 90240	(602) 978-1160
DOWNTOWN SAN DIEGO	1085	1400 6th Ave, San Diego, CA 92101	(213) 927-7702
EASTSIDE AZ	1504	3150 N 24th St, Phoenix, AZ 85016	(619) 232-2485
EL CAJON	1086	1309 Broadway, El Cajon, CA 92021	(602) 274-5835
EL CERRITO	1117	10283 San Pablo Ave, El Cerrito, CA 94530	(619) 442-0717
EL TORO, MISSION VIEJO	1055	23720 El Toro Rd, El Toro, CA 92630	(415) 528-1416
ESCONDIDO	1078	205 West Mission Ave, Escondido, CA 92025	(714) 472-4144
			(619) 480-2488

OFFICE	CODE	ADDRESS	TELEPHONE #
FLORIN WARDS	1035	5601 Florin Rd, Sacramento, CA 95823	(916) 422-1725
FREMONT	1122	38950 Blacow Rd, Fremont, CA 94536	(415) 794-5784
FULLERTON	1051	104 W Wilshire Ave, Fullerton, CA 92632	(714) 870-5312
GLENDALE, CA	1004	336 N Central Ave, Glendale, CA 91203	(818) 244-4177
HAWTHORNE WARDS	1045	12000 Hawthorne Blvd, Hawthorne, CA 90250	(213) 679-1125
HAYWARD	1119	338 Jackson, Hayward, CA 94544	(415) 537-5747
HUNTINGTON BEACH WARDS	1052	7777 Edinger Ave, Huntington Beach 92647	(714) 895-2003
INGLEWOOD	1007	238 S LaBrea Ave, Inglewood, CA 90301	(213) 673-3222
LA BANKRUPTCY	1018	510 W Sixth St, LA, CA 90014	(213) 489-4100
LA CRIMINAL		5626 Van Nuys Blvd, Van Nuys, CA 91401	(818) 901-1088
LA PROBATE		3325 Wilshire Blvd, LA, CA 90010	(213) 383-0323
LAKEWOOD	1053	141 Lakewood Center Mall, Lakewood, CA 90712	(213) 634-9744
LANCASTER	1070	44134 Tenth St West, Lancaster, CA 93534	(805) 945-9425
LONG BEACH EAST	1075	3580 E Pacific Coast Hwy, Long Beach, CA 90804	(213) 498-6448
LONG BEACH NORTH	1008	4425 Atlantic Ave, Long Beach, CA 90807	(213) 426-5541

Name	No.	Address	Phone
MARYVALE	1508	4144 N 67th Ave, Phoenix, AZ 85033	(602) 846-0200
MESA	1505	525 W Southern Ave, Mesa, AZ 85202	(602) 969-8940
MONTCLAIR WARDS	1042	9050 Central Ave, Montclair, CA 91763	(714) 625-1526
MONTGOMERY ST, SF	1114	44 Montgomery St, San Francisco, CA 94104	(415) 433-4533
NORWALK, CA WARDS	1056	12051 E Imperial Hwy, Norwalk, CA 90650	
OAKLAND, CRIMINAL	1118	3805 Broadway, Oakland, CA 94611	(213) 868-2252
OCEANSIDE	1026	2110 S Hill St, Oceanside, CA 92054	(415) 547-7201
ONTARIO, PROBATE	1027	738 N Euclid Ave, Ontario, CA 91762	(619) 439-1911
ORANGE COUNTY BANKRUPTCY		11444 South St, Cerritos, CA 90701	(714) 391-1541
PANORAMA CITY	1043	9608 Van Nuys Blvd, Panorama City, CA 91402	(714) 827-0951
PARADISE VALLEY	1503	3923 E Thunderbird Ave, Phoenix, AZ 85032	(818) 891-6775
PASADENA	1071	1055 E Green St, Pasadena, CA 91106	(602) 971-9814
PEORIA, AZ	1509	10865 N 85th Ave, Peoria, AZ 85345	(818) 449-1562
PLEASANT HILL	1108	1930 Contra Costa Blvd, Pleasant Hill, CA 94523	(602) 979-2912
PLEASANT HILL BANKRUPTCY		140 Gregory Lane, Pleasant Hill, CA 94523	(415) 689-1500
REDWOOD CITY	1111	1048 El Camino Real, Redwood City, CA 94063	(415) 689-0640
RIVERSIDE BANKRUPTCY	1064	555 N "D" St, San Bernardino, CA 92401	(415) 368-1146
			(714) 885-5616

OFFICE	CODE	ADDRESS	TELEPHONE #
RIVERSIDE NORTH	1048	7223 Magnolia Ave, Riverside, CA 92504	(714) 784-0170
RIVERSIDE TYLER	1020	3901 Tyler St, Riverside, CA 92503	(714) 785-0310
ROSEMEAD WARDS	1044	3600 N Rosemead Blvd, Rosemead, CA 91770	(818) 288-7954
SACRAMENTO	1022	1233 "J" St, Sacramento, CA 95814	(916) 441-7396
SACRAMENTO BANKRUPTCY		1233 "J" St, Sacramento, CA 95814	(916) 444-2433
SACRAMENTO CRIMINAL	1110	900 "G" St, Lower Level, Sacramento, CA 95814	(916) 448-1084
SACRAMENTO PI	1087	1776 Tribute Rd, Sacramento, CA 95815	(916) 924-1109
SACRAMENTO PROBATE		1233 "J" St, Sacramento, CA 95814	(916) 444-2433
SAN BERNARDINO	1047	144 Central City Mall, San Bernardino, CA 92401	(714) 888-7895
SAN BERNARDINO BANKRUPTCY	1064	144 Central City Mall, San Bernardino, CA 92401	(714) 885-5616
SAN DIEGO CRIMINAL		3860 Convoy St, San Diego, CA 92111	(619) 277-1472
SAN DIEGO CRIMINAL		1010 Second Ave, San Diego, CA 92101	(619) 236-9976
SAN GABRIEL	1014	722 E Valley Blvd, San Gabriel, CA 91776	(818) 572-7255
SAN RAFAEL	1116	535 Fourth St, San Rafael, CA 94901	(415) 453-6353
SANTA ANA	1057	1608 N Main St, Santa Ana, CA 92701	(714) 835-2445
SCOTTSDALE	1501	3666 N Miller Rd, Scottsdale, AZ 85251	(602) 994-8997

OFFICE	CODE	ADDRESS	TELEPHONE #
SCOTTSDALE PI		3666 N Miller Rd, Scottsdale, AZ 85251	(602) 994-8997
SOUTH PHOENIX, PI	1510	7004 S Central Ave, Phoenix, AZ 85041	(602) 243-3174
STEVENS CREEK	1124	3350 Stevens Creek Blvd, San Jose, CA 95117	(408) 246-7411
STOCKTON WARDS	1032	5400 Pacific Ave, Stockton, Ca 95207	(209) 957-5170
SUNNYVALE	1125	717 E El Camino Real, Sunnyvale, CA 94087	(408) 733-4435
TEMPE	1506	700 E Baseline, Bldg C, Tempe, AZ 85282	(602) 897-2255
THOUSAND OAKS, BANKRUPTCY	1076	171 E 1000 Oaks Blvd, Thousand Oaks, CA 91360	(805) 495-8888
TORRANCE	1011	18436 Hawthorne Blvd, Torrance, CA 90504	(213) 370-7434
TORRANCE WARDS	1058	21405 Madrona Ave, Torrance, CA 90503	(213) 370-1591
TUCSON EAST	1517	7529 E Broadway, Tucson, AZ 85710	(602) 721-7733
TUCSON NORTHWEST	1515	1650 E Fort Lowell Rd, Tucson, AZ 85719	
TUCSON PI	1519	2601 N Campbell, Tucson, AZ 85719	(602) 326-7733
TUCSON SOUTH	1518	369 W Valencia Rd, Tucson, AZ 85706	(602) 881-9472
VAN NESS SF	1115	1748 Clement St, San Francisco, CA 94121	(602) 294-7733
			(415) 387-3416

OFFICE	CODE	ADDRESS	TELEPHONE #
VAN NUYS, CRIMINAL	1003	5626 Van Nuys Blvd, Van Nuys, CA 91401	(818) 997-0216
VENTURA CRIMINAL	1049	500 S Mills Rd, Ventura, CA 93003	(805) 644-7290
WEST COVINA	1030	1329 W Garvey North, West Covina, CA 91790	
WEST LOS ANGELES	1002	2346 Westwood Blvd, LA, CA 90064	(818) 960-5467
WESTSIDE	1502	6221 N 35th Ave, Phoenix, AZ 85017	(213) 475-7393
WILSHIRE/HOLLYWOOD	1016	3325 Wilshire Blvd, LA, CA 90010	(602) 973-3266
			(213) 383-0323

EAST COAST OFFICES
Office Listing

OFFICE	CODE	ADDRESS	TELEPHONE #
150 BROADWAY	5003	150 Broadway, New York, NY 10038	(212) 267-0130
ALLERTON AVENUE	5037	751-759 Allerton Ave, Bronx, NY 10467	
ASTORIA	5030	3069 Steinway St, Astoria, NY 11103	(212) 654-6440
AUDUBON (Haddonfield)	5255	739 White Horse Pike, Audubon, NJ 08106	(718) 721-5121
BAY RIDGE	5025	537 86th St, Brooklyn, NY 11209	(609) 429-9007
BOHEMIA/RONKONKOMA	5023	3505 Vets Memorial Hwy, Ronkonkoma, NY 11779	(718) 833-4800
			(516) 471-7000
BRICKTOWN	5260	2850 Yorktowne Blvd, Bricktown, NJ 08723	(609) 255-3434

BURLINGTON	5264	2313B Mount Holly Rd, Burlington, NJ 08016	(609)386-3810
CANARSIE	5047	2348 Ralph Ave, Brooklyn, NY 11234	(718) 251-1300
CENTER CITY	5352	1535 Chestnut St, Philadelphia, PA 19102	(215) 568-3844
CENTER CITY ADMIN	5398	1535 Chestnut St, Philadelphia, PA 19102	(800) 523-1414
CENTER CITY PI		1535 Chestnut St, Philadelphia, PA 19102	(215) 568-3844
DANBURY	6144	325 Main St, Danbury, CT 06810	(203) 798-2877
DUFFIELD ST, BANKRUPTCY	5004	258 Duffield St, Brooklyn, NY 11201	(718) 858-1474
EAST 23RD STREET	5028	110 E 23rd St, New York, NY 10010	(212) 254-0181
EAST 42ND STREET	5001	51 E 42nd St, New York, NY 10017	(212) 682-3372
EAST BRUNSWICK	5140	1126 Route 18, East Brunswick, NJ 08816	
EDISON	5149	85 Lincoln Hwy, Edison, NJ 08820	(201) 238-9696
ELIZABETH	5132	1165 E Jersey St, Elizabeth, NJ 07201	(201) 549-3553
ENGLEWOOD	5139	43 W Palisades Ave, Englewood, NJ 07631	(201) 527-1120
FLUSHING	5012	136-65 Roosevelt Ave, Flushing, NY 11354	(201) 567-8030
FORDHAM ROAD	5013	One East Fordham Road, Bronx, NY 10468	(718) 961-6606
FRANKLIN SQUARE (Elmont)	5017	837 Hempstead Tpke, Franklin Square, NY 11010	(212) 365-4100
			(516) 775-6501

OFFICE	CODE	ADDRESS	TELEPHONE #
JAMKO SERVICE, NY	5098	1156 Avenue of the Americas, NY, NY 10036	(212) 536-7580
JERSEY CITY	5133	2849 Kennedy Blvd, Jersey City, NJ 07306	(201) 435-7900
KING OF PRUSSIA	5363	114 E DeKalb Pike, King of Prussia, PA 19406	(215) 265-0111
KINGS HIGHWAY	5005	1609 Kings Hwy, Brooklyn, NY 11229	(718) 998-9808
LANGHORNE	5358	203 Lincoln Hwy, Fairless Hills, PA 19030	(215) 547-0750
LAWRENCE TSS	5019	605 Rockaway Tpke, Lawrence, NY 11559	(516) 239-4200
LEVITTOWN TSS	5020	3601 Hempstead Tpke, Levittown, NY 11756	(516) 731-5200
LEXINGTON AVENUE	5031	1269 Lexington Ave, New York, NY 10028	(212) 534-1806
LINDENHURST/BABYLON	5022	215 W Hoffman Ave, Lindenhurst, NY 11757	(516) 225-5656
MEDIA	5361	140 S State Rd, Springfield, PA 19064	(215) 544-1070
MELVILLE TSS	5024	150 Broadhollow Rd., Melville, NY 11747	(516) 271-7040
MIDDLE VILLAGE TSS	5016	66-26 Metropolitan Ave, Middle Village, NY 11379	(718) 386-3770
MONTCLAIR	5135	7 Park St, Montclair, NJ 07042	(201) 746-2424
MORRISTOWN	5151	26 Park Place, Morristown, NJ 07960	(201) 644-3440

OFFICE	CODE	ADDRESS	TELEPHONE #
NANUET	5027	200 Route 59, Nanuet, NY 10954	(914) 624-3565
NEW ROCHELLE	5038	466 Main St, New Rochelle, NY 10801	(914) 633-1620
NEWARK	5136	2 Washington Place, Newark, NJ 07102	(201) 622-0084
NORTHEAST PHILADELPHIA	5353	1930 Cottman Ave, Philadelphia, PA 19111	
NORWALK, CT	6143	212 Westport Ave, Norwalk, CT 06851	(215) 742-9030
NY ADMINISTRATIVE	5098	1156 Avenue of the Americas, NY, NY 10036	(203) 846-6889
PARAMUS	5148	S 30 Route 17 North, Paramus, NJ 07652	(212) 536-7600
PARAMUS BANKRUPTCY	5191	S 30 Route 17 North, Paramus, NJ 07652	(201) 845-0300
PASSAIC	5134	694 Main Ave, Passaic, NJ 07055	(201) 845-4411
PORT RICHMOND	5362	2401 E Venango, Philadelphia, PA 19134	(201) 471-8052
REGO PARK	5006	97-45 Queens Blvd, Rego Park, NY 11374	(215) 743-7210
SMITHTOWN	5008	10 Lawrence Ave, Smithtown, NY 11787	(718) 896-5100
SOUTH PHILADELPHIA	5354	1411 Snyder Ave, Philadelphia, PA 19145	(516) 361-7240
STAMFORD	6141	184 Bedford St, Stamford, CT 06901	(215) 463-0600
STATEN ISLAND	5014	12A Barrett Ave, Staten Island, NY 10302	(203) 359-1180
			(718) 720-1000

OFFICE	CODE	ADDRESS	TELEPHONE #
TINTON FALLS, NJ	5150	980 Shrewsbury Ave, Tinton Falls, NJ 07724	(201) 389-2552
WARMINSTER	5359	75 York Rd, Warminster, PA 18974	(215) 672-5579
WEST 72ND STREET	5002	200 W 72nd St, New York, NY 10023	(212) 580-7704
WESTBURY	5045	96 Old Country Road, Westbury, NY 11590	(516) 832-9191
WHITE PLAINS	5011	200 Hamilton Ave, White Plains, NY 10601	(914) 761-9093
WOODBURY	5256	57 Cooper St, Woodbury, NJ 08096	(609) 848-1998
YONKERS	5029	6 North Upper Mall, Yonkers, NY 10704	(914) 964-0808

Index